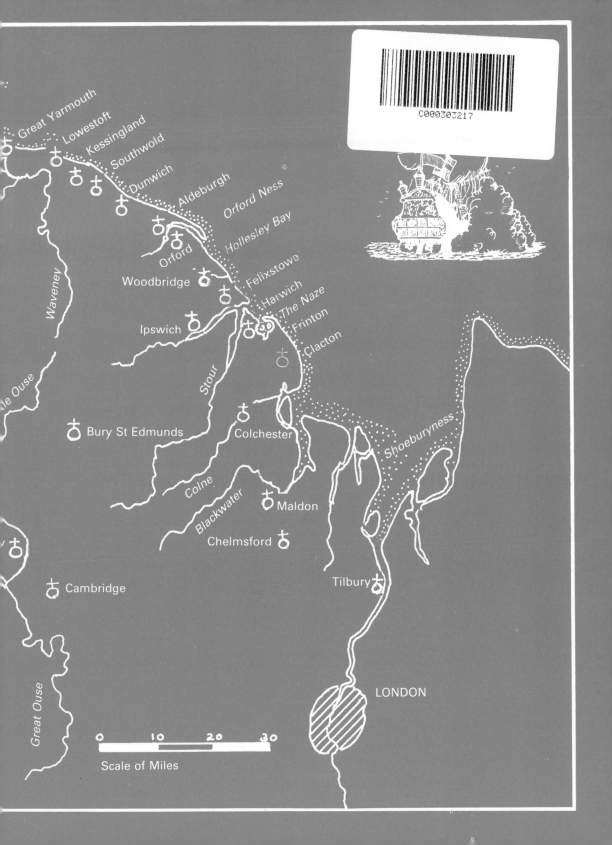

Great Yarmouth
Lowestoft
Kessingland
Southwold
Dunwich
Aldeburgh
Orford Ness
Hollesley Bay
Orford
Woodbridge
Felixstowe
Harwich
The Naze
Frinton
Ipswich
Clacton
Waveney
Stour
le Ouse
Bury St Edmunds
Colchester
Shoeburyness
Colne
Blackwater
Maldon
Chelmsford
Cambridge
Tilbury
Great Ouse
LONDON

0   10   20   30

Scale of Miles

FORTIFICATIONS OF EAST ANGLIA

Overleaf: *Landguard Fort, Felixstowe, seen from the air. There has been a fort at the entrance to Harwich harbour since the reign of Henry VIII, but the fort seen here is the casemated battery of 1875 incorporated into the ramparts of the 1745 fortress. Darell's Battery, named after the officer who commanded the fort at the time of the Dutch assault in 1667, can just be seen at upper left.*
East Anglian Daily Times

FORTIFICATIONS
OF EAST ANGLIA

PETER KENT

TERENCE DALTON LIMITED
LAVENHAM, SUFFOLK 1988

Published by
TERENCE DALTON LIMITED

ISBN 0 86138 065 7

Text photoset in 10/11pt Baskerville

Printed in Great Britain at
The Lavenham Press Limited, Lavenham, Suffolk

Contents

Acknowledgements

I would like to thank all those who have helped me in the research and writing of this book. They include Charles Trollope, who generously gave me access to his extensive collection of material; Major Tony Hill, for his information on Shoeburyness; Michael Catton, who guided me round Coalhouse Fort; Mike Osborne, for sharing his knowledge of Lincolnshire; and Robert Malster, who put the book together and tracked down extra illustrations.

Explanatory Note of Symbols used on Maps

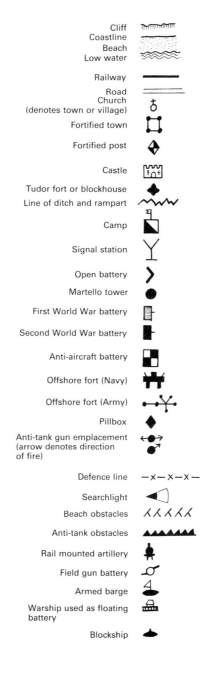

Cliff	
Coastline	
Beach	
Low water	
Railway	
Road	
Church (denotes town or village)	
Fortified town	
Fortified post	
Castle	
Tudor fort or blockhouse	
Line of ditch and rampart	
Camp	
Signal station	
Open battery	
Martello tower	
First World War battery	
Second World War battery	
Anti-aircraft battery	
Offshore fort (Navy)	
Offshore fort (Army)	
Pillbox	
Anti-tank gun emplacement (arrow denotes direction of fire)	
Defence line	
Searchlight	
Beach obstacles	
Anti-tank obstacles	
Rail mounted artillery	
Field gun battery	
Armed barge	
Warship used as floating battery	
Blockship	

The Strategic Background

1

ONLY Prince Albert and Uncle Toby have ever built forts for fun, and although military engineers would gladly have built forts on the slightest of pretexts and girded every town with ingenious variants of bastion, hornwork and ravelin, it has been on only rare occasions that the government has given them enough money to realise a tenth of their dreams[1]. Forts were the most unproductive of buildings; they were extremely expensive, uncomfortable to live in, difficult to build and by no means easy to justify in times of peace. As structures of singular purpose, they were erected only when the government could be persuaded that there was a real need for them.

Since the sixteenth century Britain's safety has rested on three lines of defence: the first was always the navy, either waiting in port or cruising off the enemy coast waiting to intercept the invasion fleet; the second was formed by coastal fortifications; and the third line was the army, ready to repel any troops that might get ashore. Generally, all agreed on the primacy of the first line. It was only when, for reasons of negligence, incompetence or rapid technological change, the country lost its confidence in the ability of its wooden walls to prevent invasion that a clamour went up for those of brick and stone; and only then was the demand met.

These occasions were rare; there have been only five substantial programmes of fort building since the sixteenth century. The first was when Henry VIII was faced by the formidable combination of France, Spain and the Holy Roman Empire; the second when the Spanish Armada threatened; the third during the American and French Revolutionary Wars; the fourth when the French developed ironclad warships and reduced the whole of Britain's vast navy to instant obsolescence; and the fifth in 1940 when the Germans controlled most of Europe and stood poised to invade. In none of these cases were the forts ever tested, for Britain retained command of the sea and the invasion never came. Because of this maritime emphasis the majority of forts were built on the coast: only twice has it been necessary to build extensive defences inland, during the Civil War of 1642–49 and in 1940.

For nearly a third of the years between 1500 and 1956, when coastal fortifications were finally abandoned, Britain was at war

Opposite page: *The impressive Water Gate of Tilbury Fort, designed by Sir Bernard de Gomme during the reign of Charles II.*

with a European power. In addition to these periods of actual hostilities there were many occasions when war and conquest, raid and invasion were considered imminent. Each period of alarm left its contribution to the collection of shore defences, so that it is possible to see a fort built by Henry VIII, modified in the seventeenth century, extended in the Napoleonic Wars, standing in the shadow of ponderous Victorian casemates and capped with an ugly jumble of twentieth-century steel and concrete.

The spur for Henry VIII's great national scheme of coast defence, the first ever undertaken in England, was the treaty of 1538 between France and the Holy Roman Empire, which ended their habitual enmity and made an invasion to re-establish the Pope's authority in England seem inevitable. These two allies controlled the whole coastline of Europe from Hamburg to Spain, enabling their combined fleets to strike any part of the English coast from Land's End to the Humber, although it was more likely that the invasion would be directed at the more accessible Channel coast and East Anglia.

In 1539 Henry directed that Commissioners "search and defend" the shore to ascertain where defences were most necessary[2]. Acting quickly on their reports, Thomas Cromwell, the Lord Great Chamberlain, drew up a document listing the places where fortifications were to be built[3]. In East Anglia they included King's Lynn, Yarmouth, Lowestoft, Aldeburgh, Orford, Landguard Point and Tilbury; further inspections added Weybourne to the list[4]. The aim was not so much to protect towns as to deny the enemy fleet the use of an anchorage where they could land troops at leisure. Yarmouth and Lowestoft Roads, Orwell Haven and Weybourne were the only places on the whole east coast that suited this purpose, and the forts planned to guard them were strategic defences designed to be components in a national scheme of defence. By 1543 more than a dozen "bulwarks" had been built on the east coast from the Thames to the Wash.

With the revival of the invasion scare in 1545 extra works were built and existing ones repaired. The forts built were a radical departure in design from previous fortifications, and the concept of a unitary scheme of coastal defence financed and directed by the Crown was also entirely new. This national plan was made possible by increased central authority, efficient administration and advances in topography and surveying. Henry's advisers had a clearer grasp of the strategic implications of their plans than previous engineers, because they had extensive and accurate maps[5].

Nothing prompted the building of any new defences until the fifteen-sixties. For most of her reign Elizabeth was threatened with invasion, but her natural parsimony prevented any improvements to the defences, beyond providing guns for those towns that pleaded for them, until the inescapable threat of the Spanish Armada forced measures to be taken. The coasts were surveyed in 1587 and 1588, the weak places noted and fortifications recommended. The strategic problem was much the same as had confronted her father. The Spanish army was at Dunkirk but the Armada that was to convey it across the Channel was capable of landing the thirty thousand troops aboard anywhere from Penzance to the Humber. Once again the effort of building defences was concentrated at the strategic anchorages: the Thames was strengthened by additional batteries and an entrenched camp at Tilbury, the bulwark at Mersea was repaired and Harwich

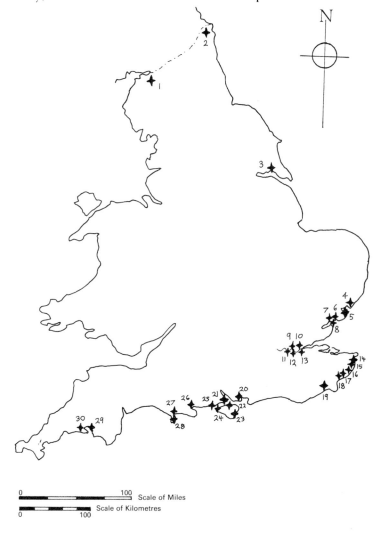

1	Carlisle
2	Berwick
3	Hull
4	Landguard
5	Harwich
6	St Osyth
7	Brightlingsea
8	Mersea
9	West Tilbury
10	East Tilbury
11	Gravesend
12	Milton
13	Higham
14	Sandown
15	Deal
16	Walmer
17	Dover
18	Sandgate
19	Camber
20	Southsea
21	Calshot
22	Cowes
23	Sandown
24	Yarmouth
25	Hurst
26	Brownsea
27	Sandsfoot
28	Portland
29	St Mawes
30	Pendennis

The major coastal fortifications built by Henry VIII to counter the threat posed by a treaty between France and the Holy Roman Empire, signed in 1538.

0   100 Scale of Miles

Scale of Kilometres
0   100

extended and regarrisoned[6]. All the coastal towns that possessed artillery built or repaired their batteries, and extensive and elaborate works of the most up-to-date design were planned for Yarmouth and Weybourne[7]. After the Armada was defeated and the danger dispersed the fortifications were again neglected, although briefly revived in 1597 when a second Armada set sail, only to be scattered by storms.

The story of fortifications in the next forty years was to become a familiar one. The coastal defences were allowed to fall into ruin without any money being spent on maintenance, until the early years of Charles I's reign brought a renewal of the war with Spain. This time the danger was not of invasion but of the continual raids of pirates based at Dunkirk and Ostend who harried the east coast, taking ships in full view of the shore, and causing the coastal towns to petition for forts and guns. The smaller towns were granted cannon on the condition that they provided the ammunition and the men to crew them, but for the principal harbour of the east coast, Orwell Haven, the Crown provided in 1626 a new fort on Landguard Point and a large battery at Harwich.

The Civil War demanded very different strategic arrangements. All the eastern counties declared for Parliament and formed a defensive alliance against the King, the Eastern Association, and took steps to fortify their frontier. Newport Pagnell became a fortified outpost on the boundary with the King's territory; Cambridge and all the crossings of the Fens were fortified[8]; King's Lynn and Yarmouth were surrounded by extensive earthworks, while the other major towns of the region, Norwich, Ipswich and Colchester, made repairs and modifications to their medieval walls. Ironically the only towns in the region to undergo a major siege, King's Lynn and Colchester, were attacked by Parliamentary forces after having declared for the King.

After the Civil War normal strategic conditions were re-established and only coastal defences were necessary. Although the First Dutch War of 1652–54 brought no fear of invasion, increased attacks on coastal shipping forced the maintenance of existing batteries and the construction of a new fort at Yarmouth[9].

The Second Dutch War of 1665–67 ended in near disaster when the premature laying up of the fleet brought the worst invasion scare since the Armada and the best chance of enemy success. A large Dutch fleet sailed up the east coast landing armed parties at will, and eventually attacked Harwich harbour. The Dutch hopes of repeating their success of a few days before, when they sailed up the Medway as far as Chatham and carried off the Royal Navy's flagship, were thwarted by the resistance of the Landguard Fort garrison. After so convincingly justifying its existence,

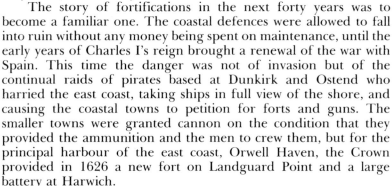

Landguard and all the rest of the forts on the coast slid into decay and ruin. There was a third war with the Dutch in 1672 with the inconclusive battle of Sole Bay, but no invasion threatened and the war quickly ended when public opinion forced Charles II to make peace.

In 1690 with William III fighting James II in Ireland, the French took advantage of England's dispersed naval forces, beat a combined English and Dutch fleet and took command of the Channel. Had Louis XIV had an army ready, a successful invasion could have been launched, but he missed his chance and the most dangerous moment since the Armada passed without incident.

Throughout the eighteenth century government policy on coast defence remained as it had been since the Tudors. Places of strategic importance were secured by works maintained by the Ordnance Office, the government department responsible for artillery and permanent fortifications, while the coastal towns were issued with guns in times of grave emergency but largely left to shift for themselves. The coast was troubled by privateers during the War of the Spanish Succession (1702–13), but British sea power secured the country from invasion as well as maintaining continental armies. Over the next seventy years the French organised four potentially formidable attempts at invasion, once in 1744, again in 1756, once more in 1759 and later in combination with Spain in 1779, when the enemy had sixty-six ships to the British thirty-nine and briefly held command of the sea. All four attempts were foiled by a combination of bad weather, decisive British naval action, and the hestitations and plain ineptitude of the enemy[10]. All these alarms had their effect on the coast defences, the most tangible being the rebuilding and extending of Landguard Fort. No attention whatsoever was given to internal defences, except very briefly during the Jacobite Rebellion of 1745 as the prospect of a rebel army marching on London momentarily alarmed the nation.

The war with the American Colonies broadened into a more serious conflict when France joined the fight against Britain in 1778, Spain in 1779 and the Dutch in 1780. The Royal Navy was outnumbered, its morale and technical proficiency reduced to a low ebb by a combination of neglect and complacency. The Dutch fleet posed a serious threat to the east coast, particularly the stretch between Harwich and Clacton, where it was thought they might land a force to march on London. A more serious threat in the long term was the war waged on British merchant ships in an attempt to cripple Britain's commerce; during the war of 1778–83 three thousand ships were lost, one third of the total[11]. To protect the east coast anchorages from the depredations of privateers and in response to anxious petitions the government provided batteries at

most of the coast towns as well as building camps and fortifications to resist an invasion[12].

In 1793 France declared war on Britain and there began the long series of wars that ended only in 1815 with the final defeat of Napoleon. Once again the east coast was threatened, for France had occupied Holland and all the Austrian Netherlands, making all the Dutch fleets and the ports of the Low Countries available to be used against Britain. The Ordnance Office ordered the coast resurveyed, as a result of which several batteries were built on the Essex coast[13]. The most acute danger came in 1797 when the Navy mutinied and the country was without maritime defence of any sort, while the French planned a triple naval assault upon Britain; themselves forming the centre, the Dutch the right and the Spanish fleet the left. The east coast was most in danger, for the French had decided to embark from the Texel, where they had assembled an army of eighty thousand men who were to sail in the Dutch fleet. The urgent demand for more forts and batteries was to be expected, although few were built before crushing defeats of the Dutch at Camperdown and the Spanish at Cape St Vincent brought relief[14].

After a brief peace, the war was renewed in 1803 and the threat of invasion became greater than ever. Most of Britain's defensive efforts were concentrated on the south coast facing Napoleon's Grand Army camped about Boulogne and the channel

Landguard Fort, Felixstowe, seen in a print of 1753 after an oil painting by Thomas Gainsborough.
Frank Hussey

ports crammed with a huge flotilla of landing craft and transports. There was, however, always the possibility of a diversionary force sailing out of the Dutch ports and landing on the east coast, and to guard against this possibility extra batteries were built from Harwich to Lincolnshire and fieldworks were sited near Chelmsford to block the road to London[15].

The danger of invasion remained, despite Napoleon breaking up the camp at Boulogne and moving the Grand Army eastwards; nor was it completely dispelled by Nelson's victory at Trafalgar. The French continued to make maritime preparations and with their allies could muster 155 ships against Britain's 113, making the prospect of invasion difficult to ignore[16]. Thus the defences continued to be strengthened. A line of martello towers was built in 1809–10 from St Osyth to Aldeburgh as well as a large circular redoubt at Harwich, and when the war ended the east coast had an impressive array of fortifications.

After Waterloo there was little concern about coastal defence for the next twenty years, until a spate of invasion scares prompted by the neglect of the Royal Navy and the introduction of steamships. It was believed in the eighteen-forties that an inferior power with a steam navy could severely jeopardise British commerce and national security. In such circumstances it was easy for trivial issues between France and Britain to be inflated to crisis proportions and "in the absence of compelling reasons for friendship or enmity Britain and France bickered like bored neighbours"[17]. Invasion scares were a novelty and sensational journalists found a fresh source of material to alarm their readers. There was a flood of pamphlets with titles like *The Peril of Portsmouth* and people began to talk of a French landing as something that was to be expected almost as a matter of course[18]. Steam warships, it was claimed, were the weapons that France would use to offset Britain's traditional naval superiority based upon a reserve of thousands of trained merchant seamen. The steamers would prey on British shipping and make sudden raids upon the coast to bombard and loot hapless seaside towns[19]. The natural protection given to the east coast by offshore winds and dangerous shoals was nullified by the greater manoeuvrability of the new steam-powered ships. In 1839 the east coast was surveyed with this particular point in mind and a recommendation was made that existing works should be repaired; additional ones were suggested at King's Lynn, Blakeney and other vulnerable points[20].

These alarms and rumours of war continued throughout the eighteen-forties until the Crimean War of 1854–56. This posed no real threat of invasion as the French were Britain's allies and it was improbable that any Russian ships would break out of the Baltic, but just in case the coast defences were once more put into order.

Above: *A martello tower.*

After this brief interlude of co-operation, Anglo-French relations deteriorated to become as strained as they had been before the war. Napoleon III's protestations of friendship and a mutual exchange of state visits overlaid gloomy predictions of future strife which came to a head in 1859, plunging Britain once more into a defensive crisis. The construction of a squadron of French ironclads, combined with the introduction of rifled artillery, changed the basis of military and naval power far more radically than the French war-steamers of twenty years before. The ironclads, invulnerable to most existing ordnance and armed with rifled guns, cancelled the Royal Navy's numerical superiority, while the increased range and penetrative power of rifled siege guns made all existing fortifications obsolete. The awful prospect loomed of an unassailable invasion force landing and demolishing all defences with contemptuous ease.

In 1858 a Royal Commission was appointed to investigate the defences of the Royal Dockyards and its report recommended the expenditure of eleven million pounds on fortifications to make the dockyards secure[21]. The government embarked on the largest and most extensive programme of fortification ever undertaken, ringing all the major naval ports with powerful land and sea forts, unjustly dubbed "Palmerston's Follies".

After the Franco-Prussian War of 1871 a new naval threat from across the North Sea was noted with some alarm. A contemporary survey noted: "In view of the recent growth of a new Northern naval power and the erection of great dockyards and arsenals at Kiel and Jahde, the latter port only three hundred miles from the mouth of the Thames, the defence of the harbours on the North Sea demands attention"[22].

By the eighteen-eighties most of the guns installed and the forts completed during the previous decade were obsolete, so fast was the onward march of military technology. Whether and how they were replaced depended on the outcome of a controversy that raged at the end of the century between two schools of thought on national defence. The navalists or the blue water school argued that this was a task best left to the Royal Navy and that the scattering of troops and guns about the coast was a waste of resources. On the other hand the militarists claimed that the navy could be lured away or temporarily outnumbered by a combination of hostile fleets, or even that a large force of one hundred to a hundred and fifty thousand men could, given the speed of modern steamers, easily be landed upon the shores of England[23]. These fears were given greater credence in 1888 by alarming revelations of the obsolete nature of the Royal Navy. Lord Wolseley, the commander-in-chief, added to the panic when he publicly stated that if one hundred thousand men were to land they could easily

Above: *The first seagoing ironclad, the French* La Gloire, *laid down at Toulon in 1858.*

8

Seamen manning a 6-pounder quick-firer on board a British warship of about 1900.

capture London[24]. The seacoast towns expressed additional fears of bombardment by armoured cruisers and clamoured for modern guns, unimpressed by the correct but callous naval response that it made little difference to the ultimate safety of the nation if a few seaside boarding houses had their windows broken and tiles cracked.

A compromise was reached by embarking on a fresh programme of coast defence, but resisting the wilder and more extravagant demands of the army. Existing forts were re-equipped with the new breech-loading artillery, if possible, and new batteries were built only if this proved impossible. The debate between the blue water school and the army went on until 1905, when it was effectively settled by Prime Minister Arthur Balfour in the navy's favour. With the *entente cordiale* relations had so improved with France that an invasion from that quarter was not a serious possibility and, providing the navy was efficient, "serious invasion of these islands is not an eventuality which we need to consider"[25].

This pronouncement did not deter authors from filling the bookshops with a stream of books on the subject of the strategic implications and domestic consequences of a German invasion. Between 1901 and the outbreak of the Great War more than forty full-length novels on such a theme were published. It seemed that the public appetite for accounts of enemy armies marching through the Home Counties to subject London to all the horrors of bombardment and pillage was insatiable. The continued expansion of German naval power kept the possibility of raids on the coast alive, but the government continued to reject demands from coastal towns for defences to protect purely local interests. Harwich alone, as a second-class naval base with a resident destroyer flotilla and oil stores, was designated a fortress and its defences kept up to date. New batteries were constructed to defend the Humber, and although many of the Thames forts were greatly reduced in armament replacement batteries were sited downstream to cover the whole estuary.

When the First World War began in 1914 troops were stationed at various points along the coast, but no trenches were dug to avoid alarming the holidaymakers who still thronged the beaches[26]. The hasty and ineffective bombardment of Yarmouth on 3rd November, 1914, only served to prove the navy's point that so long as the Grand Fleet was intact the Germans could do no more than slip across at night and fire a few salvos into an undefended town before scurrying back. It also, however, revived the fear of invasion and trenches were dug at Weybourne, Sheringham and other places along the coast. Early in 1915 a series of trench lines was begun north of London to bar the path of any invading force that might have landed in East Anglia[27].

In 1916 the Admiralty revised its stipulation that the Germans could do no more than launch a nuisance raid, warning that the Germans might land one hundred and sixty thousand men and that such an action might be decisive[28]. These fears were compounded by the inconclusive results of the Battle of Jutland and a second bombardment of Lowestoft. The important question asked was, where would the Germans land if they came? The general staff surmised that if the Germans invaded they would land between the Wash and the Thames, the Wash itself being ruled out; Norfolk was considered possible but unlikely, Essex was safeguarded by the 1st Battle Squadron anchored in the Thames, so the general staff predicted that the defenders of Suffolk would be the first to see the Germans wading through the surf. "The most favourable stretch of coast for the landing of the expedition is considered to be that between Aldeburgh and Lowestoft"[29]. The plan was to hold the coastline with the minimum of troops and, if the invaders penetrated inland, to meet them with vigorous counterstrokes from mobile forces. If these failed, then there were the field fortifications of the London Position to protect the capital, as it was assumed that any German invasion would not be an attempt to subdue the whole country, but simply a direct blow at London to bring about a quick end to the war[30].

After the Armistice all field works were abandoned and most of the permanent coastal batteries were mothballed. The defeat of Germany did not cause any radical reassessment of defence policy, the only new element needing to be considered being the development of aircraft; indeed, there was a proposal in 1921 that the air force should assume the chief responsibility for defence against invasion, but this was soon dropped[31]. The assumption continued to be that the navy would be the first line of defence, with the fixed defences playing a secondary role, while the air force would be required to combat enemy bombers.

Throughout the nineteen-twenties and early nineteen-thirties the coast defences were ignored, and what little money was available was spent on air defence until the rise of Hitler led inevitably to rearmament. In 1934, Germany was named as the "ultimate potential enemy" and the government proposed spending approximately four million pounds on bringing the fixed defences up to standard[32]. But as Germany's surface fleet was so small, and the threat still remote, it was not intended to spend the sum all at once but to complete the work within five years[33]. The risk of invasion was considered so negligible that entries bearing on the evacuation of civilians from threatened areas had been deleted from the Government War Book in 1937[34]. The Munich Crisis of the following year resulted in the first mobilisation of the coast defences since the end of the First World War and the hurrying forward of plans to update and rearm the batteries of the Thames

A large emplacement for a 2-pounder anti-tank gun built at Barton Mills, Suffolk, during the Second World War.

11

and east coast, but little of this had been completed when war broke out.

At first the small German surface fleet posed no serious challenge to either the coast defences or the Royal Navy and it was too valuable to risk in futile bombardments of seaside towns. All thought the only danger was from the air, and there was little reason to fear attacks or landings on the coast. As the war progressed the matter was reconsidered; because of German air attacks the navy was forced to use anchorages on the west coast of Scotland and this, combined with the failure of the air force to bomb German ships at sea, convinced the War Cabinet that control of the North Sea had been lost. With the approach of the long winter nights fears grew that the Germans might attempt to slip a force past the navy and land on the east coast, but the general staff considered the possibility so remote that they refused to keep extra forces in England and merely recommended that the defences of the ports and airfields be strengthened[35].

There was a rapid reassessment in 1940 with the defeat of France, the occupation of the Low Countries and the gathering on the continental shore of a vast, well-organised and victorious German army poised to invade. This was a crisis more alarming than any since the Armada, and the response was frantic. Throughout June and July the whole coast was lined with trenches and various obstacles. Hundreds of pillboxes were constructed, and road blocks sprang up at almost every junction.

In the summer of 1940 the general staff reiterated the belief that a landing on the east coast was more likely than one on the south. Churchill found this difficult to believe. He was greatly interested in the whole process of coast defence tactics and restated the doctrine of the Great War; that the coast itself be held by "sedentary" troops with mobile forces in reserve, knowing that it was impossible to guard all the beaches and that efforts should be concentrated on the most vulnerable sectors[36].

The coast was inspected, as it had been in every previous crisis, and much the same conclusions were reached. Although much of the coast was lined with marsh and cliff, a report warned that "there are few places where determined men could not get ashore and make their way inland"[37].

The commander-in-chief, General Sir Edmund Ironside, devised a defensive strategy that took into account the lack of mobility and poor equipment of the troops that had been saved from Dunkirk. Sir Edmund proposed a static defence in great depth aimed "to prevent the enemy from running riot and tearing the guts out of the country as had happened in France and Belgium"[38]. He planned a strong coastal crust, "putting up a minor Maginot Line along the coast"[39] backed by a series of blocks and

Opposite page: The planned defence lines of 1940. The GHQ Line was intended to protect the industrial Midlands and the vital factories in that region producing war supplies.

12

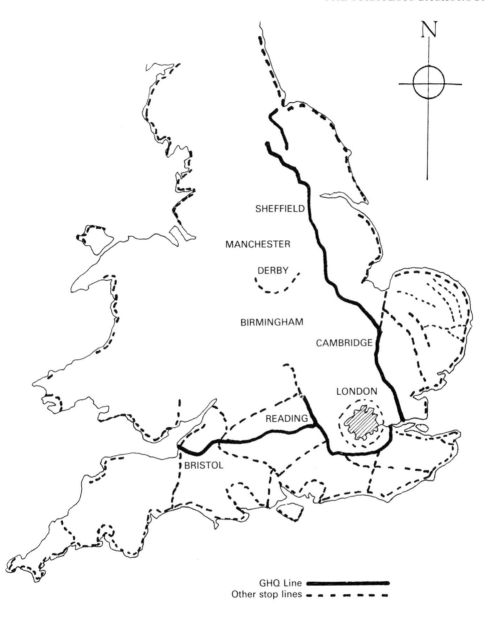

N

SHEFFIELD

MANCHESTER

DERBY

BIRMINGHAM

CAMBRIDGE

LONDON

READING

BRISTOL

GHQ Line ▬▬▬▬▬
Other stop lines ▬ ▬ ▬ ▬ ▬

0   100
        Scale of Miles

        Scale of Kilometres
0   100

13

stop lines, with every town and village a tank-proof island, designed "to restrict all movements in the country and so prevent enemy columns rushing about"[40]. The final defence position was the GHQ Line, a continuous position formed of pillboxes and anti-tank obstacles that ran from Canvey Island to Cambridge and then across the Fens into Lincolnshire, designed to protect London and the industrial Midlands. Between this and the coast were several additional defensive positions.

Much of this work was under way when Sir Edmund was abruptly replaced by General Sir Alan Brooke, who immediately abandoned much of his predecessor's system of static defence, ordering that all work on the stop lines should cease except that necessary to create nodal points for all-round defence at important road junctions. The failure of the Luftwaffe to subdue the RAF and vigorous British attacks on the assembling German invasion fleet caused Hitler to abandon the invasion in 1940. In January the next year he ordered that all preparations for "Operation Sealion" should be stopped.

New coastal batteries and defence works continued to be added throughout 1941, but once Hitler had invaded Russia and the USA had entered the war the prospect of invasion looked increasingly remote. As early as 1942 the coast defences were reduced when a number of beach batteries were closed down and others handed over to the Home Guard[41].

To counter air raids on all the principal towns of the region many batteries of anti-aircraft guns were installed. There was a formidable concentration along the Thames and to the north of London, but apart from hit and run raids on the coast German bombers were rarely seen after 1943. In 1944 AA Command was forced to move large numbers of guns to the coast to form what was known as the Diver Strip running from the Thames to Yarmouth to deal with V1 flying bombs launched from Holland and Belgium[42].

Until the end of the war the coastal defences were maintained but only a few batteries were manned. Work began on clearing the beaches before the German surrender, and as soon as the war in Europe was over the whole system was quickly dismantled. Some permanent batteries were retained, and with the advent of the Cold War were brought back into a state of operational readiness. The 6-pounder guns at Landguard Fort were adapted to be used in an anti-aircraft role, but it was a futile gesture because the political and technological changes brought by the war had made fixed defences increasingly redundant. In 1956 the coast artillery was abolished, the remaining guns scrapped and the forts abandoned. Coast defence, in a form that would have been comprehensible to Henry VIII's "sad and expert men", had ended for ever.

Tactics and Techniques 2

T HE FIRST cannon, a small tube of iron clumsily strapped to a baulk of wood, might not have looked very threatening compared with trebuchet, siege tower, mangonel and battering ram, but it drastically changed traditional ways of building castles. All the barbicans, machicolations, crenellations and towering turrets, all the ingenuity of the medieval military engineer, became obsolete.

Medieval guns had many faults: they were slow to load and aim and often proved as lethal to their operators as to their targets; but they were better than catapults and they had almost limitless potential for development, while the medieval siege engine had reached the furthest point to which contemporary mechanics and materials could take it. First introduced into warfare in the middle of the fourteenth century, early guns posed no immediate threat to castles and town walls. Castles and cannon existed together for many years and some castles, with only minor modifications, remained as effective strongholds to the very end of the age of artillery. But by the fourteen-eighties artillery had developed sufficiently to make it obvious that the art of fortification as it had been practised for centuries was outmoded.

Several factors contributed to the increased effectiveness of artillery. Stone cannonballs were replaced by cast-iron ones, resulting in a huge increase in penetrative power. Gunpowder was mixed with greater skill and consistency and cannon were cast with trunnions, enabling stronger and more manoeuvrable carriages to be built. Along with these technical improvements came tactical innovation. Commanders were learning how to use their guns more effectively, to concentrate the fire of many pieces and to train increasingly efficient crews.

At first fortifications were slow to respond both in new ways of accommodating artillery and in resisting it. The first signs of any modifications were embrasures specifically designed for handguns; these appeared towards the end of the fourteenth century. These gunports were either simple round holes or ones with a siting slit above, although some of the earliest were hardly distinguishable from ordinary cross-bow slits[1].

A fifteenth-century wrought-iron peterera, showing the removable breech-piece. Guns of this kind were often provided with several chambers to speed up the rate of fire.

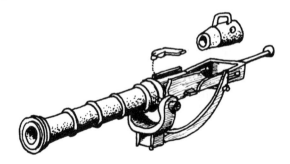

On the Continent, where the scale of warfare was so much greater than in Britain, defensive development began much earlier and the results were much more elaborate and extensive. The first response of engineers to the growing power of cannon was simply to thicken the walls. If six feet would not stop a cannonball, then it was increased to twelve and then to twenty-four. By the sixteenth century enormous thicknesses of wall had been reached, but merely increasing the mass of the structure did not increase its effectiveness in comparable proportions. The gargantuan masonry curtain wall was both extremely expensive and tactically constricting.

A very thick wall would be weakened by having too many gunports and, unless the outer opening of the ports was to be dangerously large, the lateral training of the gun would be greatly limited. Another problem was the nature of stone itself; it was not only expensive, heavy and difficult to work but was lethal when smashed into splinters by striking shot. Apart from the difficulties of making fortifications resistant in a material sense, there was the problem of how to mount artillery successfully to counter the batteries of the besieger and to defend the walls from assault. The towers of the medieval town or castle were too narrow to mount cannon as these grew from simple handguns, and therefore it proved impossible to protect the wall with flanking fire.

Three gunports from the fourteenth and fifteenth centuries. The smallness of the lower aperture indicates the small size of early medieval guns. The slits above were for sighting and for the use of bowmen.

Gradually throughout Europe solutions to these taxing problems began to take shape. The first move was to make the curtain wall less vulnerable. A high wall proved an easy target to artillery but a low one, although less conspicuous a target, was also less of an obstacle. Sufficient passive defence could be provided by a wide, deep ditch that was flanked from the walls and towers of the fortress. The search for new solutions created two distinct schools of fortification, one in north-west Europe and the other in Italy. The north-western school, one of whose most influential theorists was the German artist Albrecht Dürer, favoured rounded bastions with splayed embrasures to flank the ditch and relied on massive construction to resist attack.

16

The first major artillery forts to be built in England followed this trend. Deal and Walmer Castles and most of the important coastal forts built by Henry VIII were tall in profile with hollow, rounded and symmetrical forms. Although this appears to signify contemporary continental influence, and a Moravian engineer, Stephen Von Haschenberg, is known to have "devised" Sandgate and Camber Castles, the Henrician style seems to have been a development of the cylindrical artillery towers found in northern France and at Portsmouth, Dover and Camber. Contemporary Italian fortresses were adopting much lower profiles and more angular forms, but Henry and his advisers would have been largely unaware of this and, in any case, rounded forms of high profile were suited to the task of coastal defence[2].

As well as these major forts a number of smaller and simpler blockhouses were built where the importance of the location to be defended did not warrant anything larger. These were gun towers of no great sophistication with cannon firing through splayed letterbox embrasures. None of the great forts were built in East Anglia, but several of the blockhouses were sited on the Thames and about Harwich. A third variety of works designed for artillery were simple earthwork batteries consisting of a platform for the guns and a low parapet revetted with gabions or planks. These could only be regarded as semi-permanent works, cheap and easy to build but extremely difficult to keep in order without regular maintenance.

However sophisticated and intricate Henry VIII's coastal forts might have been, they were an offshoot of the main stem of the developing science of fortification. It was in Italy that lasting innovations were made and the basis of the geometric system laid

The German artist Albrecht Dürer published the first book on fortification in north-west Europe at Nuremberg in 1527. He advocated the use not of the angle bastions that were developing in Germany but of massive, squat gun towers or "roundels". Largely ignored in Germany, his ideas found their expression in the coastal forts of Henry VIII which closely parallel his designs in all aspects except size. Above is a small artillery blockhouse which can be seen as the precursor of Henry's later castles.

17

down. The major contribution of the Italians was the invention of the bastion, an arrowhead-shaped projection from the wall that could, if placed correctly, enfilade both the curtain wall and the face of the adjoining bastion, leaving no dead ground at all. This unique and ubiquitous defensive device was to dominate military architecture until the mid-nineteenth century.

By the middle of the sixteenth century the bastion had evolved into a form that was to endure until the end of the century. The angle of the salient was acute, the flanks recessed and protected by rounded shoulders or orillons, the purpose of which was to protect the cannon mounted in the chambers overlooking the ditch from hostile fire. Common in Italy by the fifteen-thirties, bastions arrived in England before the middle of the century. The first bastion to be built in England was added to the town wall of Portsmouth in 1547, with another at Yarmouth Castle on the Isle of Wight[3]. All subsequent works in England were built on the new Italian system. The most substantial were those at Berwick-on-Tweed designed by Sir Richard Lee, the foremost English military engineer, but with the assistance of two Italians, Giovanni Portinari and Jacopo Contio, who seem to have to have built nothing on their own account but to have acted only as consultants[4]. By the time of the Armada there was a small body of competent English engineers who produced many designs that displayed a good deal of technical assurance. The proposed fortifications at Weybourne in north Norfolk, designed by Captain Edmund Yorke, were as advanced as any to be seen in Europe.

The accumulated experience of nearly eighty years of siege warfare passed the lead in fortifications to the Dutch in the seventeenth century. The main features of their style were low earth ramparts, very broad wet ditches, a strong covered way and the extension of the fausse-braye into an independent low parapet at the foot of the counterscarp. Dutch engineers were consulted and sometimes designed English forts; John Cranvelt was specially hired from Holland to design the new fort at Landguard Point in 1626[5]. Most of the works built in the Civil War were on Dutch principles and the few that were not resulted from ignorance or the need to adapt existing defences quickly. King's Lynn and Great Yarmouth were both enclosed by bastioned enceintes and two well-engineered detached forts were sited in Huntingdonshire. The "bulwark" at Earith was an almost textbook example with fausse-braye, covered way and a small ditch at the foot of the glacis, all impeccably Dutch[6].

The great influence of the later seventeenth century and the man whose name has become synonymous with elaborate and extended fortifications was Sébastien Le Prestre Vauban. Born in 1633, he spent the whole of his life in building or besieging fortresses. More than one hundred and sixty strongpoints built to his design studded the borders of France, and although he introduced practically no new ideas he used the complex structural vocabulary of military engineering with unprecedented fluency. The main feature of his style was to put as many lines of defence as possible between the main rampart and the enemy and to ensure that every part of the ditch was swept by defensive fire. Although the basic outline, or trace, of the fortress was still that of a wall flanked by bastions, a varied collection of outworks was placed in

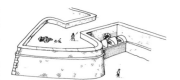

Above is an angle bastion typical of those built throughout Europe in the sixteenth century. The face of the adjoining curtain walls is covered by recessed flanking gun emplacements protected from frontal fire by orillons. Below is a section through a bastioned fortification.

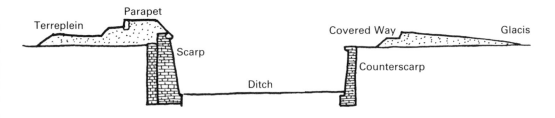

Above: *Where a larger and more expensive stone work was unnecessary earthwork batteries revetted with gabions or planks were erected. Without constant maintenance—a rare commodity in the sixteenth century—they soon reverted to shapeless heaps.*

Below: *A section through a fortification of the Dutch school.*

front; ravelins, lunettes, tenailles, hornworks and redans, all designed to deepen the defence. The only fort in eastern England that remotely approached this complexity was the new work at Tilbury, built in 1685 to supplant the old Tudor blockhouse, but Tilbury owes far more to the Dutch school than to Vauban and, despite its double ditch and ravelins, was really of quite a simple trace.

Fortifications became simpler in the eighteenth century, and while permanent forts still held to the bastioned system, field works could adopt more free forms and tended to dispense with the more elaborate methods of obtaining flanking fire. Coastal batteries were much as they had been in Elizabethan times: simple parapets with sometimes a ditch and palisade for local defence. One result of the American War of Independence was the use of timber blockhouses to guard the entrance and to act as a sort of keep.

A new solution to the problem of making coastal batteries easily defensible was adopted during the Napoleonic Wars. All along the south and east coasts as well as in Ireland and the

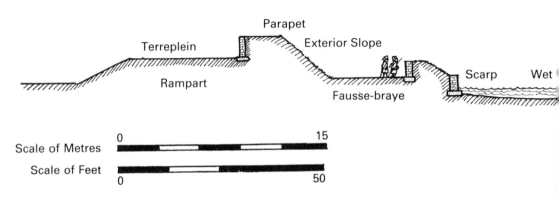

Terreplein · Parapet · Exterior Slope · Rampart · Fausse-braye · Scarp · Wet

Scale of Metres   0   15
Scale of Feet   0   50

A plan of a bastioned fortification with outworks, designed to put as many lines of defence as possible between the main rampart and the enemy and to ensure that every part of the ditch was swept by defensive fire.

a – Bastion
b – Ravelin
c – Counter-guard
d – Hornwork
e – Place-of-Arms
f – Covered Way
g – Glacis

Channel Isles masonry or brick gun towers were built to cover beaches and inlets. At first sight the martello tower seems to revert to older medieval models by abandoning the low profile of the earthwork battery, but engineers gave convincing reasons for its adoption. The first was the example of a small tower on the island of Corsica which, although mounting only three guns, had repulsed two British men-of-war with a total of 106 guns[7]. This seemed to prove the point that a ship rolling at sea could never concentrate enough of its broadside to breach a masonry wall, while the guns in the tower could easily be protected from landing parties with the absolute minimum of troops. In 1798 it was proposed to build gun-towers along the east coast, although it was not until 1808 that work began to build them[8].

The east coast towers were of a different design from those along the south coast, being larger and mounting more guns. They were built of brick covered in stucco and of two stories, the basement for stores and ammunition, the upper floor as accommodation for thirty men, with two staircases built into the thickness

21

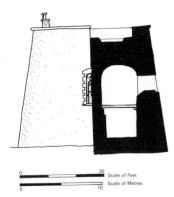

Scale of Feet
Scale of Metres

Plan and elevation of an east coast martello tower. Note how the axes of the tower are struck so as to increase the thickness of the wall on the seaward side.

Scale of Feet
Scale of Metres

of the walls. The tower was entered through a door on the first floor which was reached either by a ladder or, if the tower had a moat, by a narrow drawbridge. To ensure that the seaward wall was thicker than that on the landside an ingenious piece of construction was adopted: the towers were ovoid in shape with the inner and outer circles of the walls struck eccentrically so that the wall was thirteen feet thick facing the sea and only five facing the land[9]. The guns, normally three 24-pounders mounted on traversing carriages to gain maximum arcs of fire, were installed on the roof within a parapet shaped like a four-leafed clover.

In the mid-nineteenth century a new school of fortification developed in Germany, largely supplanting the bastion and becoming known as the Polygonal System. Its main innovatory feature was the abandonment of the bastion and its expensive and inflexible geometry and its replacement by a simpler method of flanking the ditch by caponiers or galleries built into the counterscarp wall. Although neither of these was a new feature—the rebuilt Landguard Fort of 1716 had both—they were adopted enthusiastically by English engineers.

The development of rifled artillery in the eighteen-fifties completely changed the whole technique of fortification. Guns could fire heavier projectiles further and with greater force at forts that were powerless to resist them. Coastal defences had the additional problem of needing to mount ever-larger guns to deal with ironclad warships, but the rate of fire of rifled muzzle-loading artillery was so slow that it was necessary to concentrate large numbers of guns to make sure of effectively blocking a channel. The cheapest way of installing artillery was in a barbette battery, but unless this was placed at some height above the water it was thought that the guns would be dangerously exposed[10]. The solution was a casemated fort with the guns firing through embrasures in its massive front wall. Such forts were built at all low-lying situations where heavy guns needed to be concentrated and where the attack could be expected to be by major warships.

These were the forts so characteristic of the defences built as a result of the *Report of the Commissioners Appointed to Investigate the Defence of the Dockyards.* The typical form was a row of arched casemates with the wide openings closed with wrought-iron shields fifteen inches thick. Magazines lay beneath the casemates, to which they were connected by mechanical shell hoists. All such forts had barracks and rear walls equipped for defence to protect them against seizure by landing parties. They were the last self-contained masonry forts to be built, the last of a tradition reaching back through Henry VIII to the Norman keeps of the eleventh century. Such forts combined the latest features of the industrial age, shell hoists and monster artillery mounted on intricate, finely

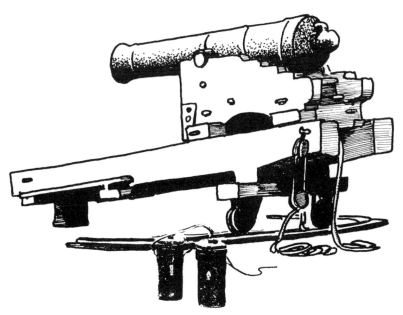

A 32-pounder smooth-bore on a traversing carriage. Guns mounted on the martello towers were on such carriages.

engineered carriages, with medieval devices like drawbridges, machicolations and murdering holes. They were expensive: one iron shield alone cost fifteen hundred pounds, and a complete fort, exclusive of armament, could cost up to a quarter of a million pounds[11]. East Anglia has two of this type: Coalhouse Fort on the Thames and the rebuilt Landguard Fort.

These were thought at the time to be the very last word in coastal fortification, but the ever-accelerating development of ships and guns reduced most of them to obsolescence before they were

The massive casemates of Landguard Fort, seen in an engraving of 1888. The wide openings for the guns were closed with wrought-iron shields fifteen inches thick.

An 8-inch breech-loading gun on a hydro-pneumatic mounting, raised in the firing position.

finished. When Coalhouse Fort was designed the largest gun in British service was the 68-pounder smooth bore; by the time it was complete there was a giant 17.72-inch RML that fired a two-thousand-pound shell. In 1882 the army converted to breech-loading guns which were both easier to work and even more powerful than the previous RMLs; both ranges and rates of fire were dramatically increased, with profound effects on the design of the next generation of forts. Longer ranges and the ability to fire faster resulted in fewer guns being needed to cover a given area. One direct result of this was a marked reduction in armaments; Harwich in 1880 had a total of thirty-two heavy guns which was reduced to twenty-one in 1900 and to eight in 1914.

The batteries for breech-loading guns were as unlike the casemate forts as it was possible to be. The longer range that the enemy ship would be firing from made the chances of hitting an individual coast gun impossibly remote, so they no longer needed the elaborate protection of casemates and armoured shields. A gun end-on provided a target of only some thirty feet square, but just in

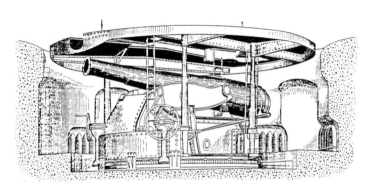

The same gun lowered for loading. The gun detachment was almost completely protected by the armoured overhead shield.

case even this minute target was too conspicuous the early breech-loaders were mounted on disappearing carriages. The gun was loaded within a pit protected by a thick concrete apron, rising only to fire before sinking down behind the parapet to be reloaded. Their only disadvantage was a slow rate of fire, although much faster than an old RML, and a range limited by their restricted elevation. By 1900 a new generation of barbette mounts had been developed that lasted, with a few minor modifications, until the end of coastal artillery.

The batteries designed for the new guns were no longer recognisable as buildings. The gun stood in a concrete emplacement that housed the hydraulic machinery to control the recoil, traverse and elevation. The magazines were underneath and covered by several feet of concrete and earth. All that could be seen from the seaward side was the low mound of the parapet and the shield of the gun. Great pains were taken to make the surroundings as natural as possible and to break up any harsh outlines. Bushes and small trees were planted behind the guns, the concrete aprons were painted and even flagpoles were hinged.

Equally revolutionary was the change in the arrangements for land defence. The development of the machine-gun and quick-firing magazine rifle convinced engineers that the deep ditches and elaborate devices to provide flanking fire could be dispensed with. The garrison was to rely on the volume of their frontal fire alone to stop an infantry assault. The traditional ditch and counterscarp

A section of a Twydall profile, a development which followed the introduction of the magazine rifle and the machine-gun.

was replaced by what was known as the Twydall Profile after an experimental redoubt constructed at Twydall near Chatham to the designs of Sir George Clarke[12]. The ground in front of the battery sloped gently forward to the bottom of a shallow depression in which was placed a spiked steel fence. The only buildings were shelters for the men and stores built under the parapet, the strength of the work lying in its ability to blend in with the landscape and its use of the minimum of exposed masonry. The coast batteries at Beacon Hill, Harwich, and East Tilbury and the redoubt at North Weald were all built on these economical principles.

In the twentieth century British engineers almost abandoned the idea of permanent land fortifications altogether. The experi-

25

ence of the Boer War reinforced the growing prejudice against elaborate works, and the conviction grew that simple trenches and barbed wire were an adequate defence. The opening shots of the Great War demonstrated the weakness of concrete and armoured land forts against heavy siege guns. The resilience of trench systems to bombardment and assault confirmed military engineers in their prejudice against permanent forts until the impressive resistance of German concrete machine-gun emplacements on the Western Front changed their minds. In 1916 the first British pill-boxes were built along the east coast. They were circular with an overhanging roof that made them look exactly like their namesakes. Their walls were thin and the most they offered their garrisons was protection against bullets and blast; later versions were hexagonal and a good deal stronger. The building material was always concrete, sometimes poured, sometimes in blocks, and most were provided with steel doors, a refinement that their successors in the Second World War rarely had.

Between the wars the French, Germans and Czechs built

A First World War pillbox at East Lane, Bawdsey, on the Suffolk coast. The resemblance to the old-fashioned cardboard pill box with its overlapped cap is apparent. At the rear is the battery observation post of a 6-inch battery dating from 1940.

extensive fortified lines of mutually supporting bunkers and underground forts, but British engineers had little reason to emulate them. As far as they were concerned permanent fortification was a lost art, but one which had to be rapidly rediscovered in 1940. The first priority was to install heavy guns to cover the beaches, and a large number of emergency gun batteries were quickly sited along the coast. The normal armament was two 6-inch ex-naval guns which had lain in armament depots since the wholescale scrappings of the nineteen-twenties. Most were well over twenty-five years old, with worn barrels and limited stocks of ammunition. They were bolted to a plate fixed in a large slab of concrete and protected by makeshift casemates of sandbags on a structure of steel girders. As time allowed the battery structures were reconstructed in brick and concrete, and all later batteries were permanent from the start. Although no two were exactly alike they all conformed to a general pattern. The two 6-inch guns were mounted in a brick casemate about thirty feet wide designed to give protection against strafing from the air but not against anything heavier. Between the gun shelters was a long, partially-buried structure containing the magazines and shelters for the crew. There were no mechanical hoists as in pre-war batteries; shells and cartridges were hauled by hand or on small trolleys. The rangefinder and fire-control equipment were placed in a tower behind. Each battery had two searchlights powered by diesel generators and the whole site was surrounded by trenches, wire, and one or two pillboxes.

The batteries for the smaller guns, 4.7-inch, 4-inch and 12-pounders, were similar but on a smaller scale. A few emergency batteries were built to mount land service guns which had a higher angle of elevation and a longer range, but the only difference was in the more substantial emplacement to take the more complex mounting.

The most widely-built fortifications of the war were pillboxes, which appeared in a bewildering variety of shapes, sizes and materials. The basic designs were formulated by the War Office but local conditions caused numerous adaptations and hybrids[13]. The standard was a small hexagon built of reinforced concrete with walls eighteen inches thick. Where timber was in short supply, brick was used as an outer and inner skin to replace shuttering. Some had doors, but most had nothing more than a blast wall covering the entrance and an anti-ricochet wall inside. Larger hexagonal and octagonal pillboxes often had a central well where a light machine-gun could be mounted in an anti-aircraft role.

Square and rectangular pillboxes were built in large numbers as well, the most common of the former having a single large embrasure for a heavy machine-gun; such a pillbox was normally

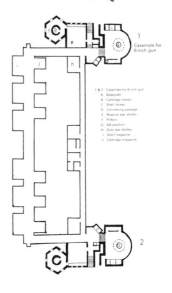

1 Casemate for 6-inch gun

1 & 2 Casemate for 6-inch gun
A Baseplate
B Cartridge recess
C Shell recess
D Connecting passage
E Reserve war shelter
F Pillbox
G AA position
H Duty war shelter
I Shell magazine
J Cartridge magazine

2

Above: *The ground plan of a typical emergency battery of 1940–42, with two 6-inch guns in casemates and a long partially-buried structure between them containing magazines and shelters.*

27

Above: *A 6-inch Mk VII gun on a central pivot mounting as installed in coastal batteries.*

Opposite page: *A Broads windpump at Ludham Bridge loopholed and internally strengthened to make an unobtrusive strongpoint. In the foreground is the mounting for a spigot mortar.*

Below: *A heavy machine-gun emplacement overlooking Salthouse, on the North Norfolk coast.*

placed to enfilade the site it was covering. The largest of the rectangular types was designed to take a 2-pounder anti-tank gun; this kind was sited only in the more important positions such as the GHQ line and particularly important beaches and junctions.

By 1941 it was realised that the hexagonal pillbox with all-round embrasures and eighteen-inch-thick walls was useless against anything other than rifle fire: "What may be called the sieve type pillbox is nothing more than a deathtrap"[14]. Later designs were therefore square, with three-foot-thick walls and a minimum of embrasures, wherever possible with a six-foot wall on the side facing the enemy. This, however, posed the problem of having either a smaller field of fire or a dangerously large opening.

As well as the conventional pillboxes of orthodox shape there were a large number of more bizarre alternatives, often produced by firms specialising in prefabricated building components. The "Norcon" was nothing more than a ten-foot diameter concrete pipe pierced with six loopholes, its light weight prompting one proposal to use it lorry-mounted as a mobile defence of airfields[15]. The Tett Turret was a concrete rotating cupola with accommodation for two men, and the Alan-Williams steel turret had mountings for most light machine-guns in either an anti-aircraft or ground role. Oddest of all was the Picket-Hamilton counter-balance fort, a small circular pillbox designed for airfield defence that popped up out of the ground. Its purpose was to cover the landing grounds without

Right: *A Norcon pillbox at Kelling Hard, in North Norfolk.*

Below: *The Tett Turret, produced by a Surrey building firm, consisted of a small concrete revolving cupola mounted on a four-foot diameter pipe. Its low profile, 13 inches, was an advantage, nullified by the cramped conditions for its two-man garrison and by its unfortunate liability to flooding.*

getting in the way of the planes, and although expensive at about two hundred and fifty pounds, it was installed at several airfields in East Anglia and seemed to work satisfactorily, although the pillbox crews expressed uneasiness about the hydraulic machinery failing and the whole thing telescoping with them inside. Another of the Picket-Hamilton's problems was the visibility of the small white circles of the roofs from the air, and it was seriously suggested that instead of trying to camouflage them the best course was to paint dozens of false white spots all over the airfield[16].

Besides these authorised designs there were numerous local variations and adaptations, barns, houses and windmills being modified by strengthening with concrete or simply by inserting loopholes; many ordinary walls were pierced with loopholes to cover road junctions.

By 1941 the building of all pillboxes, even new improved designs, had been abandoned. The War Office stated that "all experience of modern war points most strongly to the fact that the pillbox is not a suitable type of fortification for either coastal or nodal point defences" and all defensive positions in future were to rely on earthworks[17].

All these strongpoints and pillboxes were active defences with the capacity to mount weapons which could engage the enemy, but to supplement them all kinds of obstacles were erected to prevent an attacker, and particularly tanks, from getting too close. The seashore was lined with a fence of scaffolding and steel rails set at an angle to rip out the bottom of a landing craft. Anti-tank obstacles both on the coast and inland were mainly concrete blocks,

Right: *An Alan-Williams steel turret at Cley, Norfolk. Brackets were provided for Bren and Lewis machine-guns and the Boys anti-tank rifle.*

Below: *The most common type of hexagonal pillbox was based on drawings issued by the Directorate of Fortifications and designated FW3/22. The finish and details varied slightly according to the materials available. In this case the brick skin that took the place of timber shuttering has been removed to reveal the rough concrete.*

although steel rails were used extensively and V-sectioned ditches were dug across open country.

The anti-aircraft defence of the country resulted in the building of hundreds of emplacements to mount the three types of guns, 3.7-inch, 4.5-inch and 5.25-inch. All these needed extensive installations, with protective pits for the guns, a command centre with communication rooms, and platforms for predictors, range and height finders. The basic gun pit for both 3.7 and 4.5-inch guns was an octagonal pit with blast walls of concrete some five feet high, with built-in ammunition bays protected by steel doors. The 5.25-inch emplacements were much more like coast artillery positions, with a deep pit into which fitted the complex pedestal with its hydraulics, and an adjacent underground magazine. These were installed from 1943 onwards and were the last fixed defences to be built in Britain.

After the war the Royal Engineers continued to plan the next generation of coastal fortifications. Influenced by the massive German installations of the Atlantic Wall and by the knowledge that heavy bombs could be dropped with ever-increasing accuracy, they came up with suitably gargantuan solutions. A subterranean bunker with walls and roof many feet thick was to mount a turret armed with either three 16-inch, two 9.2-inch, three 6-inch or two 6-pounders according to location. The Committee on Coast Defence noted that "the final decision as to the type of emplacement recommended may well be a permanent memorial of the wisdom or foolishness of the present generation of sappers"[18]. As it was, they decided not to enter a race for protection against atomic bombs and guided missiles, and permanent fortification as practised by British engineers finally came to an end.

Two varieties of anti-tank obstacle near Holkham, Norfolk, one a massive cube of concrete and the other made of steel rail.

Tilbury and the Thames

3

$\mathbf{A}$LTHOUGH it is fifty miles from Shoeburyness to the Pool of London, the first place where the Thames could be defended with early artillery was at Tilbury and Gravesend, where the river narrows to only half a mile wide. This site was made doubly important in the sixteenth century by the ferry that plied between the Kent and Essex banks, a communications link of vital commercial and strategic importance, and by the need to protect the new Royal dockyards at Deptford and Woolwich[1].

In 1539, as part of Henry VIII's general scheme of coast defence, five blockhouses were planned for the Essex and Kent banks of the Thames, the two at West and East Tilbury being designed to cross their fire with those on the opposite bank. Work began on the blockhouses the same year that Thomas Cromwell revealed the plans, a clear indication of the vital importance of the site[2]. They were designed by James Nedeham, the Surveyor of the King's Works, and the work of construction went quickly ahead. The King himself was conveyed by Royal barge to the site in May, 1539, for a tour of inspection[3].

The completed blockhouse at West Tilbury, armed and garrisoned the following year, was a small, brick D-shaped tower with the rounded front facing the river, surrounded on the land side by a simple rampart and ditch, with an earthwork battery at the water's edge[4]. The armament was small, about five guns, with extra pieces mounted in the battery outside. East Tilbury was probably an earthwork, like those at Mersea and Harwich. More work was carried out in 1546 and during the reign of Edward VI, until in 1553 both East and West Tilbury were disarmed on the orders of the Duke of Northumberland[5]. West Tilbury was rearmed and regarrisoned shortly afterwards, but it is doubtful whether East Tilbury was ever recommissioned[6].

The small West Tilbury blockhouse had little maintenance until 1583, when one hundred pounds was allocated for some long-overdue repairs, but the money was ill spent or inadequate, as became clear four years later when it was revealed to be in a state of great disrepair[7]. West Tilbury was reported to be "further out of order than the other [Gravesend] save that there be better pieces of artillery, but not one platform to carry the least piece"[8]. The Earl

A conjectural view of the blockhouse at West Tilbury in its usual state of dilapidation. Below is a plan of the blockhouse.

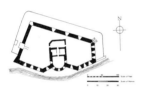

of Leicester, commander of the field army, arrived in July, 1588, and was dismayed by the state of the fortifications; although work had already been started on much-needed repairs, more was necessary. Leicester reported to the Privy Council that he needed workmen and materials to get "the forts in as good strength as time would permit"[9]. The main priority was to find timber to build platforms for the artillery, and three additional batteries were sited upriver at Grays and Purfleet to supplement Tilbury and to extend the zone of fire[10].

Tilbury was particularly important as the main camp for the army responsible for the defence of London, its choice an indication of the strategic importance of the ferry which would allow the army to counter a landing either to the north or the south of the Thames with almost equal speed. Work began on building a boom, made of great timbers and ships' masts linked with chains and supported on barges, to block the river, but as soon as it was strung out on the water it broke under its own massive weight[11].

By 8th August the situation had changed: the Armada was in flight and the danger of invasion had receded rapidly. It was on that day that the camp about Tilbury blockhouse was visited by Queen Elizabeth, arriving in the Royal barge as her father had done at the fort's building, and then riding upon a white horse wearing a glittering breastplate and crown to review her army of rustic soldiers. She brandished a miniature sword and made the most stirring speech of her reign before dismissing the army to gather in the harvest[12].

34

The extent of the Spanish defeat was not immediately appreciated; it was anticipated that the threat of invasion might recur the next year and it was advised that the still-incomplete defences of the Thames "must now be looked to"[13]. The work on the defences about Tilbury continued, strengthening the block-house and surrounding it with an additional rampart and ditch. The engineer chosen to carry out this scheme was an Italian refugee from the Spanish Netherlands, Frederico Genibelli, famed for his huge floating bomb—a ship loaded with tons of gunpowder, larded with marble tombstones—which he sailed down the River Scheldt to shatter the great bridge and barrier with which the Duke of Parma was slowly throttling the port of Antwerp. The bomb was a thunderous success but Antwerp was eventually forced to capitulate, Genibelli escaping, his reputation reverberating as loudly as his bomb, and being promptly invited to England to carry on the struggle[14]. Assisted by Thomas Bedwell and three hundred labourers, Genibelli built a new enceinte about the fort and renovated the rampart and ditch that already surrounded the blockhouse tower[15].

When the coastal defences were examined in 1620 Tilbury was in a desperate condition, the guns lying on the ground, all the platforms rotten and the ramparts virtually demolished. "This fort hath formerly been encompassed with a fair fortification as rampart, parapet, moat and counterscarp and without all this a

The defences of the Thames in 1588.

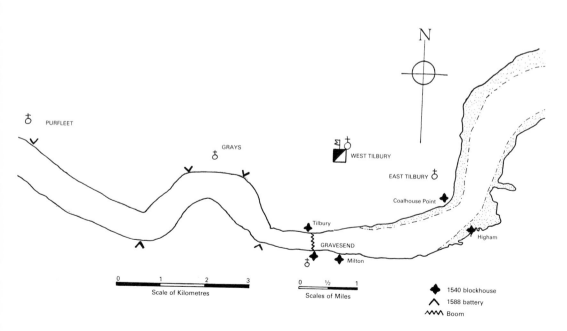

large rentrenchment for the better security of the same; all of which for want of timely reparations are now demolished, filled up and made even with the commons adjoining"[16]. Three years later the blockhouse was again surveyed and nearly four hundred pounds of repairs ordered, although all that appears to have been done was to provide some new gun carriages[17].

In 1630 the still near-derelict fortification was visited by the King's military engineer, Lieutenant-Colonel Paperill, who, after a thorough examination, recommended repairs costing over £1,200[18]. Despite this the advancing dereliction went unchecked, and in 1634 the platforms were once again quite rotten and "utterly decayed"[19]. A ferry house within the walls caused much annoyance to the garrison, and the river battery's parapet was so low and eroded that at high tide, the most likely time for an enemy to try to force the passage, the battery was flooded and the guns could not be used[20].

The responsibility for this neglect lay with the Crown and with the officers it had appointed. In 1632 the captain of the fort, Carew Saunders, was ordered to be removed on the grounds of his total and utter incompetence. Saunders was not even a soldier; he was a London merchant and shopkeeper who had taken on the captaincy, worth some ten pounds a year, as a source of income,

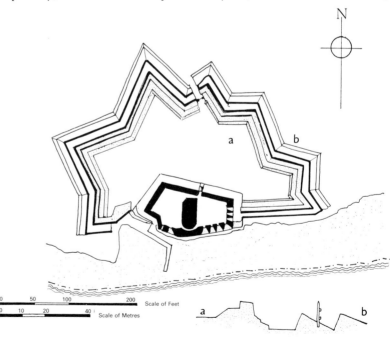

Frederico Genibelli's additional enceinte to the blockhouse at Tilbury, constructed to counter any repetition of the Spanish threat after the defeat of the Armada.

0   50   100   200 Scale of Feet
0 10 20 40 Scale of Metres

a   b

Section

regarding it as he might have done a new haberdashery counter, with no idea of any obligations as to the efficient running and maintenance of the fort. The only battle he ever fought was a tenacious legal one to hang on to his source of income. He was eventually removed and replaced by a Captain Talbot who had fought at Cadiz and La Rochelle and was authorised to fight Saunders at Tilbury, if necessary, to obtain possession[21].

During the Civil War Tilbury Blockhouse played a quiet but important part. Occupied by Parliament, it served as a checkpoint where all ships sailing up the Thames to London were examined. Its maintenance was the responsibility of the Essex Committee, which soon proved as inefficient and negligent as the Crown had been. James Temple, the captain, complained in 1643 that he had spent ten months trying to get funds to repair his fort, "which of all places concerns the City and the Kingdom"[22]. The Committee was free with promises, but little was done until eventually the blockhouse and its attendant earthworks were repaired in 1650, the cost being met from the sequestered estates of Essex royalists[23].

With the restoration of the monarchy in 1660, Charles II began a complete reorganisation of coastal defences, ordering his chief engineer, Sir Bernard de Gomme, to make a survey and draw up plans for a new fort[24]. In 1665 de Gomme proposed a large work to be built around the old blockhouse, with a rampart, double ditch and elaborately defended covered way to defend the landward side. The defence of the river, which was the main purpose of the fort, was left to the old works[25].

Above: *Sir Bernard de Gomme's first design for the new fort at Tilbury, dated 1665.*

Nothing was done for two years, until the Dutch fleet frightened the Ordnance Board into action by sailing into the Thames in search of prizes and reaching Lower Hope Point, only a few miles below Tilbury[26]. Urgent orders were given to put Tilbury into an efficient state of defence and more than eighty guns were shipped down from the Tower and rapidly mounted in temporary batteries at both Tilbury and Gravesend[27]. Forty-five Dutch ships approached within four miles of the Tilbury fort and the captain tried several shots with his newly-mounted long brass guns but failed to reach them[28].

Below: *A revised design of 1666 with the provision of a small harbour within the ramparts.*

The next year de Gomme submitted two plans, the first showing an elaborate pentagonal fort with a central bastion on the river front enclosing the old blockhouse and projecting into the Thames. Running along the water's edge was a lower tier of gun positions which, combined with emplacements on the ramparts, would have meant a main battery of well over a hundred cannon. There was a broad ditch with a covered way and another narrower ditch beyond the glacis. An interesting feature which de Gomme must have seen in Holland was the provision of a small harbour within the fortifications, entered through a tunnel under the

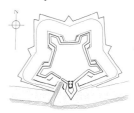

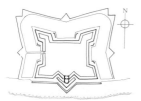

Above: *Another design of 1666 for the new fort at Tilbury, but with only four bastions.*

Below: *The final design of 1670 with a projecting river bastion enclosing the old blockhouse.*

ramparts. As no gate appears on the landward side, this may well have been envisaged as the only means of access[29].

The second plan, based on a parallelogram, replaced the centre bastion with a redan, but retained the three tiers of guns on the river front. There was the same covered way and outer ditch, but in this plan the main gate was in the middle of the west curtain[30]. Both these plans were rejected, but de Gomme was not dismayed; returning to the drawing board, he submitted yet another plan in 1670, very similar to the first but without the harbour and outer ditch[31]. The river batteries had been reduced to two tiers and the entrance had been moved to the north curtain, with the road crossing the ravelin before it reached the gate; the ramparts were to be unrevetted because of the marshy nature of the site, and the wide fausse-braye was to be retained. Within the fort an inner ditch flanked by two demi-bastions was planned to convert the river bastion and blockhouse into a self-contained citadel[32]. This plan was accepted and formed the basis, although with many modifications, of the pentagonal fort that was actually built.

Work began in the autumn of 1670, with a huge force of labourers digging out the ditches and piling up the ramparts. It went on only slowly, however, as the marshy nature of the site created difficulties. The original plan was altered to provide a brick scarp, and the weight of this demanded foundations of pile and frame[33]. Tens of thousands of individual piles had to be laboriously driven into the marshy ground before any heavy structure could be attempted. By 1676 the fort was recognisable but far from complete, and because of the increasingly evident engineering difficulties, work on the river bastion was postponed and then abandoned, but not before hundreds of massive piles had been needlessly driven into the mud at the water's edge[34].

Instead of the bastion the two curtain walls along the river front were extended to meet at the old blockhouse, which was raised by one storey and converted into a magazine. On the three landward sides the ramparts were fronted by a wide moat with a covered way at its outer edge. Beyond the foot of the glacis was an outer ditch, half as wide as the inner, and beyond that was waterlogged ground; arrangements had been provided to flood this marshy ground in an emergency. Entrance to the fort was from the north, where the road passed through a two-storey machicolated redoubt, triangular in shape, standing in the outer moat. Once through this, a causeway took the road across the outer moat, through the glacis and along the covered way, where a second bridge led to a ravelin. After this there was a long timber causeway, broken by two drawbridges, across the inner moat before the north gate was reached.

Inside the ramparts, arranged around the vast parade ground, were barracks, storehouses, a large powder magazine and a guard house with a chapel above. The red brick of the walls was picked out with quoins of white ashlar, and on the salients of the bastions de Gomme placed neat little domed sentry boxes like pepperpots. The finest architectural piece of the fort was the Water Gate, a marvellously flamboyant flourish to a utilitarian structure, like an elaborate epaulette on a dull uniform. The main armament of the fort was mounted at the water's edge in two long batteries known as the gun lines, protected only by a low parapet.

The massive appearance of the fort was a source of wonder to its many visitors. Pepys, Evelyn and Defoe came to the fort and recorded their impressions in their diaries. "A right Royal work indeed!" John Evelyn scribbled enthusiastically[35]. "A battery so terrible as well imports the consequence of the place ... so that they must be bold fellows who will venture in the biggest ships in

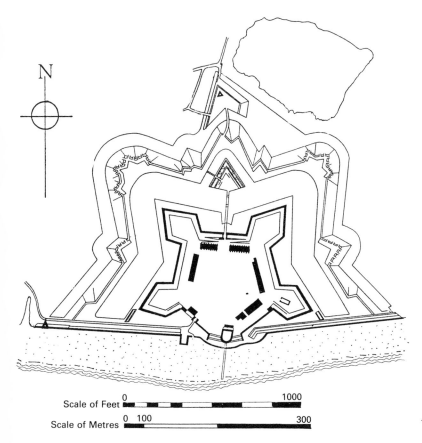

Scale of Feet 0 ▬▬▬ 1000

Scale of Metres 0 100 ▬▬▬ 300

The fort at Tilbury as finally built, without the river bastion.

39

the world to pass such a battery," enthused Daniel Defoe[36]. The cost of Tilbury Fort was undoubtedly royal. Far more than the original estimate of £47,000 had been spent before it was completed in 1682[37].

But not all were impressed; mighty and overpowering the fort might be, but was it in the right place? Lord Dartmouth, the Master-General of the Ordnance, wondered, rather late in the day, if it ought not to have been built downstream at East Tilbury[38].

Once more the familiar tale of neglect and ruin unfolded. By 1694 the platforms in the gun lines were so rotten that if a gun was fired the carriage sank into the ground and the shot flew high into the air[39]. This was remedied by installing stone platforms set diamond fashion to the riverside so they pointed not directly across but a little downstream.

Tilbury Fort in the early eighteenth century. The main defensive battery was mounted in the gun lines fronting the river but outside the main ramparts.

In 1715 there were thirty-two heavy cannon in the east gun lines and forty-three in the west, with another ninety guns planted on the ramparts and scattered about the outworks. The next year a survey discovered no fewer than 161 guns in the fort, but only ninety-two of them could be fired with any degree of confidence[40]. By 1752 the armament had been reduced and standardised to thirty 42-pounders in the gun lines and twenty-four 9-pounders on the ramparts[41].

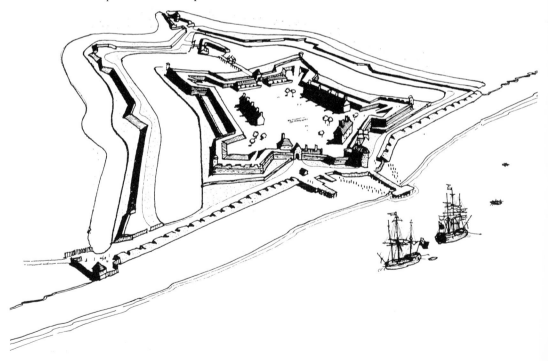

Various additions to the buildings were made throughout the century, including two massive powder magazines, storehouses and elegant barracks for both officers and soldiers. The garrison varied in size; sometimes infantry regiments were quartered there, and at other times there were no more than the master gunner and a few invalid artillerymen to look after the guns. Although Tilbury was the major defence work, the senior officers preferred to live amidst the relative civilisation of Gravesend rather than on the dank marshes across the river. The fort's gloomy reputation was enhanced when it served as a prison for some of the captured highlanders from the Battle of Culloden who were awaiting trial or transportation[42].

Throughout the eighteenth century the fort saw no action, but there was excitement of various kinds. There was a mutiny that was quelled with some severity, but the worst and most violent incident took place during a cricket match. In 1776 a match was played within the fort between the county teams of Kent and Essex. Feelings ran high, the umpire's decision was not held as final, and a fight broke out between the players that soon spread to the spectators. One of the Kentish men ran to the guardroom, seized a gun, and returning to the fray shot dead one of the Essex players. The other players abandoned their bats and overpowered the four soldiers on guard to arm themselves. An elderly invalid soldier was bayoneted and a sergeant, who was in command of the fort in the absence of an officer, was shot as he attempted to bring peace to the struggling mob. At this point, with three corpses lying on the pitch, the players panicked; the Essex men ran off over the drawbridge while the Kentish team fled across the river[43].

Tilbury was again surveyed in 1778 by the engineer Thomas Hyde Page, who declared, "The errors in the construction of this place seem to be almost past remedy without total reform"[44]. Apart from the ramparts and parapets being too thin, he saw the fort's greatest weakness as the lack of the river bastion, and proposed to remedy this by extending the gun lines out into the Thames in a redan-shaped projection to give greater fire downstream. He also recommended building a six-gun battery in the south-east corner of the covered way, again to fire downstream. Only this part of his plan was executed, but by the end of the century the fort had been rearmed and mounted fourteen 42-pounders in the east gun lines and fourteen 32-pounders in the west. The battery on the covered way was armed with six 32-pounders and there were thirty-five 9-pounders mounted on the ramparts and bastions for close defence[45].

In 1793, following the outbreak of war with France, another survey was made of the river and its defences; the subsequent report recommended an advanced battery at Coalhouse Point on

Scale of Metres
Scale of Feet

Above: *A plan of the four-gun battery at Coalhouse Point built in 1799.*

Below: *The second battery at Coalhouse Point, begun in 1847 but not finished until 1855 and incorporating most of the earlier work.*

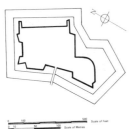

Scale of Feet
Scale of Metres

the site of the old East Tilbury Blockhouse to act in conjunction with two others on the Kent bank[46]. These proposals were approved, and the new battery was begun and quickly completed. It was a simple semi-circular earthwork battery, with a few barrack buildings forming a redan-shaped gorge, armed with four 32-pounders mounted on the new traversing carriages to give them a much wider arc of fire. Inside the battery there was a large oven for heating shot to the red-hot condition so lethal to wooden ships[47].

At the height of the invasion scare in 1803 the French refugee General Dumoirez inspected the defences, pronounced them in good order, stressed the paramount importance of Tilbury Fort and insisted that it be held to the last, for once it was taken Woolwich and all its mountains of stores and London itself were open to attack[48]. To supplement the fixed defences the Royal Trinity House Volunteer Artillery manned ten armed hulks strung across the river between Tilbury and Gravesend, troops massed, the forts were at a peak of readiness, but Napoleon never came and their efficiency and resolve were never tested[49].

Nothing very much was done until the ripples of the invasion scares and alarms of the eighteen-forties reached the forts on the Thames. It was decided to replace the small battery at Coalhouse Point with a new and more powerful fort, and work began on this in 1847[50]. The new fort was an earthwork of irregular trace built within the semi-circular moat of the 1794 battery. It had no bastions, being flanked at the gorge by caponiers, and was armed with seventeen 32-pounders, all on traversing carriages. Despite the small size of the fort and the simplicity of its construction, it was not ready for action until 1855, the eight-year delay being almost a record even among fort builders, who were notorious for their snail-like progress. Most of the problems at Coalhouse were caused by the contractor, who was described by the Royal Engineer officer in charge as a very troublesome and litigious character[51].

In 1860 the members of the Royal Commission on the Defences of the United Kingdom visited the Thames and after examining expert witnesses and tramping the ground made their report. "The defence of the Thames involves interests of vast magnitude," they stated, warning that the security of the river was imperative for the safety of the realm[52]. If any enemy ship penetrated the river above Tilbury, the huge gunpowder magazines at Purfleet, the building and victualling yard at Deptford, the Arsenal at Woolwich and all the incalculable wealth of London lay at the mercy of its guns. The commissioners regarded Tilbury as too far upriver and suggested moving the main defence line downstream, proposing two successive lines of defence. The first was to run from Coalhouse Point to Cliffe, where two new and powerful forts were to be built, and the second from Tilbury Fort across to Gravesend, where the existing works were to be modified. "We consider this second line so important that we recommend that these works [Tilbury and New Tavern Fort, Gravesend] should be put into the most thoroughly efficient state in every respect"[53].

Once funds were authorised work began. Coalhouse Fort was quickly flattened, but its successor rose at a leisurely pace. The new fort was to be one of the most powerful in the country and certainly the largest and most impressive in East Anglia. First plans revealed a line of twenty-eight casemates in a single tier, each armed with a 68-pounder smooth bore, with an equal number on the roof[54]. Work began slowly in 1861, the foundations were not finished until 1863, and more delays meant the basement was not completed until 1865. As the fort grew so did the power of artillery, and by 1869 the design had been modified several times to include iron shields in the casemate openings and much heavier guns than the original 68-pounders. The increased power of artillery following the introduction of rifled guns meant that a smaller number could be mounted, and thus by 1869 the planned armament for Coalhouse had shrunk from the original fifty-six to twenty. Twelve of the guns were to be in casemates; the remainder, mounted on Moncrieff disappearing carriages, were to be on the roof[55].

After eight years of work the fort was still far from complete. The barracks had been started only the previous year and neither guns nor shields were in place, although £52,000 had already been

An aerial view of the 1799 battery at Coalhouse Point with its four 32-pounders on traversing carriages. In the middle of the fort is the oven used for heating shot.

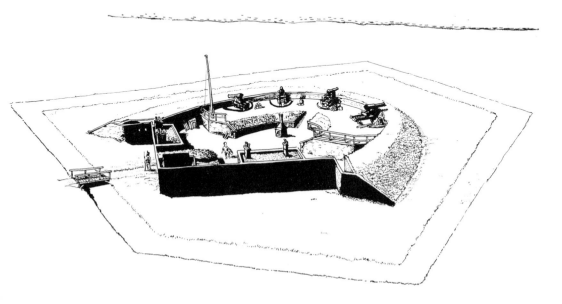

The ground plan of Coalhouse Fort. The design was revised and altered many times during the course of construction.

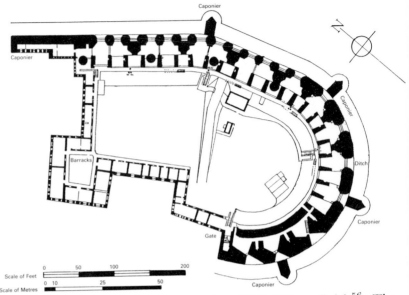

spent and estimates allowed another £158,000 to finish[56]. The fort's architect, Captain Sibourn, must have been close to despair, continually revising and altering the design following each fresh revelation of the power of artillery to punch holes through iron and granite. The idea of Moncrieff mountings was soon abandoned as prohibitively expensive and the final design was for a single tier of casemates, their embrasures closed with iron shields. By 1872 shields and artillery were installed and the fort was at last complete with a formidable armament of eleven 11-inch RMLs and four 12.5-inch RMLs in the casemates and three 9-inch RMLs in an open battery at the downriver end[57]. The enclosure was completed by the barrack block, built of Kentish ragstone and arranged to provide flanking fire from small bastion-like projections; there were even machicolations, functional enough but rather self-consciously medieval. Surrounding the fort was a sixty-foot moat, a relic of the earlier works; the efficacy of this was reduced by the old river wall that formed a causeway across the moat but was too essential a means of flood control to tamper with.

While work was slowly progressing on the forts at Cliffe, Coalhouse and Shornemead, Tilbury and Gravesend remained the only effective defence of the Thames. In 1865 Tilbury was armed with five 68-pounders, five 32-pounders, four 10-inch shell guns and fifty-two other pieces of varying size and efficiency[58]. It was a tranquil if somewhat gloomy place to be stationed; the dank air and miasmas rising from the marshes meant cases of malaria were common among the garrison and quinine was regularly issued[59].

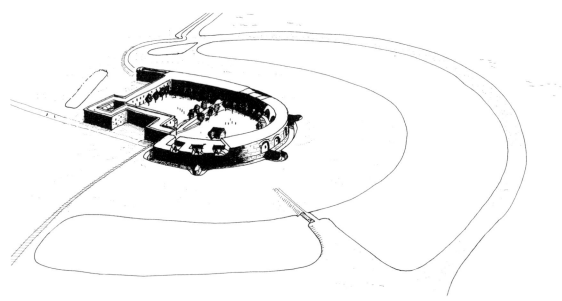

There were compensations, for in the placid depths of the moat lurked many fine fish which furnished sport for the garrison and any itinerant anglers who applied to the sergeant at the gate. To those who approached from the land along the road from West Tilbury the fort presented "an aspect of solid serviceable strength which would perhaps encourage the patriots who dread invasion"[60].

Coalhouse Fort in its original state in the eighteen-seventies.

From the land it might well have appeared impregnable to the untrained eye, but from the river it was a rather different picture. The high brick scarps of the river wall and bastion were no defence against heavy artillery, nor were the guns any threat to ironclads, and plans were made to bring Tilbury up to date. Little structural work was needed, and the modifications hardly changed its basic seventeenth-century appearance, except for the loss of the old blockhouse which was demolished in 1867[61]. The east bastion and south-east curtain were buried in earth beneath which were installed magazines and handling rooms connected to the guns above. Here, facing downriver, were emplacements for eight guns. The north-east bastion was similarly remodelled; the east flank and face were masked with earth and three emplacements were built on top. The west bastion was remodelled in exactly the same way, but with only two gun emplacements. Two years later there were positions for thirteen heavy guns, all directed on the river and heavily protected[62]. At first the guns were 7-inch RMLs, but these were soon considered too light for such an important position and were replaced by twelve 9-inch RMLs and one 12-inch RML[63].

Much of this later work was supervised by Lieutenant-Colonel Charles Gordon, who, after a spectacular interval in China as the leader of the Ever Victorious Army, had returned to the humdrum tedium of a supervising engineer's life. He was a strange man, given to the surreptitious distribution of evangelical tracts; and what were hard-headed contractors to make of a colonel of engineers who flapped his arms and proclaimed, "O that I had wings like a dove, then would I fly away and be at rest"[64]. Rest was something he did not allow his subordinates. He was on duty at eight every morning and could often be seen sitting in the stern of a four-oared gig foaming through the water propelled by a straining, sweating crew. "A little faster boys, a little faster!" he would cry as they sped by on the way to Tilbury or Coalhouse forts. Even this did not satisfy his insatiable desire for speed, and he put in a request for a steam launch, which was refused[65]. At the jetty he would leap from the boat and trot briskly through the piles of brick and over the heaps of earth, rushing out orders to masons and foremen, urging always greater and still greater haste. "Five minutes gone, boys!" he would cry. "We shall never have them

A replica 12-pounder in one of the emplacements built on top of the original casemates of Coalhouse Fort in 1903. In the background are two searchlight positions.

46

again." Promptly at two his official day ended, and he was rowed back to Gravesend where the rest of the day was spent in prayer, bible study and acts of charity[66].

Since 1859 a third artillery defence had been positioned on the Essex bank of the Thames. The experimental range and proving ground for artillery had been moved to Shoeburyness when the range of guns increased sufficiently to make Woolwich marshes too dangerous. By the mid-eighteen-sixties there was a thriving camp of two hundred and forty acres with several batteries for light and heavy guns and many targets out on the mudflats where the off-duty artillerymen went digging for mussels[67].

By the end of the eighteen-eighties the huge and impressive muzzle-loaders were entirely obsolete, although the general public did not suspect. They looked on the mighty forts from their excursion steamers and felt comforted, but this feeling was entirely illusory. Millions had been spent, the Thames was lined with rows of frowning granite casemates; could it be that they were no use at all? A chill suspicion grew in the minds of the military authorities, like a draught in a cosy parlour; a horrible certainty that the

The main gate of Coalhouse Fort, showing the barrack block built of Kentish ragstone. Outside are two 6-inch gun barrels which it is hoped will be installed in the fort during restoration.

Thames was once again defenceless. The Inspector-General of Fortifications, Sir Andrew Clarke, was asked by an incredulous parliamentary committee in 1886 if there was nothing to stop a heavy armoured ship getting up the river as far as Tilbury. "Not up the Thames," replied Sir Andrew, sadly and cryptically[68].

Major Rasch, the Member of Parliament for South-east Essex, rose in the House of Commons and demanded to know whether the public were aware that of all the guns in the Thames and Medway, of all the hundreds of supposedly formidable weapons, all but ten were useless[69]. The public was very soon aware, and then became extremely agitated. Well over eighteen million pounds had been spent on forts and guns, and now were they being asked to spend millions more? "Not at all", the War Office soothed, "a comparatively small expenditure will render this river practically safe against attack"[70].

The most urgent need was for new, heavy breech-loading guns sited downstream to take advantage of their much longer range. A new battery was planned at East Tilbury in 1887, and work began the following year[71]. Two years later, after the usual muddle, wrangles and legal difficulties over the title to the ground, it was completed and officially named Coalhouse Battery. Facing downstream and not, like the earlier forts, across the river, Coalhouse was the first of the new generation of modern batteries; it consisted of a long earth bank with magazines beneath and was armed with six new breech-loading guns. The whole work was defended not by great ditches and multi-loopholed caponiers but by a simple metal unclimbable fence in testimony to the newly appreciated power of the magazine rifle. Two 10-inch occupied the centre gunpits with two 6-inch on either side, all mounted on hydro-pneumatic disappearing carriages. These guns were designed to combat armoured cruisers and battleships, but there was also a threat of fast torpedo boats and to cope with these a battery armed with four 6-pounder QF was placed a little upstream of Coalhouse Fort[72].

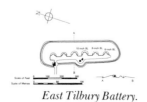

East Tilbury Battery.

The building of Coalhouse Battery moved the main defensive line of the river further downstream, and the Cliffe to Coalhouse Fort line became of secondary importance. Coalhouse Fort's armament of eighteen RMLs remained in place until the end of the century, as did the similar weapons at Tilbury Fort, but by 1900 the fact that the muzzle-loaders were of no use whatsoever could no longer be ignored. The War Office decided to scrap most of the RMLs at Coalhouse Fort, leaving only four as a secondary defence, and to replace them by 6-inch breech-loaders[73]. It was also intended to augment the heavy armament by installing two 9.2-inch guns in the fort, although it was not specified where these were to be crammed into an already overcrowded work.

By 1903 Coalhouse Fort had been substantially remodelled.

One of the 6-inch emplacements built into the south-west bastion of Tilbury Fort. The door leads into the magazine.

Alternate casemates, from which the obsolete RMLs had been removed, were filled with concrete to take the weight of four 6-inch guns which were mounted on the roof. Four of the 12.5-inch RMLs were kept as an interim anti-torpedo boat armament and were provided with case shot so they could be fired like giant blunderbusses. Four 12-pounders were placed alongside the 6-inch on the roof and two electric searchlights were installed so the guns could, for the first time, be fought at night[74]. The searchlights were an indication of the growing mechanical complexity of fortification. Batteries meant not just guns and their increasingly sophisticated mountings but extensive fire-control systems as well. These, all electrically connected to the guns, involved hidden complications undreamed of in the eighteen-sixties. Generators had to be installed to provide the power for the searchlights; primitive but robust machines powered by oil engines that could be started only with a blowtorch[75].

At the same time the 6-inch guns at Coalhouse Battery were remounted on barbette carriages, which involved rebuilding the emplacements, but the 10-inch were left on their disappearing carriages[76]. Tilbury was brought up to date for the last time when the emplacements along the south-east curtain were remodelled to take two 6-inch Mk.IV and four 12-pounders[77].

A further defence was provided by the guns at Shoeburyness. In time of war all the guns there were to be utilised for the defence of the river. This sounded better in theory than it was in practice, for the variety in size and efficiency of the guns there at any given time made them an optimistic rather than integral part of the

Thames defences. In addition to the transient collection of experimental weapons there were other regular batteries, part of the Coast Artillery School; the Heavy Quick-Firer Battery with two 4.7-inch and two 6-inch, two emplacements with 6-inch guns on hydro-pneumatic carriages, a single 9.2-inch and the Quick-Firer Gantry, an old hydraulic gantry dating from the eighteen-sixties that had been converted to a position for four 12-pounders and four 6-pounders[78]. Although Shoeburyness was not officially rated as such, it was a fort with a very formidable armament.

The Thames defences were at their peak in numbers and power in 1906. The first generation of breech-loaders were still operational and the newer models were already installed. There were twenty BL guns and four RMLs lining the Essex bank, with up to a dozen guns at Shoeburyness. With the lower estuary covered by 10-inch and 9.2-inch at Sheerness and on the Isle of Grain, the river was as impregnable as it was ever likely to be[79].

However, when the First World War broke out the number of guns had been drastically reduced. In 1912 only four 6-inch at

A 6-pounder QF emplacement in the small battery outside Coalhouse Fort. In the background can be seen the Second World War radar tower.

The heavy QF battery at Shoeburyness. The two nearer emplacements mounted 6-inch guns, the further two 4.7-inch guns. The plan below shows the position of the gun emplacements at the Coast Artillery School, Shoeburyness.

Coalhouse Fort were entered on the list of approved armaments, although the other guns might well have remained unsanctioned[80]. In August, 1914, just a few days before the outbreak of war, two of the guns at Coalhouse Fort were moved across the river to be mounted on the roof of Cliffe Fort[81]. A little later a small battery armed with two 12-pounders was built at Thameshaven to protect the petrol wharf and two naval 6-inch were added to the guns at Shoeburyness[82].

In case of the unlikely event of the Germans landing in the estuary, a number of infantry works were built along the banks and a large complex of trenches, blockhouses and pillboxes was constructed at Shoeburyness[83]. Throughout the war the only guns that fired, except in practice, were anti-aircraft guns; and a battery of these stationed on the parade ground of Tilbury Fort shot down the Zeppelin L-15 in 1916[84].

The changed conditions after the Armistice allowed a further reduction of the defences. All the older breech-loaders that had survived the war were scrapped and only the guns at Coalhouse Fort remained. In 1936 a study was made of making Shoeburyness the location of the main batteries, advancing the defence to the very mouth of the river. Plans were made to install two 6-inch and two 9.2-inch, with a twin 6-pounder to deal with fast motorboats[85]. These never materialised, but a new battery for two 6-inch was constructed at Canvey Island in 1938, enabling the guns at Coalhouse to be removed[86].

When the Second World War broke out there were only

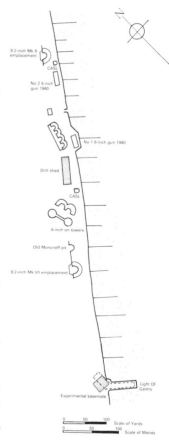

9.2-inch Mk X emplacement
CASL
No 2 6-inch gun 1940
No 1 6-inch gun 1940
Drill shed
CASL
6-inch on towers
Old Moncrieff pit
9.2-inch Mk VII emplacement
Light QF Gantry
Experimental casemate

0   50   100   Scale of Yards
0   50   100   Scale of Metres

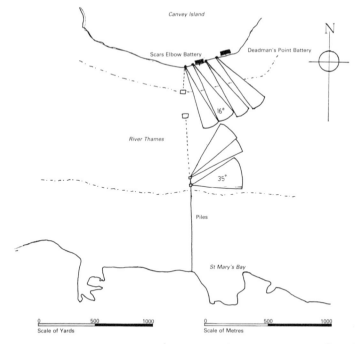

The Second World War boom defence of the Thames. The seven segments show searchlight coverage of the navigable channel; three searchlights were on platforms in mid-river.

seventeen guns protecting the whole Thames Estuary; five 9.2-inch, six 6-inch, four 12-pounders and two 3-pounders, of which only two of the 6-inch were on the Essex bank, at Canvey Island[87]. After the fall of France this provision suddenly seemed dangerously inadequate and three emergency batteries were hurriedly constructed. Two 5.5-inch ex-naval guns were mounted at Coalhouse Fort and two ex-naval 6-inch in temporary casemates on the sea wall in front of the Quick-Firer Battery at Shoeburyness. The Coast Artillery School moved to Llandudno in North Wales in September, 1940, taking with it all the regular guns. The third wartime battery was built on Canvey Island, a little upstream from the 6-inch battery at Scar's Elbow[88]. Since the First World War a new threat, that of the fast motorboat, had been recognised; none of the existing guns was fast enough to deal with such craft. In the nineteen-thirties nine twin 6-pounders, capable of firing over one hundred aimed rounds a minute, had been authorised, but none was in place at the outbreak of war[89]. Two of these were emplaced at Scar's Elbow soon after war was declared; alongside the guns were five searchlights. As an additional protection against intruding E-Boats a boom ran across the river from Canvey Island to St Mary's Bay[90].

The main threat to London during the Second World War was from the air, and the Thames provided a clear route that German bombers could follow on all but the darkest nights. To defend the capital against them large numbers of anti-aircraft guns were emplaced along the banks; some of these batteries had a dual role and could fire against enemy shipping. At Hadleigh four 4.5-inch AA guns could be brought to bear on the river, and at Bowaters Farm near East Tilbury there were a further four 4.5-inch, later supplemented with four 5.25-inch dual-purpose guns[91]. At the height of the flying bomb attack on London the Thames AA defence consisted of 208 heavy and 405 light AA guns, about half of which were stationed in Essex[92]. They had much success in shooting down both planes and flying bombs. As well as the coast and anti-aircraft guns, large numbers of pillboxes and other emplacements lined the river bank and the main defensive GHQ Line ended on the Thames at Canvey Island.

Once the war had ended the emergency batteries were dismantled and their guns removed for scrapping. Scar's Elbow and Deadman's Point were placed in care and maintenance until the final disbanding of the coastal artillery when they, too, were abandoned. Today Coalhouse Fort is being restored, and Tilbury Fort is impeccably maintained by English Heritage with an efficiency that would have been the despair and envy of the fort's seventeenth-century Governors.

A 9.2-inch Mk X at Shoeburyness in the nineteen-thirties. The gun was moved elsewhere during the Second World War. Major Tony Hill

W N E S (compass)

Col. Fothergall's quarters

Col. Gourdon's Horse quarters

Col. Har quarters

Fort Suffolk

Col. Fo ther fa Fort

Horse Guard

Horse Guard

Foot Guard

Fo rt Rainsborough

Fort Bloyes

Colne River

Horse Guard

Suffolk

Water Mill

wers

Fort In goleshy

1
2
3
11
K
P
A B
Q
4
F
19
9
12
13
N
M
14
5
6
Malden Road
Road into the
8
Merrie Road
7
Fort Essex
Fort Needham
Horse Guard

Barksteed Fort

Mr. Barrington's House

Hundreds

Horse Guard

5 Comp of Col. Barksteeds Reg. quarters

Dragoone Guard and quarters

The Generall's quarter of

2 Troops of the Lieut. Generall's Horse

Essex   4

A T FIRST sight the most vulnerable portion of the East Anglian
coast was the long indented coastline from Harwich to the
mouth of the Thames. It was both nearer to an enemy from across
the North Sea and closer to an invader's ultimate objective of
London than the coast further north. Yet, despite its flatness and
because of the natural difficulties of access to much of the
shoreline, Essex did not figure prominently in Tudor schemes of
defence. Most of the coast from Shoeburyness to Foulness Point
was a wilderness of marsh, and only the shore from St Osyth to
Walton was practical for an invading force to land upon. The only
other points of danger were the three rivers, the Crouch, the
Blackwater and the Colne.

In 1539 the commissioners charged with providing coast
defences examined the shore of Essex and made their recommendations. Apart from Harwich, they emphasised only one point
of danger in the county, the mouth of the Colne[1]. Nothing was
done at once, for Henry VIII's programme of coastal fortification
was so extensive that Essex had to await its share of scarce
resources. It was not until 1543 that Richard Lee was appointed to
supervise the building of defence works in Essex, five of which
were at Harwich and on Langer Point, the remaining three
covering the mouth of the river Colne[2]. One was sited at St Osyth,
another at the east end of Mersea Island, with the third at
Brightlingsea[3]. They were not very elaborate works, costing just
under four hundred pounds each, with a very small garrison[4].
None was built of brick or stone; Edward VI wrote of them in his
journal as "bulwarkes of earth and board"[5]. East Mersea blockhouse was a triangular work, each side three hundred feet long,
with semi-circular bastions at each apex armed with twelve guns[6].
St Osyth's may well have been the hexagonal moated enclosure of
earth revetted with gabions, and with a house for the captain and
any necessary stores, depicted in a plan in the British Library[7]. All
the forts remained operational until the summer of 1553 when, as
part of the Government's economies, the cannon were dismounted
and sent to the Tower of London[8]. Some years later Mersea was
revived and rearmed, but St Osyth's blockhouse continued to decay
and by the end of the sixteenth century had disappeared without
trace. The Mersea blockhouse was in a state of ruin by the time of
the Armada, the moat was choked, the drawbridge was decayed,

The siege of Colchester as seen in a more-or-less contemporary print. The siege lines and batteries surrounding the town can be seen, as can the forts established by the Parliament forces. Fort Whaley is mostly out of the picture to the right.

L. W. Malster

Above: *Plan of the blockhouse at East Mersea, which was in a state of ruin at the time of the Armada.*
Below: *The blockhouses erected by Henry VIII guarding the estuary of the Colne and Blackwater.*

the four remaining guns half buried in the earth and the house occupied by a poor old widow[9]. Some repairs were made, but what was the fate of the widow? Was she evicted, rehoused or simply pressed into the garrison to hobble about carrying munitions in lieu of rent?

The raids of the Dunkirkers in the early seventeenth century resulted in a proposal to build a new fort on the site of the old blockhouse, but the new work at Landguard consumed most of the available resources and Mersea was merely patched up to a sufficient state of preparedness to be pronounced efficient in 1631[10]. Eleven years later when the Civil War began Essex, deep within Parliament's territory, had little need of coastal or inland fortifications, but as a prudent measure Colchester patched up its ancient walls.

The defences were tested in 1648, when there was a widespread revival of Royalist sympathies leading to revolts against Parliament in both Kent and Essex. Colchester was occupied by a force of disaffected cavaliers under the command of Sir Charles Lucas and Sir George Lisle and quickly surrounded by units of the New Model Army, supplemented by detachments from the Essex

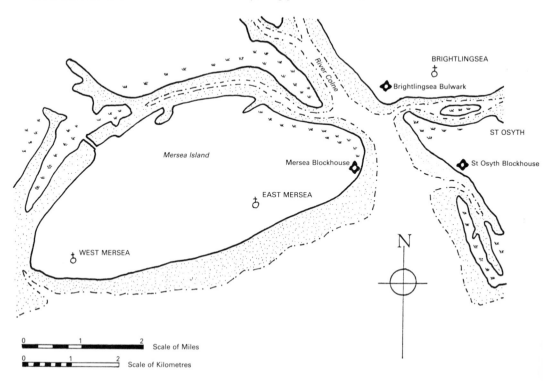

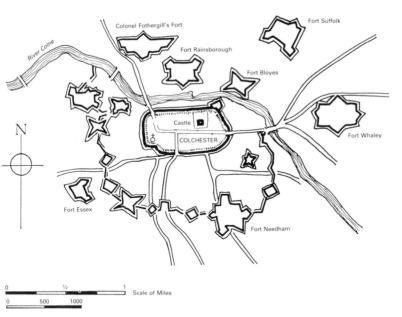

Fort Suffolk

Colonel Fothergill's Fort

Fort Rainsborough

River Colne

Fort Bloyes

Castle

COLCHESTER

Fort Whaley

N

Fort Essex

Fort Needham

0   ½   1   Scale of Miles
0   500   1000

The Civil War siege works about Colchester. The most elaborate of the fortifications were those built by the Parliamentary forces besieging the town.

and Suffolk militias. After the initial assault had failed Sir Thomas Fairfax, the Parliamentary commander, was forced to settle down to a lengthy siege. The defenders made hasty modifications to the existing works by piling up extra earth behind the walls and building a large irregular bastion at the north-east angle to command the ground before the east gate. John Evelyn was to describe the fortifications a little later as "exceeding strong, deeply trenched and filled with earth"[11]. A battery was erected in St Mary's churchyard in the south-west corner of the town and a small but lethal brass cannon placed in the belfry of the church tower, from where it greatly annoyed the besiegers until it and the gunner who served it were battered down[12].

The most interesting fortifications were built by the besiegers, who dug elaborate lines of circumvallation to seal off the town. To the south lines of trenches, strengthened by several forts and batteries, blocked all roads, while to the north, across the river, lay four large detached forts controlling the routes from Suffolk. These siege works displayed a bewildering variety of shapes to demonstrate the sophisticated pragmatism of Fairfax's engineers. As they were built quickly they were not massive structures, having a rampart about eight feet high from the bottom of the ditch. There were probably palisades and storm poles and the parapets would have been revetted with gabions and planks[13]. The result of the siege was a foregone conclusion; after a fierce bombardment hunger drove the garrison to surrender.

As a prelude to the siege the blockhouse at Mersea was captured by a troop of dragoons so that its guns might be silenced to allow four Parliamentary men-of-war to enter the river[14]. The blockhouse, mounting only five guns, two culverins, two sakers and a drake, was extensively repaired over the next three years. Turf was cut to strengthen the ramparts, a timber house was built for the garrison, additional guns were mounted and a local seamstress was commissioned to sew a fifteen-foot flag to flutter over the restored strongpoint[15]. This glory was shortlived; in 1655 Mersea was included in the list of garrisons to be reduced completely and Cromwell ordered it to be demolished[16]. It survived because the owner of the land upon which the fort stood forbade its destruction and so it remained although dismantled and disarmed[17].

For the rest of the seventeenth century and for most of the eighteenth the defences of Essex were concentrated at Harwich; it was not until the American War of Independence that any great concern was expressed for the integrity of the coast as a whole. With the Dutch Fleet opposed to Britain, Essex was particularly vulnerable. In 1781 Colonel James Bramham surveyed the coast on behalf of the commander-in-chief, Lord Amherst, and found that there were no guns at all. He proposed only two batteries; one, for two or three 12-pounders, was to be sited in the churchyard at Maldon, where it could cover the upper tidal reaches of the River Blackwater, and the other, for six 12-pounders, was to be sited on the Colne at Fingringhoe[18]. The American war ended in 1783 and the guns were withdrawn.

On the outbreak of the French Revolutionary Wars the coast was once more surveyed in 1794 and the Ordnance Board recommended an elaborate scheme of defences. A six-gun battery was proposed to defend the Crouch while the Blackwater was to be protected by no fewer than five batteries, all armed with 24-pounders. Three of these were to be sited on Mersea Island and two at Brightlingsea, with two redoubts at Clacton and two batteries at Walton; all supplemented by four floating batteries and two gunboats. In all there were to be fifteen land and five floating batteries, with eight gunboats armed with a total of 136 guns, most of them 24-pounders[19].

Only nine of the batteries were eventually built, one on the north bank of the Crouch, another on the Blackwater near Bradwell, a third at East Mersea built into the seaward face of the old fort, a fourth at Brightlingsea, and a fifth at St Osyth; all armed with six 24-pounders. Four smaller works, each with three or four guns, were sited between Clacton Wick and Walton, for that stretch of all the coast was regarded as the most inviting for an invader, offering over eight miles of sheltered beaches and an easy three days' march to London[20]. They were simple earthworks with a hot-shot oven and a wooden guardhouse that would sleep twenty men in hammocks slung from the rafters[21]. Completed by 1796, some at least were still unarmed the following year.

The false hopes raised by the Peace of Amiens in 1802 led to the guns being withdrawn from many batteries, but these were quickly restored when war was resumed the following year. Large French naval forces at Antwerp revived the concern that a landing might be attempted on the Essex coast. The fixed defences were supplemented by floating batteries, hastily improvised from Thames barges, each armed with four guns, moored at the mouths of the rivers Colne and Blackwater[22]. Two small additional batteries, each armed with two 18-pounders, were placed at Wivenhoe to defend the ferry across the Colne and at the Strood with the object of covering the causeway from Mersea Island.

To back up the front-line coast defences it was decided to

The defences of Essex, 1778–1815. The chain of martello towers from St Osyth Stone to Walton-on-the-Naze can be seen, and also the signal stations which provided a line of communication by which information could be passed over considerable distances in a surprisingly short time.

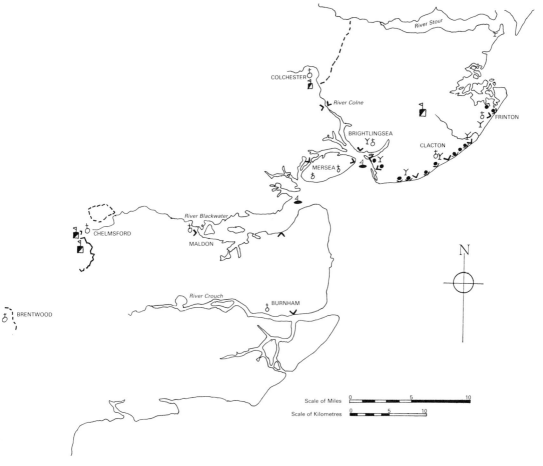

create a strong position blocking the approach to London; the enemy could not capture such a position without his advance being delayed and could not ignore it without leaving a large force to threaten his communications. The commander-in-chief, the Duke of York, suggested a six-mile-long position near Colchester, running from Greenstead Church to Stratford Bridge on the river Stour, to be occupied by thirty thousand men. The Duke chose this line from a glance at the map and without any knowledge of the ground; the proposal was challenged by Sir James Craig, the Commander of the Eastern District, who protested that the site was bad and the proposed garrison needlessly extravagant[23]. He recommended a location just south of Chelmsford, and after much dithering and several counter-suggestions that included entrenched camps at Sudbury, Braintree and Dunmow, this was approved and work began in September, 1803[24].

Designed by Major Bryce, the field fortifications could not be turned by the enemy; they covered all the roads. The intended garrison was fifteen thousand men with 224 guns, and the position ran from Widford southwards through Galleywood Common and

Below: *The entrenched camp proposed in 1795 to block the approach to London of an enemy force which had landed near Harwich. The site, to the north of Chelmsford, lay athwart the main Ipswich–London road.*

Right: *The entrenched position built in 1803–04 south of Chelmsford. It was never armed.*

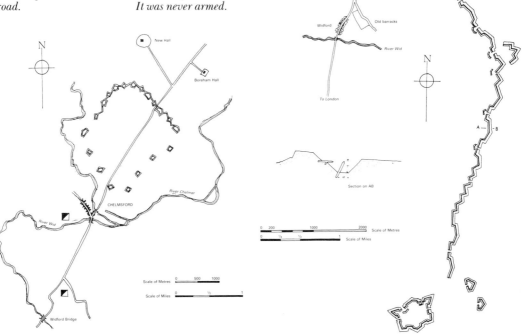

consisted of an earth rampart fronted by a shallow ditch and secured at the ends by two detached forts and a pair of small redoubts; the trace of the lines and the forts was a flexible combination of bastions and tenailles. The work was mainly completed by the following year, though there were problems of settlement probably aggravated by the winter rains[25].

Three years later Bryce was back in Essex examining the coast. He proposed building two strong forts on either bank of the Crouch and more batteries along the coast, some to complement the existing works and others to replace batteries like that at Walton which were already threatened by erosion[26]. At this point General Morse, the Inspector-General of Fortifications, intervened and suggested that masonry towers would be a better means of defence, especially at river mouths where they could be combined with booms. He proposed more than forty towers in Essex, beginning at the mouth of the Crouch and ending at Harwich[27]. In May, 1808, a further survey was made and as a result of this only eleven sites were purchased[28]. Work began on the towers the following year, and they were completed and armed by 1812. The chain began much further north than originally intended. The first tower A stood at St Osyth's Stone near Brightlingsea Ferry, and the last martello in Essex, K, overlooked the marshes and inlets behind Walton-on-the-Naze. All the towers apart from H had auxiliary batteries armed with three 24-pounders, except batteries A and D, which had five, giving a total of fourteen batteries and eleven towers armed with eighty-five cannon[29].

The towers were never occupied by troops, for it was soon discovered that they were most unhealthy. After the war ended they were occupied by pensioners, who found the damp air of their massive homes a greater threat to their health than the bullets and bayonets of Waterloo[30]. In 1818 some of the towers were turned over to the Customs and Excise, who sallied out to do battle with boats laden with contraband[31].

The sea proved to be the martello's greatest enemy; G, H and I were sold and pulled down in 1819, while J was so dangerously eroded that it had to be demolished in 1835[32]. The rest of the towers and their associated batteries remained in reasonable repair and fully armed until the middle of the nineteenth century. There was a plan in 1839 to repair the towers and build a new battery on Osea Island[33], but this moderate ambition to maintain the linear defence of the coast was never implemented, and not revived until the early eighteen-seventies when concern about the defence of the coast was prompted by the emergence of a powerful German Empire.

Once again groups of Royal Engineers unrolled their maps and surveyed the beaches and estuaries. They proposed a modern battery at West Mersea and another by tower A equipped with three guns mounted on Moncrieff carriages as well as a field of electrically-fired observation mines, with the martello tower as a control point. The rest of the remaining towers were to be retained in case they might serve some useful purpose, although the report did not specify what that might be[34].

Nothing came of these plans except that Battery A was handed over to the Royal Naval Reserve for use as a practice battery and rearmed with a 7-inch RML. It was not until the end of the century that fears of invasion began to grow again. No one then proposed building new permanent fortifications, although some still envisaged a useful and active role for the martellos, but official policy designated the defence of the coast to mobile columns of cavalry and bands of enthusiastic volunteer cyclists[35].

Concern for the safety of London, in case an enemy should land in East Anglia and march on the capital, prompted various schemes to build fortifications in the county to the north and east of the city[36]. In the eighteen-eighties the vague proposals began to take substance and the idea of fortifying London began to be taken very seriously. The sheer size of London and the subsequent length of the defensive perimeter precluded any major forts, and most schemes proposed fieldworks or semi-permanent redoubts. In 1887 Lieutenant-Colonel Ardargh, the Deputy-Director of Military Intelligence, drew up a memorandum that suggested building entrenched camps at Epping and Brentwood to counter the secondary threat of a landing on the east coast[37].

The plans were realised in the form of a series of small permanent redoubts which were intended to be the storehouses and magazines for the lines of fieldworks that would link them in an emergency. Most were sited to the south of London along the crest of the North Downs, but two were planned for Essex, on either side of the main road from the east at Epping and North Weald[38]. The first of these was never built, but work began on the North Weald redoubt in September, 1889, and was complete by the end of the next year. It was neither a large nor a complex work, and cost just under eleven thousand pounds[39]. It was never referred to as a fort, always as a redoubt or mobilisation centre, because of the need to allay the prejudice against permanent land fortifications that had always existed in Britain.

It stood to the east of North Weald village near the railway station and was a regular earthwork of simple trace with no flanking arrangements apart from a caponier in the gorge. The defence of the unrevetted ditch was left to a sunken metal fence covered by rifle fire from the parapet. There were bomb-proof casemates beneath the ramparts and another set of casemates with windows opening out on to the gorge. There was no provision for mounting artillery within the redoubt, for its role was envisaged as both a store and strongpoint for the temporary fieldworks and batteries that would be built if London were to be threatened. The sites for these and connecting trenchlines were planned and all arrangements made for their construction in time of war[40].

These plans were put into operation when the First World War broke out. Trenches were eventually dug along the coast after the initial reluctance to alarm the holidaymakers and in February, 1915, the London Defence Position was built, largely following the plans of the eighteen-nineties, to bar the road to the capital to any force that landed in East Anglia. Eventually there were three trench systems, the outer running north of Chelmsford by Maldon and Danbury Hill, the inner by Ongar and Epping, incorporating the redoubt at North Weald[41]. These would be manned, when the Germans landed, by fifty-three battalions of second line troops[42].

On the coast among the fieldworks two batteries of light coast defence guns were emplaced. There were four 15-pounders at Frinton and a further four at Clacton[43]. Inland, for the first time, anti-aircraft guns were mounted to counter the Zeppelins coming

One of the Essex martello towers, tower G, built to command the landing place at Clacton Wash. The seaside resort of Clacton-on-Sea has almost engulfed the old defences.

The defences of Essex, 1914–18, with the fieldworks of the London Defence Position running from the North Weald redoubt towards the coast.

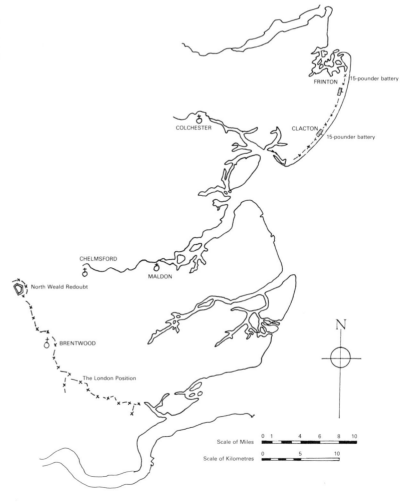

in from the coast. There was a single 3-inch at Romford, another at Chadwell and then four at intervals until the last on the Thames at Barking Creek[44].

In 1940 the distribution of the coast defences was almost exactly the same as that of all the previous invasion scares. The most vulnerable stretch was again seen to be between Walton and St Osyth; the wild shore between Bradwell and Shoeburyness with its mudflats and marshes had sufficient natural defences to deter an invader. Large numbers of troops, contractors and volunteers dug trenches, laid obstacles and built concrete fortifications. Pillboxes covered all likely landing places and the surviving

martello towers were recalled to service as observation posts or
light gun positions.

To provide heavy artillery fire to cover the coast and river
mouths, five emergency batteries were built. On the cliffs of
genteel Frinton the concrete casemates of a twin 6-inch battery
intruded, and further down the coast at Clacton there was a similar
battery armed with two elderly ex-naval 6-inch guns covering the
most likely approach through the offshore sandbanks[45]. There
were two batteries at either end of Mersea Island covering the
entrances to the Colne and Blackwater, each armed with two
4.7-inch guns.

The last and most shortlived of the coastal batteries was on
Foulness Point[46]. In July, 1940, it was armed with one 6-inch and
one 6-pounder, but as more guns became available it was brought
up to standard strength[47]. Early in 1941 it was closed and the guns
sent to arm the new battery at Bawdsey in Suffolk[48]. With the
removal of the guns the Crouch was without protection until the
installation of a controlled minefield[49]. In addition to the permanent batteries there were large numbers of field guns and four 6-

Below: *This pillbox,
fallen on the beach at
Walton-on-the-Naze as a
result of cliff erosion,
clearly shows the thickening
added to the lower walls
when it was realised that
15-inch walls afforded
insufficient protection.*

FORTIFICATIONS OF EAST ANGLIA

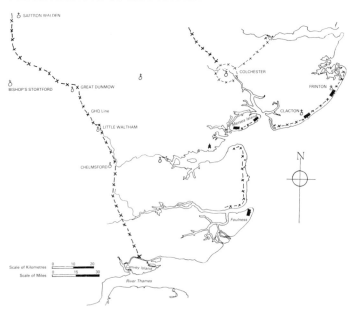

The Second World War defences. The major component was the GHQ Line running right across Essex from Canvey Island to Newport and thence through Cambridgeshire into Lincolnshire.

nch rail guns stationed on the rickety branch line at Tollesbury[50].

Throughout the county, especially at road and rail junctions, roadblocks and pillboxes proliferated. In addition to these there were two continuous defensive positions. The major of these was the GHQ Line, the Essex section of which ran from Great Chesterford south-east through Great Dunmow, Chelmsford, Battlesbridge and Benfleet to reach the Thames at Canvey Island. Before this was a stop line that began at Wivenhoe, continued around Colchester and then ran north to Sudbury and Bury St Edmunds. The GHQ Line in particular was a dense combination of anti-tank emplacements, pillboxes, trenches and anti-tank obstacles following, as much as was possible, rivers, streams and other natural barriers.

Colchester assumed great tactical importance, barring the way of an invasion force that had landed on the peninsula between Harwich and Brightlingsea. The River Colne served as a form-dable anti-tank obstacle and the town was surrounded by a defensive perimeter strengthened by pillboxes and buildings that had been hurriedly adapted. The railway line from Colchester to

Above: *The Crouch was defended by a minefield controlled from this tower on the north bank.*

Opposite page: *The remaining casemate of the 4.7-inch battery at West Mersea, still serving a useful purpose in peacetime.*

Right: *The searchlight emplacement of the West Mersea battery, now used as an ice-cream kiosk.*

Manningtree, running for most of its course either in a cutting or on an embankment, provided a ready-made line of defence with the bridges over the Stour at Manningtree secured by fieldworks and pillboxes[51]. It is fortunate that these fortifications were never put to the test, for it was admitted that the pillboxes were "non-tankproof"[52]. A good deal of effort was expended on thickening their walls, and many can still be seen with a kind of plinth up to the level of the embrasures.

After 1942 the attention paid to the coast defences lessened. By 1943 the batteries at Frinton and East and West Mersea had been turned over to the Home Guard, leaving only Clacton to be manned by regulars until they were all finally closed in early 1945[53].

The most extensive addition to the coast defences was made in 1944 to combat the flying bombs launched from the Low Countries to outflank the south coast defences. The work of shifting numerous heavy anti-aircraft guns and their attendant equipment to the wastes of the Essex coast was enormous, but the job was quickly accomplished. It was these that fired the last shots; as soon as the war had ended the guns were removed, leaving nothing but a string of derelict emplacements.

Holland Battery, Clacton, built in 1941 and armed with two six-inch guns.

A	CASL
B	Engine room
C	Pillbox
D	Battery observation post
E	6-inch gun casemate
F	Shelter and magazines

0   100   200   300
Scale of Feet

0   50   100
Scale of Metres

The Sea Forts   5

THE MOST unusual and inaccessible of all the east coast defences were the sea forts built in 1942–43 to plug an easily exploitable gap in the area's defences. Low-flying aircraft, dropping mines and swooping in for hit-and-run raids on coastal towns, had combined with marauding E-boats to make the approaches to Harwich and the Thames Estuary extremely dangerous[1].

The gap was partly plugged by the employment of a number of small vessels, mainly paddle steamers, as auxiliary anti-aircraft ships for operations in coastal waters, but a more permanent solution was needed and it was suggested that several gun platforms could be sited on the shoals off the coast and in the estuary[2]. The siting of forts in shallow offshore waters presented no real difficulties if tackled in a conventional way. Four huge forts stood in the Solent guarding the approach to Portsmouth, but they had taken several years to raise above the waterline and many more before they were fully complete and armed; even the two smaller forts in the Humber had taken two years to build, and that with a measure of prefabrication.

The problem in 1942 was how to build solid works miles out to sea, with all the dangers presented by a construction site battered by wind and waves in a sea infested by enemy torpedo boats. The solution was deceptively simple; to build the forts in the sheltered waters of the Thames and then to tow them out to be sunk in their allotted positions. As they were rather like permanently moored ships it was appropriate that they should be manned and administered by the Royal Navy.

They were designed by G. A. Maunsell, who had been chosen by the Admiralty because of his experience of similar projects using concrete structures in deep waters, like the Aalstrom Bridge in Denmark[3].

Although the concept was imaginative, the actual structure was simple. On a wide, flat concrete barge one hundred and seventy feet long were set two tall cylindrical towers sixty feet high and twenty feet in diameter. Each tower had seven decks, most of which were designed to be below sea level. The lower three held water tanks, stores and magazines, while the crew of one hundred sailors and marines were crammed into the upper four. Joining the two towers was a steel superstructure, very like the deck of a sawn-off ship, with two 3.7-inch AA guns at each end. Between the guns was a deckhouse housing the officers' quarters, with two 40mm Bofors guns on top. Completing the impression of a badly modelled ship was the bridgelike control room festooned with radio and radar aerials[4].

Four forts were built quickly at Gravesend, using the most advanced techniques of poured concrete prefabrication; then, when completely fitted out down to the last piece of utility cutlery in the galley, they were towed out to their allotted sites. When the spot was reached the pontoon was flooded and the fort sank to the seabed. All that remained was to lay a communication cable to the shore and the fort was ready for action[5]. Three of the forts were sunk off the Essex coast; HMF Rough Sands lay seven miles off Harwich, HMF Sunk Head eleven miles off Clacton, with HMF Knock John a little to the south. The fourth, HMF Tongue Sand, was even further to the south, nearer the Kent coast than the Essex shore. Once installed, they soon proved their worth by extending accurate low-level radar cover over the Thames approaches so that the course of minelaying aircraft could be easily plotted.

Duty on these forts must have been the most tedious of all. The crews had all the disadvantages of being on a ship without ever seeing anything but the same expanse of sea and, on very clear

The anti-aircraft forts in the Thames Estuary.

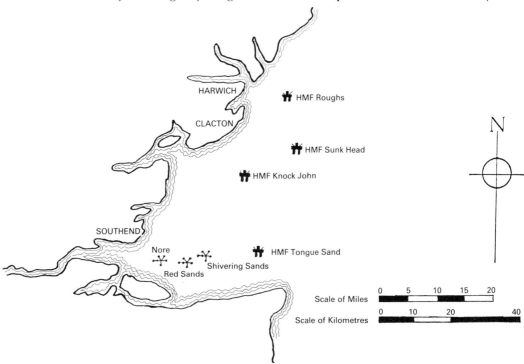

days, the barrage balloons glittering above distant Harwich. The original crews of one hundred officers and ratings were soon reduced by half without any loss in efficiency, but with a great gain in space and the number of permitted showers. The forts proved to be dangerous to German aircraft, and later in the war provided a welcome additional outer gun defence against flying bombs launched from Holland. At the end of the war their tally was one E-boat sunk, twenty-two aircraft and thirty V1s downed; by far the most successful and actively engaged of all the east coast's defences. After 1945 they were stripped of all equipment except the 3.7-inch guns and left to rust and crumble.

Their later history was to prove far more bizarre than could have been dreamed of at the time of their construction. Presumably the Admiralty imagined they would fall to pieces within a few years, but it was a tribute to their designer and builders that they survived twenty-five years without any maintenance and were still there, outside territorial waters, when pirate radio stations boomed in the nineteen-sixties. Suddenly squatters boarded them with grand plans to turn them into television stations, with visions of an aquatic version of Radio Luxembourg beaming its music from a hulk of ancient but free concrete.

A section through one of the naval forts.

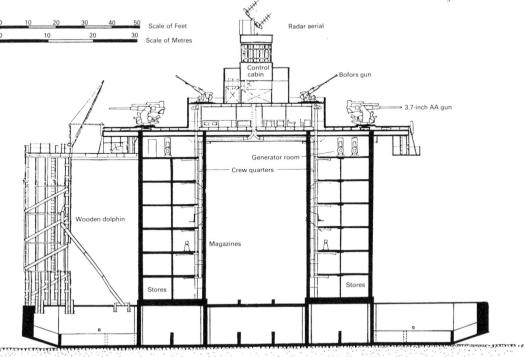

71

In 1966 the Rough Sands fort was annexed by an ex-Major, Roy Bates, who proceeded to name the fort "Sealand" and proclaimed himself Prince of Sealand. He installed his "royal family" in the uninviting cabins of the new principality, and from then on the history of the fort was sheer farce; there began convoluted legal wrangling as to the exact status of "Sealand". Was the new principality, having been built of British concrete, still part of Britain? Had it ever been formally abandoned? Could the new monarch issue his own stamps? How long before "Sealand" was admitted to the United Nations?

There were even minor wars. "Sealand" was briefly invaded and captured by two Germans; a relieving force arrived and retook it; petrol bombs flared in the night. Rifle shots were reportedly fired at a Trinity House tender, detectives in macintoshes went out in small boats to interview Bates through a megaphone, and there were dark reports of mercenaries massing in Harwich. While this went on the Government resolved to avoid any further embarrassments and to prevent the creation of any more offshore kingdoms; on 20th August, 1967, a helicopter landed a squad of Royal Engineers on the Sunk Head Fort with orders to destroy it[6]. "Sealand" still remains, but so far the dreams of its "prince" remain unrealised.

The Roughs Tower after the "Sealand" takeover.

Harwich   6

FOR OVER four hundred years Harwich was the only major fortress in East Anglia and a vital link in the chain of national defences. The estuary of the rivers Stour and Orwell formed the largest and safest haven between the Thames and the Humber, essential as both a harbour of refuge for merchant shipping and a base for men-of-war. As a commercial port Harwich's importance was minor, its main traffic being passengers, and until well into the twentieth century Ipswich always had the greater volume of trade[1]. Yet to an invader the haven was of great value, providing an ideal sheltered anchorage in which to disembark an army within three days' march of London.

Standing at the tip of a small peninsula jutting out into the waters of the estuary, Harwich was in an ideal defensive position, needing fortifications only to the south and east. "It is strong by situation and may be made more so by art,"[2] it was said in 1792. The defence of the haven entrance was made easy by a constricted navigation channel that swept close to the Suffolk shore within point-blank range of the guns on Landguard Point. The town was defended on the south and east sides by a stone wall dating from the fourteenth century, with a castle at the north end, although this was hardly more than a large strong tower[3].

In 1539 the town was visited by Henry VIII's commissioners, who found that the townspeople in an unusual display of enthusiasm had already dug two trenches and built two earthwork batteries[4]. The Earl of Oxford wrote approvingly, "Ye should have seen the women and children work with the shovels at the bulwarks there"[5]. These were soon completed, and guns to arm the new works were sent from the Tower in April, 1539.

Harwich, from a sixteenth-century manuscript.

In 1543 Harwich became more important when Henry VIII chose it as the site of a new naval base[6]. The new yard, situated at the north-east tip of the town, was small, consisting of no more than a few sheds, a sawpit, light-tower, and two jetties; to protect these new and important facilities something a little more ambitious than the two amateur batteries was necessary. Two large artillery forts, both symmetrical works with central keeps, were designed in that year by Richard Lee; one was to be on Beacon Hill and the other on Landguard Point[7]. Neither was built; instead three small blockhouses were sited along the shore, one on Beacon

Hill, another several hundred yards nearer the town and the third near the castle. Called the "Bulwark on the Hill", "The Middle House" and the "Blockhouse of the Tower", they were largely earthworks revetted with gabions, although the third might well have been an adaptation of the old castle[8]. The permanent garrisons were small, just a captain, a gunner and three porters for each blockhouse, but even this proved too expensive for the Crown and the forts were abandoned in 1553 and the guns returned to the Tower[9].

Later in the same year a domestic political crisis prompted the construction of further defences. Mary Tudor established herself at Framlingham Castle after the death of her brother, Edward VI, and prepared to fight the Duke of Northumberland for her right to the throne. Harwich declared in her favour and to secure the town against attack the guns of the blockhouse on Landguard Point were carried across the harbour[10]. The townsfolk took up their shovels once more, began to widen and deepen the ditches before the medieval wall and raised a large mound around the tower at the south-east angle to cover both land and sea approaches to the

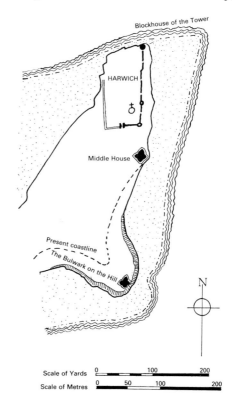

Above: *The fort designed by Richard Lee to be sited on Beacon Hill, Harwich, in 1543.*

Right: *The three blockhouses at Harwich, abandoned in 1553.*

74

town[11]. Either at this time or shortly afterwards a roughly triangular ravelin was built to the west of the town gate in an attempt to outflank the small hill that overlooked the walls.

Little else seems to have been done during the next two decades except that the walls were backed with earth. When Queen Elizabeth arrived in 1561 she was surprised to find that Harwich wanted nothing from her, not even the new fortifications so obviously needed, and four years later the town was regarded as being wholly defenceless[12]. Appeals to the Crown were met with customary inertia, and nothing was done until the aftermath of the Ridolfi conspiracy of 1571 raised fears of troops landing from the Low Countries[13]. These focused the Crown's attention on Harwich, but nothing resulted until the town petitioned the Privy Council for artillery in 1576[14]. Just how low Harwich was on the list of the Crown's priorities was made clear in 1584, when Harwich's portion of an allotted eleven thousand pounds for coast defences was a mere twenty; but as England's relations with Spain moved towards open war a fresh assessment was soon made[15]. New defence works were proposed; the blockhouse on Beacon Hill was

A conjectural view of Richard Lee's fort.

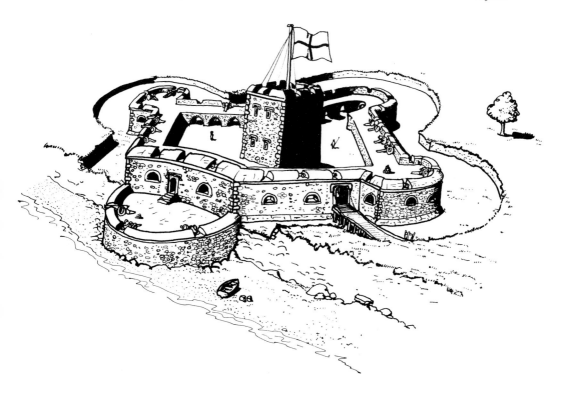

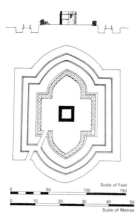

Scale of Feet
0   50   100   150

Scale of Metres
0   10   20   30   40   50

to be supplemented with another at the foot of the cliff, a bulwark was to be built at the south-east corner of the town and a platform raised on the walls to cover the town quay[16].

The following year Harwich was reported as still being weak and under-protected; in November, 1587, an estimate was sent to the Privy Council by the Earl of Warwick, the lord lieutenant of Essex, for £1,288 accompanied by a demand for nineteen guns. The Crown agreed to provide one thousand pounds "upon consideration had of the weak estate and open situation of the town", leaving the Earl to find the rest[17]. The money was to be used to repair the old walls, to construct a palisade along the quays and to build a strong bulwark[18].

Much more ambitious plans to turn Harwich into a modern fortress were drawn up at the same time, but were never

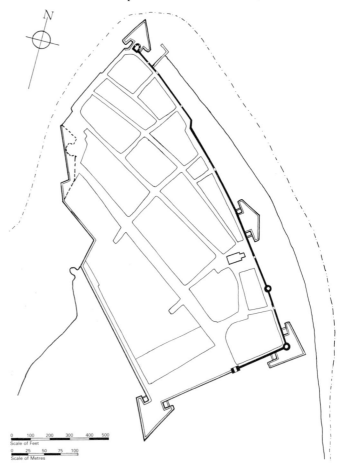

Above: *A plan of a bulwark in the Cottonian Collection marked "Harwich"; it is probably that on Beacon Hill.*

Right: *The planned fortifications of 1588, intended to transform Harwich into a powerful fortress.*

Scale of Feet
0   100   200   300   400   500

Scale of Metres
0   25   50   75   100

implemented. About the south-east corner a large bastion with an acute-angled salient and recessed flankers was to be set, with a very large and obtuse-angled bastion with similar flankers midway along the east wall. A third bastion was planned to enclose the tower next to the dockyard; this was more acutely angled than the first and jutted out into the harbour. The western ditch was to be strengthened with a line of rampart flanked at either end with a demi-bastion. Instead of these elegant examples of military geometry the rudimentary bastion built about the south-east tower was strengthened, a demi-bastion was formed at the south-west corner to enfilade the approaches to the gate and, in an attempt to deny the high ground to the south to the enemy, a bank and ditch was dug from the south-west corner of the walls to Beacon Hill[19]. The remaining blockhouses were brought back into service and forty-six guns mounted in them and along the walls[20]. After 1588 the ramparts were allowed to crumble, the platforms to rot and the guns to rust.

This state of affairs lasted well into the seventeenth century, when the attacks of Dunkirkers virtually halted all coastal trade. At one point there were fifty-eight Ipswich ships crammed into the haven, too scared to set sail for fear of capture[21]. The Privy Council was informed that Harwich was completely defenceless. "The ancient fortifications are now by reason of the many years of happy peace become wholly wasted and unserviceable"[22]. Sir John Coke

Harwich Castle in 1585; note the artillery embrasures.

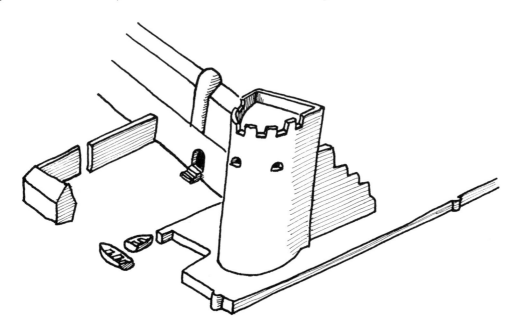

noted that "all the ordnance is dismounted and the platforms decayed and the forts so abandoned that a few Dunkirkers may, without interruption, enter that harbour and burn that rich town"[23]. News that a Flemish pirate ship was to be seen nonchalantly taking soundings in the approaches to the harbour prompted the Crown to send three hundred pounds to be spent on new defences, on which work began in 1626[24]. An earthwork battery with emplacements for nine guns was raised on the King's Quay while a further sixteen guns were placed in the semi-circular Dunn's Bulwark built in front of the walls facing the harbour. But once they were in position the familiar tale of neglect and ruin began, and within eight years the guns were described as "lying all growling and groaning as if they were bed-rid"[25].

These were the only fortifications that guarded Harwich when the Civil War broke out in 1642 and the town declared for Parliament. Three years later Parliament ordered new works to be built, although all this seems to have entailed was the mounting of twelve large cannon[26]. In 1653 the governor of Landguard Fort was ordered to remove the guns and demolish two old forts in

Below left: *The Harwich fortifications of 1626, which suffered so much from neglect that within eight years the guns were said to be "lying all growling and groaning as if they were bed-rid".*

Below right: *The fortifications designed by Sir Bernard de Gomme during the Second Dutch War.*

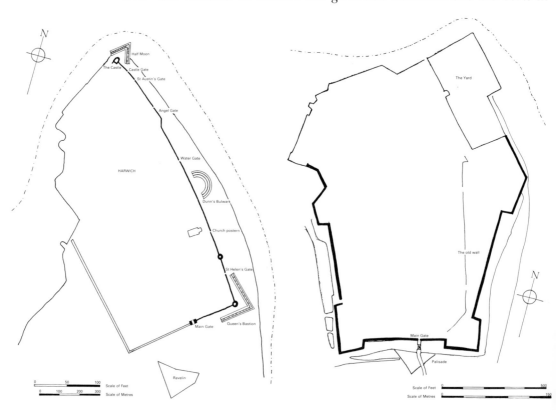

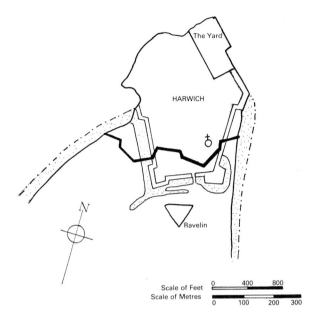

The planned new Harwich fortifications of 1708 rationalising but reducing the defended area.

Harwich, probably the Half-moon Battery and the remains of one of the Henrician blockhouses, which he did so thoroughly that he removed the garrison's only guardroom[27].

During the Second Dutch War, which began in 1665, Harwich stood in the front line, and so great were the fears for the town's safety that the Duke of York and Sir Bernard de Gomme arrived with the urgent task of reforming the defences[28]. A small battery was built on Beacon Hill and the town was surrounded by a completely new enceinte. The Queen's Bastion and the south rampart were remodelled and a new curtain wall facing the harbour was built, which involved demolishing one of the remaining medieval towers and a stretch of wall. Work on the new fortifications was continued into 1668, when Charles II descended on Harwich to examine the existing fortifications and to inspect the site of further works. Accompanied by a train of admiring local worthies, he processed round the defences; taking de Gomme's plan, he corrected it before them all "in his own hand with a black lead pen", thus demonstrating that his ample talents extended to the field of military engineering[29].

As none of these remodelled defences were revetted they rapidly deteriorated. In 1708 the works were so neglected that not a single gun was mounted; the curtain wall on the east had apparently disappeared and the ravelin was a ruin[30]. In 1708 yet another set of plans was drawn up to refortify the town with a new two-bastioned rampart, built behind the old wall and cutting off the peninsula completely[31]. Land was bought on the marshes to the west and a farm purchased on Beacon Hill, where it was planned to build a small fort[32]. But once the land was bought the decline in the importance of the naval yard made the Government change its mind, and it was many years before possession was taken of the land; then it was leased for other purposes[33]. In 1713 the yard was leased to a shipwright, although it continued to build warships.

For the rest of the eighteenth century the rebuilt fort across the water on Landguard Point was regarded as sufficient defence for both harbour and town, while the depredations on the old works continued; in 1732 the battery on the ness was demolished[34]. In 1745, to save the trouble and expense of new works, the old frigate HMS *Winchester* was moored in the harbour to act as a floating battery, and a small stockaded battery armed with four 9-pounders was built on the site later occupied by the redoubt[35].

To secure the high ground, a defensive position was planned at Dovercourt in 1781 consisting of a line of rampart secured at each end by a redoubt[36]. The American War ended before anything could be done, and when war broke out with Revolution-

ary France all Harwich had in the way of defences was its small four-gun battery[37]. To protect the still-vulnerable landward approaches it was proposed in 1798 to site a masonry tower on Beacon Hill, but nothing was done until six years later when General Craig recommended building a tower there armed with "as many guns as possible", as well two smaller towers built on shoals in the harbour to prevent shallow-draught ships slipping in[38].

Two years later yet another report proposed building "a considerable work" of "a nature to be perfectly secure from assault" near the lighthouse to co-operate with Landguard Fort in defending the harbour and to act as a citadel for the town[39]. The first proposal was for a martello tower with a circular battery, but this subsequently evolved into a firm plan to build an eight-gun polygonal redoubt which was changed just before work was to begin to a circular work mounting ten guns[40]. Work began in the spring of 1807 and after various difficulties was completed in 1810 at a final cost of just under sixty thousand pounds[41].

It was a circular work two hundred feet in diameter sur-

Two views of the Redoubt, built into the top of the low hill outside the walls of Harwich between 1807 and 1810. On the opposite page is the courtyard, and on the right is the ditch into which some of the Redoubt's muzzle-loaders were tipped when they became obsolete.

rounded by a thirty-foot-wide and twenty-foot-deep ditch, very similar to the contemporary redoubts at Eastbourne and Dymchurch. Inside was a parade eight-five feet across, around which were arranged eighteen bomb-proof arched casemates to house the garrison and stores. Entrance was gained from a drawbridge leading from the lip of the ditch to the roof of the redoubt, from where three staircases descended into the interior. Around the roof were mounted the guns, 24-pounders, firing through stone-lined embrasures in the parapet. The outer walls were eight foot thick on granite foundations and consumed millions of bricks, the products of brickfields as far away as the Thames Estuary, from where they were brought by barge and delivered to the shore by the site.

In addition to the Redoubt three other batteries were built around Harwich. In 1811 a small semi-circular work armed with three 24-pounders was built on the west side of the town, while on the harbour front the Angel Gate battery armed with five 24-pounders was constructed. The next year the third was built on Beacon Hill and armed with five 12-pounders. After the peace in 1815 the defences were maintained and it was erosion, not neglect, that removed the Beacon Hill battery in 1822. The practice of quarrying the septaria rock at the foot of the cliff to make Roman cement soon led to the sea devouring the cliff and the battery on it. Once it had gone the difficulty of adequately covering the wide harbour entrance reasserted itself and a replacement, armed with five 32-pounders, was planned in 1839 but never built[42].

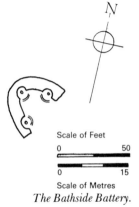

N

Scale of Feet

0   50

0   15

Scale of Metres

The Bathside Battery.

Occupied by a small company of infantry and several gunners, the Redoubt remained the main defence of the harbour; as time passed it assumed a municipal park-like aspect; the grassy hill, with a thick close hedge about the brink of the ditch to prevent cattle and children from falling in, was much frequented by the inhabitants of Harwich who regarded its slopes as a civic amenity. There children played, artillerymen courted nurserymaids, old men sat and watched the ships and occasionally the guns boomed in practice[43].

General Burgoyne, the Inspector-General of Fortifications, visited Harwich in 1853 and wrote an unfavourable report on the defences. He found the "only work of any construction that can be called at all respectable is the Circular Redoubt and that has the very essential defect of being entirely unflanked" and recommended building caponiers in the ditch and replacing the 24-pounders with heavier guns. He proposed siting a powerful battery for thirty or forty guns on the shoal in the middle of the harbour entrance, but rejected that in favour of rebuilding Landguard Fort[44].

In all, General Burgoyne intended spending one hundred and

fifty thousand pounds on new fortifications, but not a penny was spent until after the Royal Commission reported in 1860. Its findings ignored Harwich completely, which prompted anxious letters to General Burgoyne and the asking of questions in the House of Commons[45]. Eventually fifteen thousand pounds was voted to bring the defences up to date and, despite an attempt in Parliament to stop it, work went ahead in 1862. The Redoubt was rearmed with three 8-inch SB and seven 68-pounders while Angel Gate Battery was remodelled to take three 68-pounders[46].

In 1870 a fresh examination of the defences recommended replacing the smooth-bores, which had been virtually obsolete from the day they had been mounted, with heavy RMLs and giving the Redoubt some flanking fire by placing small caponiers made of boiler plate in the ditch[47]. The caponiers never materialised, but three embrasures in the redoubt were widened and cut down to accommodate three twelve-ton 9-inch RMLs, large and bulky guns with an effective range of two thousand yards and the ability to pierce armour plate. They co-operated with the guns of Shotley Battery and the rebuilt Landguard Fort which, when fully armed, gave a total of more than thirty RMLs ranging in size from 12.5-inch to 7-inch.

These works remained adequate until the eighteen-eighties when the rapid advance of military science overtook them, leaving them obsolete and antiquated; Harwich faced the possibility of being bombarded by ships that its guns could not reach. When this threat became impossible to ignore a secret defence committee was convened in 1887 to examine the defences once more. Both Sir Andrew Clarke, the Inspector-General of Fortifications, and General Brackenbury, the Director of Army Intelligence, regarded Harwich as of the utmost importance, for any enemy that disembarked there could rapidly march on London[48]. How much was needed to put things right? the committee was asked; it suggested one hundred thousand pounds to pay for two com-

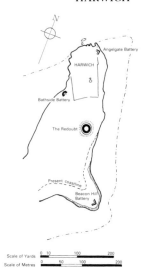

Scale of Yards
0 10   100   200

Scale of Metres
0   50   100   200

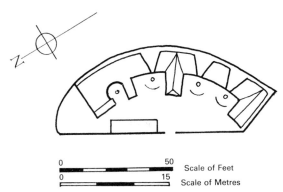

0   50
Scale of Feet

0   15
Scale of Metres

Above: *The Napoleonic batteries.*

Left: *Plan of the Angel Gate Battery after its reconstruction in 1863.*

83

Plan of Beacon Hill Battery, the first of a new generation of fortifications designed to mount breech-loading guns.

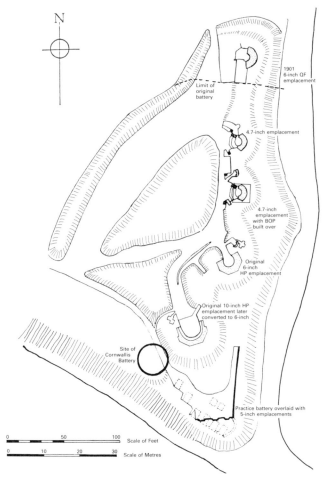

N

1901
6-inch QF
emplacement

Limit of
original
battery

4.7-inch emplacement

4.7-inch
emplacement
with BOP
built over

Original
6-inch
HP emplacement

Original 10-inch HP
emplacement later
converted to 6-inch

Site of
Cornwallis
Battery

Practice battery overlaid with
5-inch emplacements

0   50   100   Scale of Feet

0   10   20   30   Scale of Metres

pletely new batteries armed with the most modern large-calibre guns, one to be sited at Landguard Fort and the other on Beacon Hill. Plans were quickly completed, the work was approved, the money—reduced to forty-two thousand pounds—was voted and in 1889 construction began[49]. The new battery was the first of the new generation of fortifications designed to mount the new breech-loading guns. It was made as inconspicuous as possible; all that could be seen from the sea was a grass bank, and only close to did the shallow ditch of the Twydall Profile reveal itself. Within the fortified enclosure there were positions for four guns; the largest contained a 10-inch BL on an Elswick HP mount, with a 6-inch BL on a similar carriage in the adjoining emplacement, separated by a deep subterranean magazine. Beside these were two 4.7-inch QF to combat fast torpedo-boats. By 1892 the battery was fully armed, with searchlights and position finders, and ready for action. Despite its inconspicuous and modest appearance it cost twenty-five thousand pounds, of which thirteen thousand were for the guns and their attendant machinery[50].

The guns were manned by a brigade of Garrison Artillery, supplemented by visiting militia and volunteer units who came for training. The commanding officer of the new battery was Major Panzera, later to become famous as the commander of the scratch collection of antique guns that defended Mafeking during the siege by the Boers. An odder contrast in circumstances can hardly be imagined as Panzera exchanged his giant 10-inch BL and the mists of the North Sea for miniature 7-pounders out on the veldt[51]. More guns were added over the next few years. Two 3-pounders were emplaced for practice to the south of the 10-inch emplacement and four 5-inch BL were placed in a practice battery below it.

Throughout the eighteen-nineties and for the first years of the twentieth century Harwich was a fortress maintained at peak efficiency. Although the main defensive emphasis was seaward, provision was made to protect the town and batteries from landward attack. Two battalions of volunteers and four field guns were allocated to Harwich with a defensive line, to be dug when necessary, running across the peninsula at Dovercourt. The total garrison, including troops at Felixstowe and Shotley, was five thousand men[52].

The expansion of German naval power at the end of the nineteenth century led to a fresh examination of the Harwich defences. In 1899 yet another committee considered the newly anticipated threat and the ability of the existing guns to protect the harbour[53]. The single 6-inch on its disappearing carriage was condemned as too slow, and the next year a 6-inch QF was installed in a new emplacement sited just outside the original battery; the defences were extended to accommodate it[54].

The Redoubt had been rearmed in 1890 with two 12-pounder QF; the three old 9-inch RMLs were ignominiously heaved over the parapet into the ditch, where they lay to be gently buried in falling rubbish. Two of the vacated emplacements were then built up and filled with a raised concrete base in which expense lockers were fitted[55].

The zenith of Harwich's artillery defences was reached in 1904 when it bristled with one 10-inch, two 6-inch, four 5-inch, two 4.7-inch, two 12-pounders and two 3-pounders, but the Owen Report on the armament of the Military Ports recommended scrapping all but the 6-inch and 4.7-inch[56]. The two original BL emplacements were rebuilt to take two 6-inch Mk VII on standard Mk II mountings. The following year Harwich became even more strategically important when HMS *Audacious* and a destroyer

A view over Beacon Hill Battery. In the foreground is a casemate over the old 10-inch emplacement later converted to 6-inch. In the background are the second 6-inch emplacement and the battery observation post.

flotilla made the harbour their headquarters, the facilities of which included a floating dock, a coal hulk and oil tanks. The flotilla made regular sham attacks on the harbour entrance, when the searchlights flickered and the guns cracked and boomed their mock defiance. Harwich Council was not altogether happy about the thunder of artillery on summer days, which annoyed and occasionally alarmed visitors, but it was prepared to accept the inconvenience in return for the security offered by the garrison and fortifications[57].

On the outbreak of the Great War, Harwich was in the front line at once. The guns on Beacon Hill were augmented with a pair of 1-pounder automatics, the first anti-aircraft guns to be installed[58]. The harbour was packed with the destroyers of Admiral Tyrwhitt's Harwich Force and a Royal Naval Air Station was established at Felixstowe. The town and surrounding area was designated a class A fortress, a set of trenches and wired strongpoints was built across the peninsula at Dovercourt, and the district was closed to all but those who either lived or were stationed there. Strangers were an object of deep suspicion; a young Scotsman discovered sketching waterside scenes was arrested and dragged off to the Redoubt, where he was briefly imprisoned until his mother arrived to rescue him[59]. For the four years of the war the guns were ready and waiting, but no target ever presented itself and the only shots fired were in practice. The only German warships to penetrate the harbour were the surrendered U-boats that congregated in dismal queues after the Armistice awaiting the breaker's torch.

After the war the Redoubt and the surrounding land was sold to the town council and the 12-pounders and the 4.7-inch guns at Beacon Hill were removed. Rearmament programmes in the nineteen-thirties considered installing twin 6-pounders and re-mounting the 6-inch on long-range carriages, but nothing had been done by the outbreak of the Second World War[60]. In April, 1940, work began on building an emplacement for a twin 6-pounder, which was finished in July. This, the Cornwallis Battery, was a bleak structure of reinforced concrete with a high tower to hold the rangefinder and predictor[61].

The small size of the German surface fleet in 1939 made bombardment a most unlikely proposition, although all the guns were maintained at peak levels of readiness. The greatest immediate danger, once war had broken out, was air attack, particularly aerial minelaying, which claimed an early victim when HMS *Gipsy* was blown apart by a magnetic mine just outside the harbour entrance[62]. Heavy and light AA guns were emplaced all around the town, which had been designated a gun-defended area within the

Destroyers in Harwich harbour about 1914. Approaching them is a Sopwith Bat Boat from the Royal Naval Air Station that had just opened at Felixstowe.

Gordon Kinsey

Left: *The rear of one of the casemates constructed in 1940 to give overhead protection to the Beacon Hill guns.*

Below: *Cornwallis Battery, completed in 1940, mounted a single twin 6-pounder. This battery remained until Beacon Hill Fort closed in 1956, its 6-pounders being then the only armament.*

Two fixed-beam searchlight emplacements on the shore below Beacon Hill.

general schemes of AA defence[63]. Not only did the Luftwaffe attack but on eight separate occasions in the autumn and winter of 1940–41 the Italian air force struck blows of incomparable feebleness and incompetence[64]. The AA defences were increased and in July, 1940, there were seventeen heavy AA guns in the town as well as numerous light weapons; but by September the pressure of the Luftwaffe's assault on other areas of the country had forced a reduction to eight[65].

The guns at Beacon Hill, two 6-inch Mk VIIs, began the war in open emplacements, but as the threat of low-level attacks by aircraft grew they were provided with semi-circular flat-roofed casemates. These look exceptionally modern today, stark and massive, with a highly textured surface showing the shuttering rather like some unfinished seaside exercise by a particularly austere new brutalist. Two tall slab-sided towers were built, one in the old right 4.7-inch emplacement as a BOP and the other outside the perimeter for radar[66].

In late 1940 the Angel Gate Battery was rebuilt, mounting two 12-pounders in brick gunhouses disguised as small cottages, one hundred and twenty feet apart with the BOP built between them[67]. Two searchlights completed the battery, together with a set of air-raid shelters that were originally destined for Beacon Hill but were built at Angel Gate by some inexplicable piece of bungling. While these works were being built the Admiralty installed a temporary battery of 4-inch guns on Harwich Green[68].

The only subsequent alteration to the guns of Beacon Hill was to move the right-hand 6-inch gun to the reconstructed QF emplacement in 1941, giving the confusing impression that three guns were mounted instead of only two. Plans to replace the guns with three 6-inch Mk XXIV were delayed and then cancelled in favour of two 5.25-inch on dual-purpose mountings which were never installed[69].

A line of pillboxes, machine-gun posts and anti-tank obstacles ran from the south of Dovercourt to the Stour near Parkeston Quay with 25-pounders, 75 mm guns, and 6 and 2-pounder anti-tank guns. The Redoubt was reoccupied by the army but played no crucial role in the defences, being used to imprison unruly soldiers whose obscene scrawls on the cell walls remain as uncouth testimony to their lack of education and of enthusiasm for the war effort.

In 1945 the Angel Gate Battery was closed; the 6-inch on Beacon Hill were withdrawn in 1947, but the 6-pounder remained, although adapted for AA fire. In 1956 the last of all the hundreds of pieces of artillery that had defended Harwich were taken away to be scrapped and, after more than four hundred years, Harwich was no longer a fortress[70].

This massive blockhouse and observation post controlled the minefield guarding the entrance to Harwich harbour.

Shotley and Felixstowe 7

APART FROM one small battery armed with three 32-pounders at the foot of Bull's Cliff, all the main defences of Harwich harbour were concentrated about the entrance until 1798, when it was proposed to build three masonry towers along the cliffs at Felixstowe to prevent an enemy landing and attacking Landguard Fort from the rear[1]. This scheme came to nothing but was revived five years later with the addition of a strong fort on Shotley Point to cover the interior of the harbour and to stop armed boats going upstream to attack Ipswich and Manningtree[2].

It took a further five years before the plans were realised and ten martello towers and six batteries were built. Three towers and three batteries were sited on the banks of the harbour, with the rest along the coast from the tip of Landguard Point to the mouth of the river Deben. All the towers were of the standard east coast design, armed with three guns, and all but towers O, P, S and U supported small batteries. Towers L and M with attendant batteries were placed on Shotley Point instead of the planned fort, crossing their fire with the Bathside Battery at Harwich and tower N at Walton. All ten towers and attendant batteries were completed and armed by 1811, but almost as soon as the Napoleonic Wars had ended in 1815 some became redundant or were threatened by erosion. Tower P was handed over to the coastguard in 1816 and O and S were abandoned to the sea in the eighteen-thirties[3].

Nothing more was planned until 1862 when, in the wake of the Royal Commission, the fort at Shotley was finally built and towers L to Q rearmed with one 68-pounder and two 8-inch SB each[4]. Captain Jones, the local RE officer, seized his chance to design a major fort with enthusiasm and planned an ambitious polygonal fort with a deep scarped ditch generously flanked by two double caponiers and a single caponier. The lines of the fort were actually staked out on the ground when Colonel Jervois, the secretary to the Royal Commission, realised that it was far too elaborate and expensive and substituted a much simpler defensible battery[5]. This was an irregular seven-sided work with an unrevetted ditch and loop-holed Carnot wall. Finished in 1863 at a cost of ten thousand pounds, it was armed with fourteen 68-pounders[6].

Ten years later the fort was rearmed with 7-inch RMLs and Walton Battery was rebuilt to take three heavier 9-inch RMLs[7]. Firing a 112-pound shell, the guns at Shotley were rather smaller

The projected fort at Shotley designed by Captain R. Jones. An elaborate and extensive design, it had two double caponiers and a single caponier as well as generous casemated accommodation.

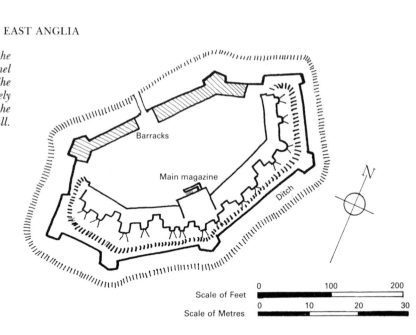

Shotley Fort as built to the designs of Colonel W. F. D. Jervois. The caponiers were merely loopholed projections of the scarp wall.

Barracks

Main magazine

Ditch

N

Scale of Feet

0   100   200

Scale of Metres

0   10   20   30

than would normally be emplaced by that time; but by then the decision had been taken to rebuild Landguard Fort, relegating Shotley to a minor role, despite the fact that both Ardargh and G. S. Clarke firmly stated that, if properly armed, it made Landguard Fort and Beacon Hill superfluous[8].

In 1887 it was necessary to upgrade the armament at Landguard Fort and build the new battery at Beacon Hill, which left the remaining towers and their attendant batteries without military significance. The guns, by then totally obsolete, were withdrawn from 1880, the last to go being the 9-inch at Walton Battery. In order that Shotley Fort could still play a useful role in the defences it was planned in 1891 to replace the 7-inch with four 10-inch RMLs on long-range mountings; these were already obsolete, and the replacement can only have been regarded as a temporary expedient[9]. Only half this scheme was eventually carried out; the two new emplacements with connecting magazines obliterated six of the original emplacements, and the ditch was filled in and earth heaped up to give extra protection. The guns, which had an active life of less than ten years, were last used in 1901[10]. Three years later the fort and adjoining land were transferred to the Admiralty to become part of the shore establishment of HMS *Ganges*, and the right-hand emplacement and whole south-east corner of the fort were demolished to make room for new accommodation blocks.

With hindsight, Shotley Fort appears to have been the most successful of all Harwich's nineteenth-century defences. It mounted more guns than Landguard Fort at a fraction of the cost, could not be bombarded from the sea, and covered the harbour so effectively that no enemy ship could have anchored there with the fort in action. The only task beyond Shotley Fort's capability was stopping Harwich from being bombarded, but that was, in brutal strategic terms, an unimportant one. What did matter was to deny the use of the harbour to an invading fleet.

The martello towers, although obsolete as active defences, still continued to serve military functions. Tower L became a signal station at HMS *Ganges*, P was adapted as a naval wireless station when Harwich became a destroyer base[11], and Q and R were used as position-finding stations for the new batteries at Landguard Fort, only becoming redundant in 1909 when Landguard's 10-inch guns were removed[12].

After the removal of the RMLs at Shotley there were no effective modern weapons outside the two defensive complexes at Landguard Fort and Beacon Hill until the Committee of Imperial Defence recommended in 1913 that two powerful new guns, intended to replace the scrapped 10-inch BLs and to eliminate an area of dead water, should be sited at North Felixstowe[13]. If an armoured cruiser lay to the north-east of Landguard Fort it could not be fired on by the guns at Beacon Hill, and only the solitary 6-inch left-hand gun at Landguard Fort could engage it. The committee's suggestions were repeated in 1914 and work began on the new battery at North Felixstowe in April, 1915[14]. The guns, two 9.2-inch Mk X brought from Berehaven in Ireland, were in place and ready for firing by the end of the year[15]. Firing a 380-pound shell to seventeen thousand yards, they were the most powerful weapons ever to be mounted upon the east coast; although the 10-inch BLs at Landguard, East Tilbury and Beacon Hill fired a five-hundred-pound shell, they had a smaller range and less penetrative power.

The new battery, named after General Brackenbury, was a simple but strong structure, the guns and their complex carriages

Tower N at Walton Ferry, near Felixstowe. It has the distinction, shared with tower 30 at Rye, Sussex, of having a cunette—a wet ditch at the foot of the glacis—twenty feet wide. The moat around the tower was, at seventy feet, one of the broadest of all those around the martello towers. The tower itself was demolished in the early years of this century and the surrounding battery disappeared under dock extensions in 1980.

The Felixstowe and Shotley area, showing the defences on the Suffolk side of Harwich harbour.

being set in concrete pits with magazines and shelters beneath. The earth parapet curved round behind the guns to give some rearward protection, and the whole battery was surrounded by a shallow ditch and iron fence. Separate barracks for the garrisons were built one hundred yards behind.

During the First World War Shotley and Felixstowe were included within the land defences of Harwich fortress, and the

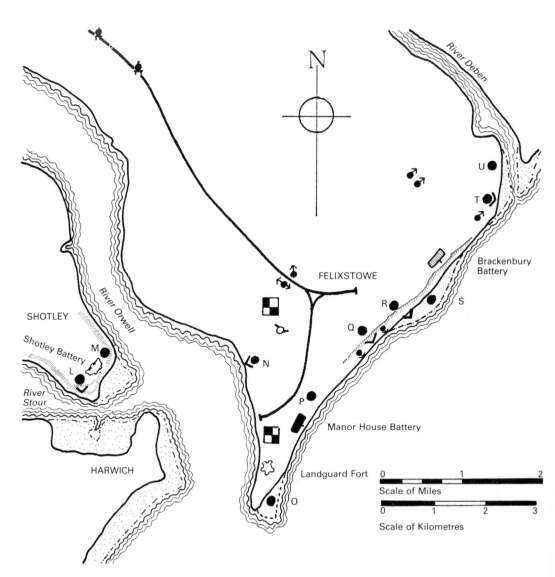

N

River Deben

River Orwell

SHOTLEY

Shotley Battery

River Stour

HARWICH

FELIXSTOWE

U

T

Brackenbury Battery

R

S

Q

M

L

N

P

Manor House Battery

Landguard Fort

O

| 0 | | 1 | | 2 |
Scale of Miles

| 0 | 1 | 2 | 3 |
Scale of Kilometres

94

positions of the trenches and wire entanglements generally followed those laid out in pre-war defence plans[16]. The main positions were at Walton, to defend the rear of Landguard Fort, and on the high ground overlooking Bawdsey Ferry, while machine-guns were installed on N, P and Q towers[17].

After the Armistice Brackenbury Battery was retained and used for training by Territorial Army units. They tended to practise on summer Sunday afternoons to the maximum discomfort of the neighbouring residents, the concussion of the guns rattling windows and shaking loose plaster to such an extent that the local MP was moved to ask a question in Parliament. He asked if the firing could be stopped, because Felixstowe was a resort largely used by people with shattered nerves whose convalescence was ruined by the thud of heavy artillery. The War Office rejected his complaints, offering only sympathy and mild regrets to those whose nerves remained unsteady and whose ceilings continued to crack[18].

In 1930 the worn-out barrels of the guns at Brackenbury Battery were replaced and the next year a change from 15-degree

One of the two 10-inch RML emplacements installed at Shotley Fort in the early eighteen-nineties.

to 35-degree long-range carriages was approved, but never implemented. After the new barrels had been fitted the battery was placed in care and maintenance; the guns were covered in grease and the breech, firing mechanisms and all electrical equipment were removed. In 1936, with a renewed German threat looming once more from across the North Sea, it was proposed to add another gun to the battery, but this, like so many other plans, came to nothing[19]. The guns were reactivated at the time of the Munich crisis and resumed practice firings, but this time there were no complaints to Parliament. It was on a practice shoot in July, 1939, that the battery unwittingly contributed to the development of coast artillery radar. Purely by chance the shoot coincided with radar trials from nearby Bawdsey Manor, and the splashes of the heavy shells striking the sea were large enough to appear on the radar screens. Further experiments were quickly conducted to determine the feasibility of obtaining range and bearing[20].

With the outbreak of the Second World War Brackenbury Battery was ready for action. The only alteration to the physical structure was the building of blast walls about the emplacements, which reduced their arcs of fire, and surrounding the whole

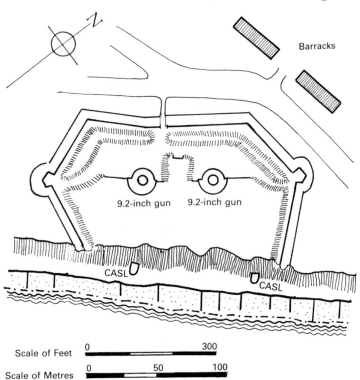

Brackenbury Battery, Felixstowe.

*One of Brackenbury
Battery's two searchlight
emplacements at beach
level, added in 1941.*
East Anglian Daily Times

position with trenches and strongpoints. The main disadvantage of
the battery was that it had no capacity to fire at night, a defect
which was not remedied until 1941 when two 90 cm searchlights
were installed in emplacements at the foot of the cliff. At the same
time the fire control system was reorganised by installing a
thirty-foot Barr and Stroud rangefinder[21]. Despite these improvements the battery's wartime service was brief. By the middle of the
war the possibility of a German ship worthy of the battery's heavy
shells appearing was extremely remote, and the battery was again
placed in care and maintenance after the first general reduction of
coast artillery in 1943[22].

The only other coast defence work, and the last major
fortification to be built in the area, was an emergency battery sited
one thousand five hundred yards to the north of Landguard Fort,
directly in front of the Manor House Hotel, after which it was
called. The guns, two 6-inch Mk XII ex-naval guns, were mounted
in standard concrete casemates built on the edge of the beach. This
battery was allotted a close-defence role, long-range counter-
bombardment being left to the land service guns at Landguard and
Brackenbury[23]. In addition to the already heavy armament of the
area, two 12-inch rail guns were stationed at Levington Bridge and
Wallgates Farm, Trimley, during 1940.

Extensive land defences were built around Felixstowe in 1940,
with anti-tank guns covering the main entrance to the town and the
marshes toward the Deben. A battery of 25-pounders was sited on

the heights at Walton, and the beach was sown with mines and blocked by scaffolding and barbed wire. A 75 mm field gun was installed at the mouth of the Deben and two batteries of 3.7-inch AA guns were emplaced, one on Landguard Common near the fort and the other to the north of the town near the railway line[24]. Q tower was brought back into service as the AA operations room for the Harwich defended area and directly linked to No 11 Group's operations room at Uxbridge[25].

When the war ended the mines were grubbed up, the scaffolding and wire removed, Manor House Battery abandoned and Q tower sold to become a private house. Brackenbury Battery alone remained active, occasionally firing for the benefit of territorial units, until 1952 when it was ordered to be dismantled. It was sold to Felixstowe Council, who demolished it with great difficulty in 1969.

Felixstowe in 1837, from an etching by Henry Davy. Tower P can be seen at left and the cliffs of Felixstowe are in the background; towers Q and R were built on the cliffs.

Frank Hussey

Landguard Fort 8

LANDGUARD POINT was the key to Harwich Harbour, secured by a fortification since the reign of Henry VIII, for guns placed there dominated at close range the only available channel for large ships. The latest fort, an architectural amalgam of eighteenth-century bastions, Victorian iron armour-plate and twentieth-century utilitarian concrete, still stands as a monument to its strategic importance.

The first defensive work was recommended for the point in 1539, when John de Vere, Earl of Oxford, proposed building a fort there, a decision confirmed by Thomas Cromwell[1]. As a temporary measure entrenchments were dug but no further work was done until the summer of 1543, when a visit by the King was followed by a firm decision to fortify Harwich harbour properly[2]. Richard Lee, the Surveyor of the King's Works, drew up plans for two large artillery forts, one on Beacon Hill and the other on Landguard Point. The work on the point, armed with more than forty guns, was diamond shaped, with two projecting oblong artillery platforms, a square central keep and two small flanking bastions; in almost all respects identical to Southsea Castle, built the following year[3]. This ambitious proposal remained on parchment, and instead the following year two small blockhouses or bulwarks were sited at "Langer Point" and "Langer Rood"[4]. The site of the bulwark on the point is obvious, but the location of "Langer Rood" remains a mystery. Major Leslie, in his history of the fort, supposed that it was located at a place then known as Garrison Rood two miles away on high ground at Walton[5]. This is unlikely, as a fort there would be too far from the harbour to be of much use except to cover the rear of its neighbour on the point. It is more likely that "Langer Rood" was located at Walton Ferry, where it could cross fire with the blockhouse at Harwich and worry any ship that penetrated the harbour. When Royal Engineers were searching for a suitable location for martello towers in 1808 local fishermen pointed out the site of an old fortification at Walton Ferry where tower N was eventually built[6]. The bulwarks were little more than semi-permanent batteries, revetted with timber and gabions, described by Edward VI as "bulwarks of earth and wood"[7], a description confirmed by two contemporary plans[8].

They did not remain as active military posts for long, and within ten years were reduced to ruin by a parsimonious

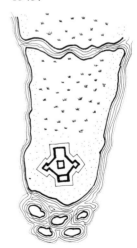

Richard Lee's proposed fort on "Langer Point", 1543.

A conjectural view of the proposed fort on "Langer Point".

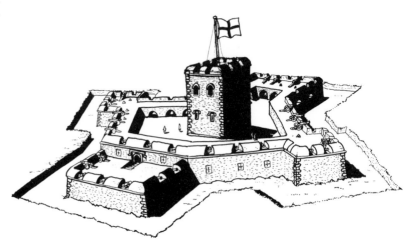

administration that refused to maintain any but the most essential defences in peacetime. Both bulwarks were ordered to be dismantled in October, 1552, and the next year the guns were taken to the Tower of London[9]. Shortly afterwards the works were pulled down by John Jennyn, the lieutenant of the point bulwark, probably so that he could sell or use for private purposes the timber from the gun platforms and revetments[10].

Over the next four decades what remained of the two earthworks was eroded by the elements, until the prospect of war with Spain prompted inquiries into their condition. Lord Darcey was directed to examine the "decayed fort beside Harwich" in 1578, but nothing tangible resulted from his visit[11]. In the year before the Armada the point was surveyed again and reported to be extremely vulnerable. The Privy Council was warned that the Spanish might bring large ships close to the point and, having seized it, entrench themselves to bombard Harwich and raid throughout the county; only a new sconce, built of turf and armed with six guns, could prevent this[12]. This report was supported by the deputy-lieutenants of Suffolk, who asked for one thousand pounds and some field guns[13]. The military engineer Arthur Gregory was commissioned to draw a plan for a new fort, yet all that was done was to repair and re-form the old bulwarks[14]. Both were regarrisoned in 1588 and appeared in the list of establishments under their old names of "Langerside Bulwark" and "Langer Rood"[15]. A map of 1715 showing the remains of the "Langer Point" work reveal it to have been a simple hexagon, each face about one hundred feet long, with no flanking defences[16]. For just a few months Landguard Point and its fortifications were the

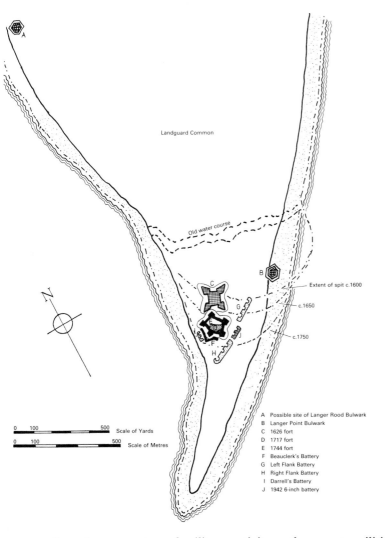

Landguard Common

Old water course

Extent of spit c.1600

c.1650

c.1750

A Possible site of Langer Rood Bulwark
B Langer Point Bulwark
C 1626 fort
D 1717 fort
E 1744 fort
F Beauclerk's Battery
G Left Flank Battery
H Right Flank Battery
I Darrell's Battery
J 1942 6-inch battery

0   100   500
Scale of Yards
0   100   500
Scale of Metres

N

centre of much unaccustomed military activity as the county militia
gathered to repel the Spanish threat, but after the Armada had
fled, battered and demoralised, the defences were abandoned.

By the beginning of the seventeenth century Landguard Point
was without any adequate fortifications, and when the activities of
the Dunkirkers became a serious threat Harwich appealed to the
Crown; as a result a decision was made to build a completely new
fort a little to the south of the ruins of the old bulwark, but nothing
was done until 1625 when the Crown allocated three hundred
pounds[17]. Later in that year the Earl of Warwick, lord lieutenant of

101

Essex, gathered troops to protect the harbour while the new fort was being constructed. He commandeered six guns from a ship, installed them in a temporary battery, pressed into service a large body of labourers and set to work on building the fort[18].

Although Warwick took the credit for building Landguard Fort, and his name is still commemorated in one of the bastions, he did not design it; that was done by Simon Van Cranvelt, a Dutchman who had been recruited from Holland[19]. He started work on the new fort in November, 1625, and continued until the end of the year when he was ordered to Newcastle, where he died[20]. An Englishman, Richard Scott, took over the work of supervising construction until superseded by Master Heath, the designer of Sandown Fort in the Isle of Wight[21].

The new fort was a simple square with an acute-angled bastion at each corner. The ramparts, forty feet thick and twenty-five feet high, were made of turves laid like bricks, giving a steeper profile than would have been possible with heaped earth. The dry ditch sixty feet wide and twelve deep was crossed by a timber causeway and drawbridge. At each corner of the fort was what was described as a "batterie" but was probably a raised mound or cavalier on which some of the guns were mounted to gain increased command. Within the walls were two brick barrack blocks for the soldiers, a vaulted magazine, a chapel, a house for the captain and a gatehouse complete with portcullis[22]. On the ramparts was a formidable armament of sixty-two iron and brass guns, their names

The bulwark at "Langer Point" was a sconce of earth and board, as in this reconstruction. Such a fortification had no permanence.

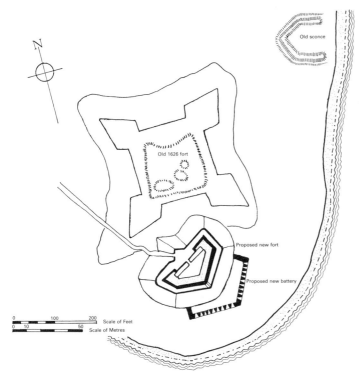

*This plan of 1715 shows
the remains of the
hexagonal sconce built in
1540 and recommissioned
in 1588, though by this
time there would be no
more than a low bank of
earth to be seen.*

like the inventory of some fabulous zoo: basilisks, sakers, drakes
and demi-culverin all poked their muzzles from the embrasures of
the new fort[23].

The guns' first target was not a predatory Dunkirker but one
of the King's own ships. It was the practice that ships passing a
Royal fort should lower their flags in salute, and when one
obstinately refused to do so the lieutenant-governor, Robert
Gosnold, threatened to open fire. It was not a good indication of
the fort's powers that it gained the worst of the encounter[24].

Richard Plumleighe, captain of the offending vessel, later
reported to the Admiralty Secretary:

> I told them that without an Order from the Counsell or Commissioners
> of the Admiralty I durst doe noe such obeisance, they answered that if I
> refused it they would sinke me and that they had warrant from my Ld.
> of Warwick soe to doe. I slighted that Authority and replyed that I
> thought my selfe as able to beate their paper fort to pecies with my
> Ordinance as they to sink me, and bidde them take heed how they made
> the first shott, upon this wee fell to worse wordes and at length to some
> blowes in which they had nothing the better.

Gosnold was the start of a long tradition of eccentric and
irascible commanders. The year before this "battle" he had quelled

The fort of 1626, with its ramparts made of turves laid like bricks.

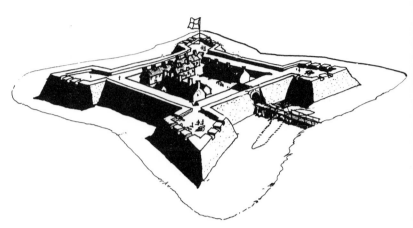

a mutiny, or what he deemed a mutiny, by seizing six men at random, defining them as ringleaders, forcing them to draw straws and then condemning the trembling clutcher of the shortest to death. The prisoner was not immediately executed but was ordered to be sent back to his home, where the sentence was to be carried out. The prisoner got only as far as Trimley where the constable, knowing the law far better than the lieutenant-governor, released him[25].

The condition of the fort rapidly declined: Charles I was chronically short of money and had none to spare for Landguard Fort. In 1635 grave concern was expressed over the state of the fort; more than twenty guns had disappeared and the remainder lay useless and rusting on the ground amidst the remains of their rotten carriages. The moat was unfinished, the bastions and ramparts slumped in a state of almost irremediable dereliction, while the unfortunate garrison was in danger of starving to death[26]. The next year, the surveyor-general found the fort "decayed and ruined"; the ramparts were so eroded by the weather that it was possible to ride into the fort at several points. The only solution was to encase it with a twelve-foot-high brick revetment, for which the money was never found[27].

When the Civil War began in 1642 the ill-treated garrison not surprisingly declared for Parliament; their Royal master owed them seven years' back pay. The war hardly affected the fort, beyond a mysterious plot to subvert the garrison in which the chaplain was strongly suspected[28] and the execution of the governor, the Earl of Holland, for treason against Parliament[29]. Throughout the Civil War and the First Dutch War Landguard was well maintained but by 1656 it was decayed once more and the

104

garrison forced to sleep out in the nearby villages for want of bedding[30].

The year 1660 saw Charles II enjoying his restoration and Landguard Fort, as ruinous as ever, needing one. Despairing of ever seeing it efficient, the Duke of Albemarle ordered it to be demolished in 1663, but the Master-General of the Ordnance protested so strongly that the decision was revoked and the fort provided with six new culverins, twelve new demi-culverins and two minions[31].

The Second Dutch War began in 1665, and Landguard Fort was prepared for action as enemy ships began to cruise off the coast. The next year the fort amply justified the time and labour expended upon it when a Dutch squadron anchored off the point and a culverin was fired from the fort at a sloop that ventured close to the shore[32]. This incident served as a timely warning; the gun platforms were repaired and palisades brought from Ipswich to be placed in the ditch as an extra defence. Early in 1667 the Council of State ordered that the fort, which was still largely unrevetted, be cased in brick and stone, with extra outworks and a redoubt to protect the landward approaches[33]. The renovations were planned by Sir Bernard de Gomme, but there was only time to build a low brick scarp to form a fausse-braye; the ramparts and bastions themselves were not completely revetted and the outworks never materialised. Slight though the fausse-braye was, only some ten feet high from the bottom of the ditch, it proved a formidable and decisive obstacle to the assaulting Dutch[34] when the attack did come in July that year.

For several days the Dutch fleet did nothing but cruise up and down the coast until, on 2nd July, the long-expected attack took place. The Dutch ships came close in to the shore and drew up off North Felixstowe out of range of Landguard Fort. Their intention was simple; to land troops to capture the fort so that they might enter the harbour unopposed. Forty-seven ships, the bulk of the fleet, were to remain off Felixstowe while two squadrons were to move south to lie off the fort. One squadron, commanded by Admiral Jan van Nes, was ordered to try to force the harbour entrance and bombard the fort from the west while the other, under Admiral Cornelis Evertsen, was to lie to the east and attempt to cover the infantry attack with rolling clouds of gunsmoke[35].

Inside the fort were about five hundred men under the command of Captain Nathaniel Darell, two companies of infantry and some artillerymen, while outside on the heights at Walton the Suffolk trained bands and some cavalry were waiting. Had the Dutch attacked at once and then pressed on with a resolute assault they might have succeeded in their designs, but their commander, Admiral de Ruyter, held off until the afternoon due to the failure

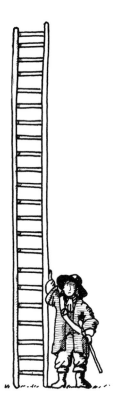

of van Nes and Evertsen to reach their allotted positions. It was not until two in the afternoon that about two thousand Dutch soldiers and marines with three small cannon landed on the beach at the foot of Felixstowe cliff. The delay had allowed the English troops at Walton time to advance, forcing the Dutch to leave a sizeable portion of the landing party as a rearguard to protect the boats. The rest advanced down the spit to the fort carrying fascines and scaling ladders. Led by the English traitor Colonel Dolman, they rushed at the fort derisively crying, "peace! peace!"[36]. When they reached the edge of the ditch the Dutch ships ceased firing for fear of hitting their own men, and the Dutch troops established themselves on the shingle about the fort. There was a brisk exchange of fire and then the Dutch launched an assault; for about three-quarters of an hour they tried to get their ladders against the wall, but were driven off. They tried again but met with such a fierce response from the fort and from two small English ships, the *Truelove* and *Lennox*, which fired across the spit from the waters of the harbour, that they retreated in haste and disorder[37].

The fort's garrison emerged from the gate to find a litter of abandoned scaling ladders, some hand-grenades, a case of handsome pistols and four Dutchmen dead on the sand[38]. When the fleeing Dutch reached their landing place and were united with the rearguard they found that the tide was out and the heavy boats had grounded on the shingle; they were forced to remain under fire from the trained bands until darkness fell. It was not until two the following morning that the last of the assault force regained the safety of their ships[39].

The Dutch fleet continued to lie close in to the shore and in the next few days more English troops marched in to secure Land-

The fort as reconstructed by Sir Bernard de Gomme in 1667 with a brick revetment. Although the revetment was not completed at the time, de Gomme's fausse-braye proved a formidable obstacle to the Dutch attackers that year; they failed to get their scaling ladders, above, against the ramparts.

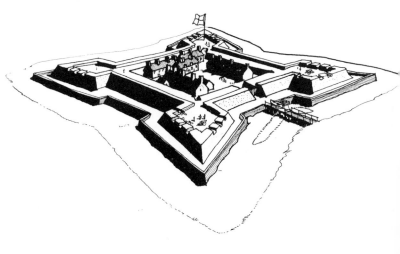

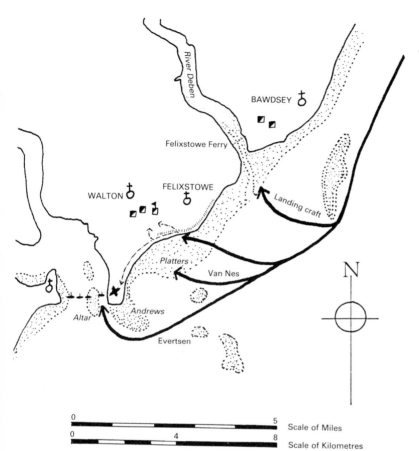

The Dutch attack on the fort, July, 1667.

River Deben

BAWDSEY

Felixstowe Ferry

WALTON   FELIXSTOWE

Landing craft

Platters

Van Nes

N

Andrews

Altar

Evertsen

0					5

Scale of Miles

0			4		8

Scale of Kilometres

guard Fort. The whole county was busy with alarums, and the trained bands treated every stranger with deep suspicion, knocking out the brains of a Frenchman whose accent they took for Dutch[40]. Several more days went by before the Dutch fleet finally sailed off, leaving many grim mementoes; every tide rolled ashore the corpses of Dutch sailors, and close by the fort the sea uncovered two hastily buried attackers[41]. The Dutch had altogether some seventy men killed and twice that number wounded, while the garrison lost only one man dead and four wounded, including Captain Darell, shot in the shoulder. Had the Dutch pressed their attack with more vigour and had better luck they might well have succeeded.

When the Third Dutch War began in 1672 another attack on Harwich harbour was anticipated, and the inevitable complaints about the condition of Landguard Fort were made. "This place is in the most miserable condition of any fort in Europe," it was reported at this time. "Everyone who sees it and considers its importance wonders that no greater care is taken to secure it"[42]. The drawbridge had fallen down, the ramparts were ruinous and the garrison was unpaid. Repairs were made, and towards the end of the seventeenth century the fort, until then largely unrevetted, was finished in brick. This was accomplished piece by piece; a report of 1683 stated that "if the two remaining curtains were finished, the moat cleansed and a counterscarp made . . . this fortress would be no less strong than considerable"[43]. But despite this intermittent work the fort was hardly more than a ruin in 1715[44]. The walls were decayed and one of the bastions had partly tumbled into the moat, in which the sea had made two substantial breaches[45]. As if to emphasise the fort's decrepit state, the garrison was composed of a company of invalids, hobbling and wheezing about their duties[46]. Seventy guns lined the ramparts, too many to work efficiently; and most were as old and corroded as the garrison. It was obvious to even the most optimistic observer that Landguard in its existing state could never be defended.

In 1708 plans were made to expand the dockyard across the water at Harwich, and in anticipation of this Landguard Fort was once more surveyed. The Ordnance Office thought that, enlarged and repaired, it might serve a useful purpose and an order was made to refortify Harwich and rebuild the fort at a total cost of £10,801[47]. Plans for the new Harwich fortifications were soon shelved and those for Landguard modified. Instead of rebuilding the fort it was suggested that it be demolished and replaced by a simple defensible battery for sixteen or twenty guns with a barrack for twenty soldiers. At £2,975 this was a much cheaper alternative; a full-sized fort would have cost over £21,000[48].

Below left: *A plan of the fort in 1715.*

Below right: *A 1725 plan of the second Landguard Fort.*
A *Counterscarp gallery*
B *Caponier*
C *Barrack rooms*
D *Guard room*
E *Gunners' room*
F *Stores*
G *Powder magazine*
H *Yard*

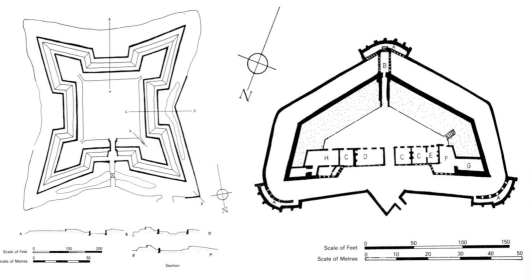

Scale of Feet
Scale of Metres
Section

Scale of Feet
Scale of Metres

The new fort, begun in 1717, was an unusual, economical and surprisingly modern design with no bastions, the ditch being flanked by counterscarp galleries and a caponier at the salient; there was a small barrack at the gorge, and an initial armament of twenty cannon, ten each of 18 and 9-pounders[49]. In 1730–31 the barrack block was extended and enlarged by an extra storey[50] and five years later a new battery armed with another ten guns was built on the glacis in front of the fort[51].

In 1744 the second fort was again rebuilt, this time as a much larger regular pentagon with standard bastions. It incorporated the two main faces and barrack block of the superseded work, but the greater part was completely new. The new fort was largely finished by 1749, when it was described as "refitting and greatly enlarging for the convenience of the officers of the ordnance", but the interior buildings, a long barrack block for the soldiers and a large house divided up for the officers and lieutenant-governor, were not completed until 1751[52]. Standing over the gate was an elegant chapel flanked by the guardroom and cookhouse. Built of warm red brick picked out with ashlar dressings, with long lines of sash windows, a delicate cupola crowning the barrack block and the arched window of the chapel overlooking the courtyard, the interior of the fort looked more like the quad of a college than a military post.

For the remainder of the eighteenth century the fort's history was uneventful, with small groups of bored soldiers living in bleak isolation pining for the day when they would be sufficiently invalid to retire to Chelsea Hospital. Only the eccentricities of the governors and chaplains can have lightened the stale monotony of

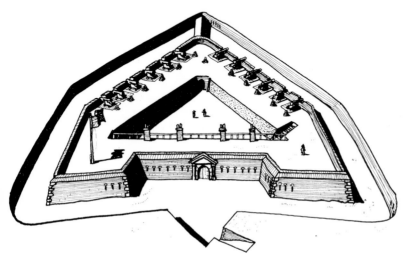

The fort of 1717.

Captain Philip Thicknesse, from Major J. H. Leslie's The History of Landguard Fort in Suffolk.

The new fort of 1749 seen from the south-east.

garrison duty. The holders of these offices were an odd crew, but the maddest of all was Philip Thicknesse, lieutenant-governor from 1753 to 1766, who was notorious for his scandalous behaviour; his temper was as unstable as ancient nitro glycerene. After setting the officers of the fort at one another in virtual civil war, he was convicted of libel and then charged with a comprehensive list of offences including brewing beer to sell within the fort for his own profit and ordering several of the invalid soldiers to march to London for some private and unspecified purpose[53]. He was found guilty of two offences and was later either dismissed or forced to resign. Apart from this ignominy, his only other claim to fame was that he discovered the young Thomas Gainsborough, whom he commissioned to paint the fort, and whom he eventually persuaded to go to Bath to pursue his career[54].

The main strength of the fort lay, throughout the eighteenth century, outside its brick bastions in the battery built on the glacis. This had been demolished when the second fort was reconstructed and then reinstated some time after 1749. Although it may not have been built exactly during his term of office it became known as Beauclerk's Battery after Lord George Beauclerk, who was governor from 1753 to 1768. In 1766 the fort was surveyed and its condition, unlike so many others whose state varied from the bad to the ruined, was pronounced as "good"[55]. Its armament was still that of 1752, the promised increase never having materialised.

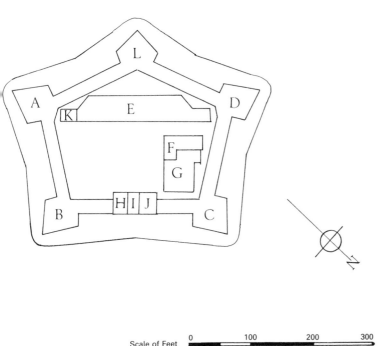

A plan of the third
Landguard Fort.
A King's Bastion
B Holland's Bastion
C Chapel or Warwick's
   Bastion
D Queen's Bastion
E Soldiers' barracks
F Officers' quarters
G Lieutenant-governor's
   house
H Guard room
I Gate (chapel over)
J Cookhouse
K Hospital
L Harwich Bastion

Scale of Feet
Scale of Metres

Twelve years later there was more cause for concern. At the
outbreak of the American War the coastal defences were examined
and as usual found to be in a poor state of repair. Landguard Fort
was surrounded by rotten palisades, its parapets were too thin and
Beauclerk's Battery was obscured and overlooked by a bank of
sand and shingle heaped up by the sea[56]. A large military camp was
formed on Landguard Common and work began to extend the
fort. On either side, facing the harbour, two large enclosed
earthwork wing batteries were built, surrounded by a wet ditch on
all sides except where they joined the glacis. Behind the fort, a little
way up the beach towards Felixstowe, there was a strong square
redoubt, sycophantically named after the country seat of the
Master-General of the Ordnance, Lord Townshend. A line of
ramparts ran from the redoubt to the harbour, converting the
whole tip of the point into an entrenched camp of many acres.
Ireton's Ditch, an ancient watercourse that almost made the point
into an island, was utilized as an advanced ditch and its further
shore occupied by a *tête du pont* to defend the entrance[57]. One
thousand yards north of the Raynham Redoubt there was a smaller
redoubt and two short lengths of rampart blocking the way along

111

the beach from Felixstowe[58]. The armament of the fort remained as it had been in the seventeen-sixties, the only real change being the substitution of 42-pounders for the 32-pounders in Beauclerk's Battery[59].

This defensive complex was never completed, and all work stopped in 1783 at the war's end. In the interval between the American and French Revolutionary Wars nothing else was done, and when Sir John Moore visited the fort in 1797 he noted that "the position of Landguard Fort is strong but the works are injudicious"; they were too extended and needed too large a garrison. All that was required in his opinion was a strong work for no more than a thousand men, capable of holding out against a regular siege for up to three weeks[60]. But instead of aiding the garrison in this objective the earthworks were a positive hindrance. Their only function seemed to be to give cover to the enemy, the Raynham Redoubt being "so ingeniously placed that it could not be covered from the fort", which was itself judged to be little better: "the smallness of the work, bad construction of the parapet and the imperfect state of the covered way render it unequal to make any resistance against an attack on the landward side"[61]. On the seaward side it was proposed to re-form Beauclerk's Battery by filling in the embrasures and remounting the guns on traversing carriages. As for the land works, nothing could be done except to level them; work began on the levelling in 1803[62]. Despite this,

The third Landguard Fort. The main strength of the work lay in the battery on the glacis covering the channel into the harbour.

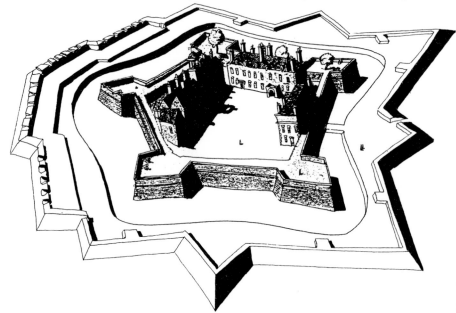

General Craig had begun to despair of ever getting the fort into a defensible state. "We have done what could be done to it in its present state, but I by no means consider it as secure against a *coup-de-main*; on the contrary, I think a resolute enemy would carry it by escalade ... I fear nothing short of pulling it down and erecting a new one of larger dimensions in all its parts would be effectual"[63].

One major improvement that resulted was the strengthening of the ramparts in 1807 so that they could withstand the recoil of

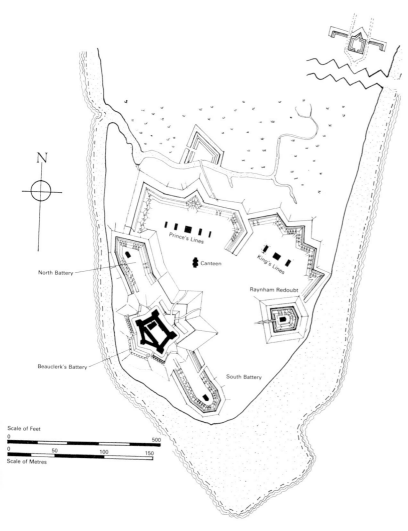

Landguard Fort and the additional fieldworks of 1782. Ireton's Ditch which almost cut off the point from the Felixstowe direction was utilised as an advanced moat. The redoubt at the top of the plan lay one thousand yards north of the Raynham Redoubt and blocked the way along the beach from Felixstowe.

113

32-pounders, fourteen of which were mounted in the fort, with thirty-one 18-pounders, two 12-pounders, one 6-pounder and twenty 12-pounder carronades for flank defence[64]. Despite this, the governor was still not satisfied and complained that the work of demolition had extended to "destroying everything that was comfortable or useful in the place, pulling down all the hospitals and guardhouses" and replacing them with temporary wooden huts in the courtyard which were a "nuisance to the healthy and injurious to the sick"[65]. These were all cleared away at the peace in 1815, and by 1817 the armament had been greatly reduced with the withdrawal of the 18-pounders.

In 1831 the eleven 42-pounders in Beauclerk's Battery were replaced in the interests of standardisation by an equal number of 32-pounders on traversing carriages[66], while on the ramparts and bastions of the fort itself were twelve 32-pounders and twenty 12-pounder carronades[67]. By 1847 the armament had been reduced to three guns in the battery and twenty-one in the fort[68], but it was brought back to strength in 1851–52 by installing four 32-pounders, four 8-inch shell guns, a 10-inch mortar and one portable iron furnace for heating shot[69].

The next year Sir John Burgoyne visited the fort, and his views were very much the same as General Craig's half a century before. Only the complete replacement of the "old and very defective work" could ensure the proper defence of the harbour[70]. Throughout the nineteenth century the fort must have presented a mellow, almost domesticated appearance. A magnificent garden complete with fountain stood on the north of the fort, the ditch was laid out in the style of a formal garden with lawns and ornamental paths, while on the south-west bastion there grew a wide-spreading tamarisk. Other trees peeped above the ramparts and spread their shade upon the barrack square, making it look even more like a college quad.

Despite the isolation—there was no road to the fort until 1850, and it could be reached easily only by boat from Harwich—life was not unpleasant in the military community on the point. There were some consolations in this lonely exile, especially for the officers. They shot golden plover, snipe and wildfowl with enthusiasm, played billiards and fives, and were in great demand at all the local parties and dances. The soldiers stalked the beach in search of coprolites, which they found and sold in large quantities, and on the clear bright days after a gale there were sharks' teeth, amber and jet to be found on the shingle[71]. Occasionally they ran out the guns, as if remembering the true purpose of their life in the fort, and the dull boom of artillery was heard as the unfurling clouds of smoke slowly drifted across the waters of the harbour.

The splendours of the garden declined throughout the

century and a visitor who struggled across the sands to visit the fort shortly before it was reconstructed saw only a "small garden and few ragged looking tamarisks but the general aspect is bleak and cheerless"[72]. The number of guns mounted in the fort declined remorselessly until by the end of the eighteen-sixties there were only five used for saluting[73]. The Royal Commission had not considered Harwich, and the modest upgrading of the harbour defences in the early eighteen-sixties did not affect the fort.

A fresh examination of Harwich and its defences in 1870 saw no further use for the antiquated fort; it was vulnerable to increasingly accurate long-range fire and, providing the battery at Shotley remained active, completely superfluous. "If Shotley be perfectly secure there would be so little to gain by reducing or even destroying Landguard that an enemy would not undertake any extensive operations for that purpose . . . As long as the [Shotley] position is held it will be practically impossible for an enemy to make any use of the port"[74]. The only defences this report allowed on the point was a small advanced battery. However, this accurate and economical solution to the harbour's defences was overruled, and the next year work began on a massive and extremely expensive reconstruction of the old fort into a monumental casemated battery.

The first step was to clear the interior of the old fort of all existing buildings; the barracks, the governor's house, the chapel, even the tamarisk trees were all torn down, leaving only the outer ramparts. The south-west curtain and centre bastion were demolished and replaced by the new casemate battery, contained in an elliptical keep which had seven casemates facing the harbour,

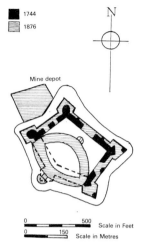

1744
1876

N

Mine depot

0   500
        Scale in Feet
0   150
        Scale in Metres

*The reconstruction of
1871–76.*

with outer walls of granite and embrasures closed by wrought-iron shields twenty-five inches thick. The rest of the keep was filled with barrack rooms and offices housed in bombproof casemates and opening out into a courtyard, in the centre of which stood a well. The outer wall of the keep was blank and windowless, pierced only by a gateway. The fort's new squat and utilitarian appearance, in comparison with the tall chimneys and tiled roofs of the demolished buildings, was a grimly significant reminder of the vastly increased destructive power of artillery. The keep was enormously expensive, extremely strong, a masterpiece of spatial organisation but tactically a blunder. It expressed an idealised conception of what a fort should be rather than being an efficient solution to a military problem. Despite the modern artillery installed, the line of descent from the turreted medieval stronghold was faintly discernible in a drawbridge and a murdering hole hidden beneath the ornamental keystone of the gate.

To replace the lost flanking fire of the demolished centre bastion, a small pitched-roof caponier was built out from the wall directly beneath the centre casemate with several loop-holes on either side. To protect the caponier from the shells of an enemy ship in the harbour, a huge quarter-spherical shield, like a giant petrified fruit buried in the earth, was built at the seaward end. This was a folly, a completely useless construction more like sculpture than serious military engineering, although completely true to its own dotty logic. If a caponier had to be built in that position, then it had to be strong enough to resist very heavy shells fired from warships; but a caponier was not necessary at all. Two small galleries in the flanks of the remaining bastions would have given ample covering fire if an enemy were so suicidally inclined as to land beneath the fort's main battery and to try to storm it.

The rest of the fort was little altered; its basic trace and four of the five bastions remained intact. The ramparts were heightened by a thick concrete parapet into which three separate casemates were built; one stood in the centre of the south-east curtain and the other two in the salients of the seaward-facing bastions. Two circular barbette emplacements were made in the other two bastions and two embrasures cut in the parapet, one on either side of the gate.

The rebuilding of the fort did not go smoothly. None of the usual problems of shifting sands, tilting foundations and bankrupt contractors delayed the work; but the antics of one local landowner certainly did. He utilised the tangled complexities of medieval land tenure to delay the fort, and to make himself a good deal of money and the War Office a laughing stock. The dispute arose when, in 1867, Colonel George Tomline bought some six thousand acres of land in the Felixstowe area and became lord of the manor of

Walton-cum-Trimley. By this time the title of lord of the manor was little more than a mere courtesy, though the lord retained certain residual rights over Landguard Common. These had been a source of some acrimony between the Board of Ordnance and previous lords of the manor, earlier disputes having been solved by one lord granting to the Crown a lease of 999 years which allowed the army to use the common for military purposes while not usurping the lord's tenure[75].

With the arrival of Tomline this mutually satisfactory state of affairs ended. When he saw the enormous amounts of equipment and building material arriving for the reconstruction of the fort he disinterred an ancient manorial right. The foreshore was his and all that passed over it was charged a toll at the rate of 6d per ton. As every brick and bolt had to be brought by barge to the fort's jetty this added a sizeable amount to Tomline's already substantial fortune. The War Office, confronted with this outrageous demand, meekly paid. The colonel raised the toll to a shilling a ton, and this was paid; then to 1s 6d and it was still paid; then to two shillings for every ton. Building materials, munitions, cement and shells, all were taxed by the implacable colonel, and still the War Office paid![76]

At last public opinion demanded that this legalised robbery be stopped. The War Office sternly refused to pay a penny more and work ceased, the new guns lying rusting on the shore, the fort

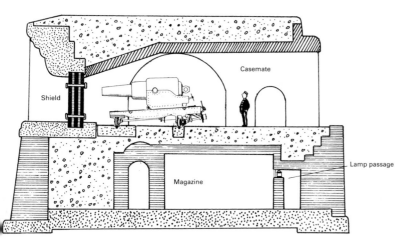

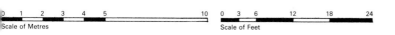

Scale of Metres

Scale of Feet

Section through the new casemate battery showing one of the massive RMLs on its traversing carriage.

117

incomplete and empty. Then Colonel Tomline, as if in a final assault, severed the lead pipe that had carried water to the garrison for over two hundred years, and from then water was brought to the fort in a cart[77]. At last the Government awoke to the futility of its tolerance of such absurd rights and invoked the terms of the Defence Act to acquire absolute ownership of all the common land and foreshore. Before this could be enforced a week-long enquiry was held in the Shire Hall at Ipswich. The colonel claimed that only the vast sum of forty thousand pounds could compensate him for his loss of manorial rights, but he had to be content with a little under two thousand[78]. The fort's access was restored, and Tomline set about building Felixstowe dock and railway and being offensive to the officers of the fort whenever he met them.

With Tomline defeated, work on the fort continued and was completed by 1876, but the armament was slow in being installed.

The gate of the keep, with the date 1875 on the keystone. Originally there was a drawbridge.

Three 10-inch RMLs and five 12-inch RMLs had been promised in 1874, but two years later there were only four 9-inch RMLs in place. These were removed in the early eighteen-eighties and replaced by heavier guns; it was not until 1886 that the fort was fully armed with four 12.5-inch RMLs and three 10-inch RMLs in the keep and two 10-inch RMLs and another 12.5-inch RML in the three seaward casemates. The remaining guns were for land defence and were a mixture of smooth-bores and palliser converted rifles[79].

The rebuilt fort was a far more massive and grim-looking structure than its predecessor; no-one ever claimed it was beautiful. Major J. H. Leslie, the commanding officer in 1897, was interested enough in Landguard Fort to write its history, but even he saw nothing in it to please the eye. "It presents no feature of architectural beauty, it is in fact a picture of ugliness whilst its

The front of the casemate battery with the caponier and its shield. In the background can be seen the Right Flank Battery.

*The reconstructed fort,
with the new casemate
battery on the left.*

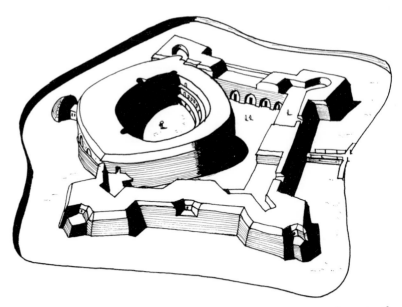

internal arrangements are by no means such as to conduce to the extreme comfort of its occupants," he said[80]. There were others who found more serious defects in Landguard Fort than a want of beauty. Sir George Clarke singled it out as a particularly glaring example of monumental incompetence and was unimpressed by its frowning embrasures, its masses of granite and its armour plate. Clarke saw the new keep as a shell-trap, sharing the same fate as the Malakoff Tower at Sevastopol. "In Landguard Fort the vicious principles on account of which the Russians paid so dearly are faithfully reproduced," he said[81]. An enemy ship could lie out to sea off P martello tower without a single gun in the fort being able to bear and, as safely as if at a review, methodically demolish the exposed masonry of the expensive and supposedly impregnable fort. What should have been built was an earthwork like Shotley which would have mounted more guns, with greater protection at far less cost. The rebuilt Landguard Fort was no more than a great brick box to be shot at, even if it looked massive and strong; it appeared to be the mighty protector of the harbour, but it was really something of a sham.

One might have thought that this formidable and very expensive battery would have sufficed to allay the fears of the most nervous military commanders, but it did not. The experiences of the American Civil War, during which several ships had been sunk by mines, prompted busy experimentation with this new and cheap form of harbour defence. By the late eighteen-seventies a number of suitably lethal devices had been perfected, and the Royal Engineers began to look for harbours which they might defend. Harwich was one of those selected because of its narrow entrance and sheltered waters, and by 1879 a Submarine Mining Depot had been completed on the west side of the fort[82]. There, in a low single-storey brick building, several dozen mines were stored on trolleys ready to be wheeled out along the narrow gauge railway track to a small jetty where they could be loaded on to lighters, taken out into the harbour and moored in predetermined positions. Electric cables connected them to the fort, where an observer waited to explode the mines when his calibrated sights told him a ship was in the right place. Such controlled mines had the advantage of blocking the channel without any of the dangers to friendly ships associated with contact mines. There were certain problems which remained unsolved; what would happen if an enemy ship attacked before the lengthy process of laying the mines was completed? And if the guns of the fort were adequate, what was the point of the mines? No-one ever fully answered either of these questions, but a company of Royal Engineer Submarine Miners wheeled their trolleys back and forth between depot and jetty until the early years of the twentieth century.

The new guns had been in place for only five years before they were obsolete; as useless as the basilisks and demi-culverins of the first fort. Within ten years it was obvious, even to the War Office, that Landguard Fort was once again unable to defend the harbour or even itself. The increased range of guns mounted in contemporary warships enabled them to remain several miles out at sea and to destroy the fort at their leisure. Despite all the thousands of pounds expended, the Inspector-General of Fortifications, Sir Andrew Clarke, sadly revealed in 1887 that Harwich was the weakest point in the nation's defences. Landguard Fort, the key to Harwich, he admitted was "weak; the design of the work itself is not the most judicious in the world"[83]. The main problem was insufficient guns to cover the sea approaches, and for once the War Office acted with urgency and proposed installing two each of the new 10-inch and 6-inch breech-loaders. As these guns could not be fitted within the fort a completely new battery was necessary; the War Office gritted its teeth and resolved that, whatever the cost, Landguard would be efficient.

In December, 1888, work began on the new battery. Standing to the north of the fort just beyond the main gate, it was called the Left Flank Battery, and consisted of two gunpits facing the sea buried in an earth bank twenty feet high. In the larger pit, nearest the fort, was a 10-inch BL, and in the other a 6-inch Mk IV BL, both on hydro-pneumatic disappearing carriages. The work was finished by January, 1891, at a cost of £7,252; nearly seventy-five

Above: *An observation mine with its electric firing cables on the trolley which ran on the narrow gauge railway within the fort. These mines contained a charge that varied from 250 to 1,000 lb of guncotton, depending on the depth of water in which they were to be laid.*

121

per cent over budget[84]. The 10-inch proved a troublesome piece of equipment, and it was not fully operational until nearly three years later[85].

Above: *A 6-inch gun on an HP mount in the Left Flank Battery.*

Once more vain hopes were expressed that the fort had reached a peak of military efficiency and was fully equipped to deal with whatever threat presented itself. Major Leslie wrote in 1897: "Its present construction and armament are both such that a modern enemy would still find the bulwark of the most important harbour between the Thames and the Humber as hard a nut to crack as was discovered by our Dutch foemen"[86]. Yet even as he wrote this testimonial, a committee of the Royal Artillery and Royal Engineers was noting that the guns of the fort had "all the worst defects of small arcs of fire, low angles of elevation and slow fire common to all guns mounted in these antiquated works"[87]. The main problem was still the lack of guns firing out to sea. Ships entering the harbour approached from the east and then, because of shoals, turned north, taking them beyond the field of fire of Beacon Hill Battery, resulting in the harbour entrance being

Left: *A rear view of the Right Flank Battery. The rounded structure is one of the casemates built over the 6-inch guns in 1940 to give overhead protection.*

Opposite page: *The 10-inch gun in the Left Flank Battery was mounted on Easton and Anderson's disappearing carriage, a type that was not adopted for service; the Landguard installation was the sole example in Britain.*

The Royal Artillery Institution, Woolwich

effectively protected by only two breech-loading guns. As the RMLs were useless, it was proposed to remove them and build a second battery for another 10-inch and two 6-inch[88]; and to protect the harbour entrance from light craft speeding through, a pair of 4.7-inch QF was planned and a second 6-inch on an HP mounting was to be added to the Left Flank Battery[89].

The new Right Flank Battery, begun in 1898, lay to the south-east of the old fort facing the sea. Like its elder companion, it mounted one 10-inch and two 6-inch BL, but these were on barbette mountings. From the sea it appeared as a low, gently sloping earth bank, the long barrels of the guns peeping over the top, but from the rear it presented a sheer face of concrete pierced with the windows and doors of the magazines and shelters. There was then, in effect, one long battery facing the sea, with two 10-inch in the centre flanked on either side by two 6-inch[90]. Work was completed in 1900 and in the same year construction began of two emplacements for 4.7-inch QF on the site of Beauclerk's Battery and directly in front of the casemates. Unlike its predecessors it was

By 1945 the original fort was almost surrounded by the complex of batteries that had superseded the Victorian emplacements.

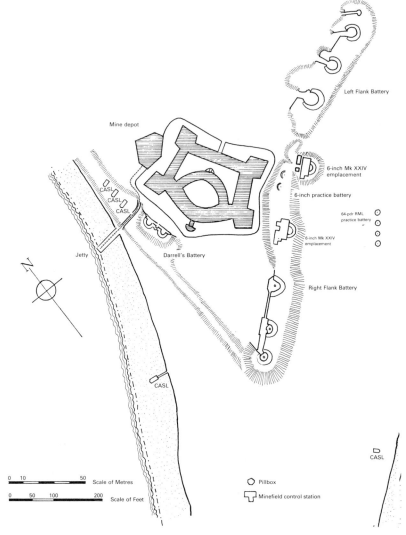

Left Flank Battery

Mine depot

6-inch Mk XXIV emplacement

6-inch practice battery

64-pdr RML practice battery

6-inch Mk XXIV emplacement

Darrell's Battery

Right Flank Battery

Jetty

CASL
CASL
CASL

CASL

CASL

| 0 | 10 | | 50 | Scale of Metres |
| 0 | 50 | 100 | 200 | Scale of Feet |

○ Pillbox

⌂ Minefield control station

given a proper name, Darell's, after the defender of the fort in 1667[91]. This departure from the previous utilitarian practice was made in response to an appeal from the fort's historian, Major Leslie, who regretted that the names of the old bastions redolent with the fort's history were no longer remembered and pointed out that there was no commemoration of the heroic defence against the Dutch. "Surely some part of the existing fort might be called after Darell, so that the name, at least, of a fine soldier shall not be entirely lost to recollection. A Darell Battery, with a suitable inscription on one of the fort's bastions, would be a fitting tribute to the memory of a distinguished and brave man"[92].

In the early years of the twentieth century Landguard Fort was at the zenith of its power. Between the two flank batteries was a practice battery armed with two 6-inch Mk II on slide carriages and two 3-pounder QF[93]. The RMLs were still in position in the fort and equipped with canister to prevent torpedo boats running past, although the building of Darell's Battery partially masked their fire and ended their usefulness in this role. The guns in the Left Flank Battery, however, were already obsolete; the disappearing mounts might have been mechanically ingenious but the rate of fire of the guns was slow and, because of the restricted elevation imposed by the carriage, their range was limited. An expensive plan to remedy these defects was proposed in 1903 involving remounting the 10-inch on a barbette carriage and the 6-inch on central-pivot mountings as well as installing extensive underground magazines and shelters[94]. The work was not carried out and in 1909 the guns were withdrawn[95]. At the same time the Committee of Imperial Defence quite rightly decided that the submarine mining systems were superfluous and they were scrapped as well. The remaining 10-inch in the Right Flank Battery was also withdrawn, but the loss of the heavy armament was made good with the building of Brackenbury Battery in 1915.

At the outbreak of war in 1914 Landguard faced the enemy with two 6-inch and two 4.7-inch, the smallest complement of guns that it had ever mounted, but these were far more powerful than the dozens of ancient cannon that had once lined the ramparts; as well as the guns there were four searchlights to illuminate the harbour entrance. Throughout the war the guns guarded a harbour busy with destroyers and light cruisers, but they were never called upon to fire at the enemy, and the only addition to the armament was a 3-inch AA gun. The fort gained a sinister reputation during the war as a prison in which conscientious objectors were held before being shipped over to France, where they would be subject to the discipline of an army in the field. Several dozen objectors were confined there before the practice was stopped[96].

After the armistice the fort remained a coast defence post garrisoned by regular and Territorial Army units. The activity at Felixstowe that caught the public eye centred on the elegant flying boats based next to the fort and not on the guns that occasionally boomed out in practice. No alterations or additions were made to the fort's armament in the inter-war years, although there was a plan to install experimental high-angle 6-inch guns in the disused Left Flank Battery and a proposal in 1936 to replace the guns in

Left: *A twin 6-pounder in Darell's Battery. A skilled detachment could maintain a rate of fire of 120 rounds per minute.*

Below: *Darell's Battery was converted to twin 6-pounders in 1940. The towers held directors for the guns and the searchlights.*

Darell's Battery with two twin 6-pounders to deal with fast motor boats[97].

In 1939 the armament was as it had been in 1918, two 6-inch and two 4.7-inch, but the guns of Darell's Battery had been earmarked for conversion. Work began in January, 1940, when the 4.7-inch were removed and replaced by two 12-pounders which were mounted beside the battery[98]. The twin 6-pounders were in place and ready for action by July, 1940[99]. The gun emplacements were modified by building a concrete gunhouse about the original emplacement with a magazine below. Over each gunhouse was built a tall and gaunt director tower to mount the predictor, rangefinder and searchlight control equipment. Seen today, angular and sinister against the light, they look like dinosaurs in profile, crouching on the bank ready to wade into the harbour to sink their teeth into the gleaming flanks of a passing car ferry. To the right of the rebuilt battery three fixed-beam searchlights were installed in concrete shelters, and a further three were placed to the east of the fort between the Right Flank Battery and Landguard Point. The 6-inch guns were given additional protec-

The 10-inch emplacement in the Right Flank Battery showing one of the ammunition recesses originally fitted with armoured doors. This emplacement was converted to a battery command post in 1912 and is now part of a bird observatory.

tion against air attack when in July and August, 1940, gunhouses identical to those at Beacon Hill, even down to the details of the shuttering, were built about them.

These alterations increased the security of the guns but could not give them more range. The forty-year-old 6-inch Mk VIIs on their Mk II CP mountings could elevate to a maximum of 15 degrees, which limited them to 14,000 yards. In order to extend the area of water covered by Landguard Fort it was proposed to replace the two existing guns in the Right Flank Battery with three 6-inch Mk XXIV on Mk V 45-degree mountings with a range of 24,000 yards. The original plan, on which work began in 1942, was to build two new emplacements to the left of the battery for two of the new guns and to put the third in the old number two position. This caused so many problems, however, that eventually new guns were installed only in the two new emplacements and the old Mk VIIs were removed the following year[100].

The fort itself was used as barrack accommodation, and a plotting room was established in the magazines after Trinity House had been persuaded to remove the fifteen tons of explosive which that organisation had stored there[101].

When the war ended the fort continued as an active component of the coast defences, while the rest of the temporary batteries along the coast were dismantled. Landguard Fort was the headquarters of the local artillery command and acted as a depot for the reception of the abandoned batteries' guns before they were hauled off to ordnance stores and eventually scrapped. For the next ten years the fort was still manned and, in the hope that its guns could still be of some use, the 6-pounders were adapted for an anti-aircraft role[102]. They were not withdrawn until 1956 when coast artillery was abolished. The long and occasionally distinguished service of Landguard Fort came to an end when the last soldiers marched out in 1957.

A 6-inch gun in the Right Flank Battery with overhead protection and wartime camouflage.

Suffolk 9

THE FIRST defensive work in Suffolk specifically designed for artillery was a "bulwark" built at the mouth of Dunwich haven in 1479, an insubstantial structure costing only four shillings that on foggy days fired its guns to guide the lost seafarer[1]. There is no evidence of any other artillery fortifications until the early sixteenth century when, some time in the fifteen-twenties, gun-ports were added to the gatehouses of West Stow and Gedding Halls near Bury St Edmunds. West Stow had cross-slits and Gedding the more common small circular gunports, both intended for small handguns only[2].

After this fortifications were, almost without exception, to be built on the coast, for the qualities that now make the Suffolk coast so alluring to the weekender, a gentle stretch of beaches and low cliffs close to London, were exactly those that made it attractive to any potential invader. There are three anchorages where an invading fleet might lie offshore and disembark an army; Hollesley Bay, Sole Bay and Lowestoft Roads. In 1539 the commissioners appointed by Henry VIII drew up a list of vulnerable places, and a chain of batteries was planned to cover the whole coast[3], but apart from the coastal towns only Minsmere was fortified with a line of entrenchments to defend its small haven[4].

The Duke of Norfolk surveyed the coast six years later and suggested building a small fort at Corton to cover the north end of Lowestoft Roads[5]. He also made a significant addition to his own castle at Framlingham by placing before the main gate a half-moon-shaped outwork, solidly built in stone[6].

The blockhouse planned for Corton, from the Cotton Manuscript.

In 1571, in the wake of the Ridolfi Plot, the coast was surveyed again but nothing was done, although by this time the slight works about Minsmere had long since decayed and the whole coast was completely unfortified. Dunwich had been granted some artillery in 1569, but neglected to maintain the guns or even to mount them, and when the threat of the Armada caused the coast to be examined in 1586 Dunwich's guns were still unusable[7]. A detailed survey of 1587 recommended an extensive scheme of defence. Bawdsey, although partly protected by the sand bar across the mouth of the River Deben, needed two or three small guns for an adequate defence; Orford, with its old and crumbling castle useless as a defence, needed four guns on Finbury Point and two on the

The early Tudor defences of Suffolk, including those which were proposed but never built.

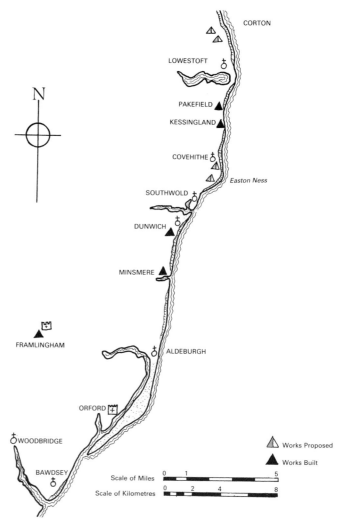

quay in the town. Minsmere and Dunwich had the remnants of old entrenchments that were to be repaired, and small batteries were planned for Dunwich and Walberswick. The stretch of coast between Lowestoft and Gorleston was seen as particularly exposed to troops who might land from ships anchored in Lowestoft Roads, and it was intended to dig a line of trenches along the cliff top and to build a small earthwork fort at Gorleston overlooking the Yare[8].

None of this had been carried out by the beginning of 1588 when twenty-nine dangerous points were listed and the estimated cost of protecting them with sufficient fortifications was estimated at one thousand pounds[9]. Not all activity could have been concentrated on the coast. There must have been plans to construct new or renovate old fortifications inland. Instructions had been sent to the lords lieutenant of all the most threatened counties giving detailed plans of how to counter invasion. The town wall of Ipswich, consisting of a medieval bank and ditch, was repaired, and, if the instructions to the lords lieutenant were like those sent to Norfolk, orders were given to defend the main river crossings to prevent the invaders pushing inland.

Once the danger of the Armada was past, whatever had been built was abandoned and nothing remained by the end of the century. The activities of the Dunkirkers in the seventeenth century caused a flurry of alarm; when Sir John Coke surveyed the coast he found it without any defences except two old and useless guns at Dunwich[10].

The Civil War touched Suffolk very little. The county was so far from all the main areas of action that any major fortifications were unnecessary, although the initial uncertainties of 1642 resulted in some minor works. As early as January, 1642, long before the King raised his standard at Nottingham and the official outbreak of the war, an order was made for fortifying Ipswich[11]. The earth bank and ditch were repaired and a small bulwark or two might have been added, for the town council sent to Colchester to ask for the services of a military engineer, which they would hardly trouble to do if they only intended to clean out the ditch; the treasurer was given orders to buy sixty wheelbarrows for the use of the townspeople in building breastworks about the town[12].

For the rest of the seventeenth century and most of the eighteenth the defences of Suffolk were concentrated about the ports. When the war with the American Colonies began renewed attention was paid to the coast defences as invasion from Holland seemed possible. From 1779 troops were posted along the shore and a chain of signal stations built from Lowestoft to Bawdsey[13]. Signal guns were positioned at these and a message could be sent from one end to the other in sixteen minutes. No elaborate fortifications were planned, only a few light works; more durable ones were not only expensive but ran the risk of being held against the home forces if captured by the enemy[14]. The only use envisaged for Orford Castle was as a barracks for two or three hundred men; its days as a serious defensive post were over[15].

The same concerns were expressed when the French Revolutionary Wars began and an invasion from Holland was feared once more. In 1798 Captain Reynolds surveyed the coast and recommended building, instead of ordinary batteries, twelve brick towers at regular intervals from Bawdsey to Lowestoft[16]. Positions were planned inland to make enemy movement difficult; Bungay was designated a "strong point and receptacle for troops" intended to block the advance of an invader either marching up the Waveney valley or attempting to cross the river from Norfolk[17].

The danger of invasion was never greater than in 1803 after the war had been rekindled, and the demands for defences of all kinds became insistent. Floating batteries, hurriedly improvised from Thames barges, armed with four guns each and manned by sea fencibles, were moored at the mouths of the rivers Alde and Deben. A sixty-four-gun man-of-war was anchored in Hollesley Bay, which was described as "the most desirable object for an enemy as far as the naval operation of invasion is concerned"[18]. The numerous disadvantages of floating batteries made them only a temporary solution, and in 1806 local demands for more substantial defences were stimulated by the news that martello towers were to be built along the south coast. In May that year

Tower AA at Hollesley Bay, one of the chain of martello towers built on the Suffolk coast between 1808 and 1810.

General Morse, the Inspector-General of Fortifications, initiated a survey which was carried out by Major Bryce. He recommended building conventional forts and batteries, but was overruled by General Morse who decided that towers were a better solution, proposing that ten be built from the Deben to the mouth of the Alde, with two extra large eight-gun towers at Orford and Slaughden near Aldeburgh[19]. Work on the towers began in 1809, but only seven were eventually built. The eight-gun tower at Orford was never started and that at Slaughden reduced to a four-gun tower to help pay for the Redoubt at Harwich. Tower V

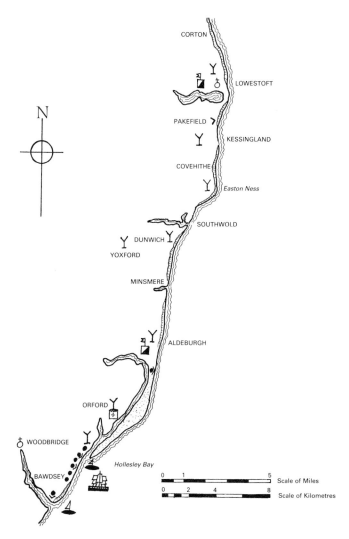

stood on the north bank of the Deben, towers W and X were behind the beach at Bawdsey village, Y, Z and AA at Shingle Street to defend Hollesley Bay and BB half a mile further north on a shingle bank near the mouth of the river Ore. Towers V, Y and AA also supported small batteries each armed with three 24-pounders. After the war ended some of the towers were handed over to the Customs and Excise, while others were demolished either by man or by the sea[20]. The remainder were maintained and armed up to the eighteen-seventies.

The invasion scare of 1859 had its most visible response in the volunteer units that were raised throughout the county; no new defences were built, but numerous suggestions were put forward of the best methods of resisting the anticipated arrival of the French. One drawn up by Lieutenant-Colonel Shafto Adair, of Flixton Hall near Bungay, proposed entrusting the defence of the county to volunteers and militia artillery. He planned three major lines of defence: one along the coast, the second resting on the course of the Waveney and the third running through mid-Suffolk from Ipswich through Debenham to Eye. The towns on the Waveney were to be enclosed by simple fortifications, and the river itself was to be patrolled by armed wherries; the central citadel for the county was to be Framlingham[21].

In 1870 a report on the coast defences, prompted by the growth in German naval power, concluded that Suffolk was likely to be attacked and suggested a small four-gun battery at Bawdsey and one armed with heavy guns at Orford, while the remaining martello towers were regarded as still being of some use[22]. The alarm died down without anything being done and for the rest of the century the War Office's plans envisaged nothing more than a minor raid on the coast, the defence of which was left to mobile columns of cavalry and cyclists[23].

On the outbreak of the First World War in response to new threats of invasion trenches were dug quite early, to be supplemented by numbers of concrete pillboxes at Hollesley, Sizewell, Bawdsey and Kessingland. No permanent coastal batteries were built but field guns were emplaced at various times, although their value as an effective defence was slight. Field artillery with little range and penetrative power was unable to fight warships; its only effective use was against infantry attempting to land in open boats. Guns on fixed mountings were much more efficient, but by 1917 there were only eight such guns sited along the whole coast: four at Bawdsey, two at Dunwich, one at Thorpeness and one at

The martello towers and batteries on the short stretch of coast between the Deben and Orford Haven. Further to the north at Slaughden was the last of the chain, Tower CC.

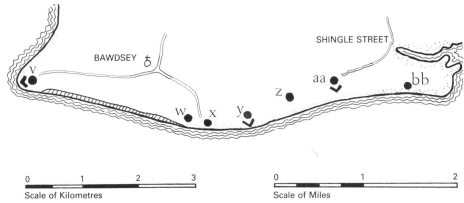

Covehithe. All were 15-pounder BLCs on pedestal mounts in small open batteries[24]. A more dangerous and obvious threat was that of the Zeppelin, and attempts were made to counter it by siting guns and searchlights about Felixstowe, Ipswich and important points like the explosives factory at Stowmarket[25]. Mobile batteries of AA guns were stationed in the villages in the east of the county, but they had little success and the only Zeppelin to be shot down in Suffolk fell victim to fighters from Orfordness; it crashed at Theberton, near Leiston.

The first nine months of the Second World War did not change the assumption that no coast defences were needed, and apart from the institution of routine coastal patrols nothing was done. It was the collapse of France and the prospect of imminent invasion that spurred a frenetic bout of fortification all over the county. The main priority was to construct a thick crust of coastal defences, but there was hardly a village or road junction without some sort of defence work.

The most important provision was heavy coastal artillery. By July, 1940, there were five emergency beach batteries, at Pakefield, Covehithe, Dunwich, Sizewell and Minsmere. All but Dunwich, with two 4-inch, were equipped with two 6-inch guns and two searchlights. The next year additional batteries were built at Kessingland, Hopton and Bawdsey, and the guns at Covehithe were moved to Easton Woods, a mile to the south. All were typical of batteries built at the time, the guns in concrete casemates with

Above: *Light coastal defence guns improvised from 15-pounder field guns and mounted in small open batteries.*

Left: *A First World War pillbox at Ringsfield, near Beccles, guarding a crossing of the Hundred River.*

Left: *A 6-inch gun in the Easton Woods Battery. Its camouflage was particularly elaborate and effective.*

Below: *Bawdsey Battery, built on the site of tower X, was armed with two 6-inch guns taken from the redundant battery at Foulness in Essex.*

magazines and shelters underground. No two were exactly alike, all had their individual distinctions; Hopton, for instance, had a gunhouse roof of plastic armour plates[26]. All had a secondary armament for close defence, normally a 75mm gun as well as light AA guns and rocket projectors. The main armament consisted of old naval guns; the Mk XI 6-inch guns at Easton Woods had started life afloat aboard the cruiser HMS *Dartmouth*[27], built in 1910 and sold for scrapping in 1930.

Between the batteries ran strings of pillboxes, with mines, lines

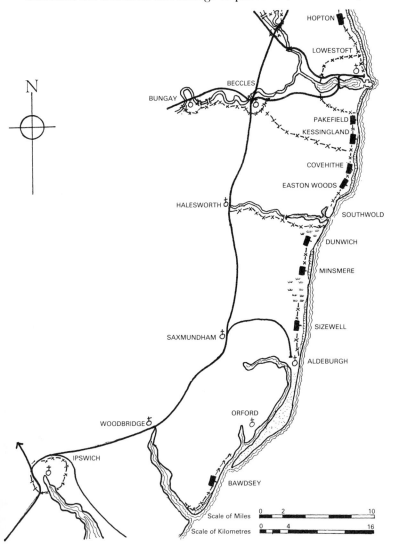

The coastal defences of Suffolk, 1940–45.

of scaffolding and other obstacles along the beaches. The pillboxes, mainly built in the summer of 1940, were of two distinct types: north of Thorpeness most were square, while south of Orford most were hexagonal. The martello towers were recalled to service, some as observation posts and gun positions; the ruins of Tower X at Bawdsey provided the foundations for part of the new battery. As well as the towers other seaside buildings were pressed into service. An old flint chapel at Minsmere was converted into a disguised machine-gun post and a small blockhouse was incorporated into the artificial rock cliffs at Bawdsey Manor.

Away from the coast fortifications were concentrated along river lines to prevent the invading forces pushing inland. Every crossing of the Waveney was provided with a pillbox, and a second line of defence was formed by the Hundred River from Beccles to Kessingland. The river Blyth from Halesworth to Southwold formed another stop line, and Ipswich was surrounded by a ring of roadblocks and pillboxes. The major internal defence position ran right through the middle of the county from Mildenhall through Bury St Edmunds, Lavenham, Sudbury and Bures to Colchester. This line consisted of a variety of pillboxes, including the one-man Tett Turret and numbers of 2-pounder anti-tank bunkers. For most of its length this line used the rivers Lark and Stour, and all

To the left of this standard pillbox at Hollesley Bay can be seen a line of concrete anti-tank blocks. In the background is tower Z.

Right: *A searchlight emplacement at Bawdsey, with a pillbox and martello towers visible in the background.*

Below: *Almost buried in the shingle is a First World War machine-gun emplacement, with a 1940 pillbox standing up clear of the beach behind.*

crossing points were heavily defended. The airfields and radar stations were provided with defences in 1940 to combat the fear of paratroops. Most of these were pillboxes of orthodox design, but Martlesham Heath airfield was selected for the installation of the Picket-Hamilton disappearing pillbox[28].

After 1943 the coastal batteries were placed on a reduced level of operational readiness, and the following year all were handed over to the Home Guard except Easton Woods, Minsmere and Bawdsey, which were shut down, although retained on care and maintenance. Although the danger from the sea might have receded, that from the air was greater than ever. After the allies had overrun the V1 launching sites in northern France the Germans began to launch these flying bombs from aircraft flying over the North Sea from bases in Holland, and they began to cross the east coast in increasing numbers on their way to London and the Midlands. Several hundred light and heavy AA guns were hurriedly moved to the coast as part of the "Diver Strip"; these guns shot down many bombs before they crossed the coast[29]. It was a 3.7-inch battery at Orfordness that shot down the last V1 on 28th March, 1945.

That was the last action of the coast defences, and at the end of the war they were rapidly dismantled. The guns were removed for scrapping, the steel obstacles were cut up, the barbed wire coiled and the mines, or those that could be found, lifted. Despite all efforts some still remained buried in the sand, and nine years after the end of the war no fewer than forty-three Kessingland children were injured in one summer by the old defences[30].

Not all the Suffolk pillboxes were hexagonal. This example of a local variant, oblong in shape and with a cavity wall of concrete blocks packed with earth, is at Friston near Aldeburgh.

Aldeburgh   10

ALDEBURGH's only defensive necessity was to protect itself
from bombardment or a sudden raid, for it had no real
harbour and the beach was not the first choice of an invading army,
although there was a good anchorage offshore.

The first simple defences were planned in 1539; one three-
gun earthwork battery was intended to be sited at Thorpeness and
another similar work on Aldeburgh beach, and there was to have
been a long entrenchment at the south end of the town running
from the Alde to the sea, each end being secured by a two-gun
battery[1]. These were never built.

Six years later the Duke of Norfolk, who had been commanded by Henry VIII to examine the coast once more, found
neither guns nor fortifications, even though he designated Aldeburgh the only spot where an enemy might land between
Orfordness and Lowestoft Roads. His concern for the town's
defence seems to have been almost entirely selfish, as he wrote to
the King: "The enemy will not land any great number there; and a
small number could do little hurt, and that chiefly to the writer,
whose poor town of Alboroughe and lands thereabouts should be
burnt"[2]. Despite this report, no guns were sent nor bulwarks
raised.

Aldeburgh remained undefended for another twenty-three
years until in 1569 the Earl of Warwick, in answer to a petition,
agreed to supply artillery, but only on the condition that the town
maintained the guns and supplied them with ammunition[3]. Eight
cannon were sent: three demi-culverins, three sakers and two
minions[4]. Five years later a gunner was despatched to teach the
townsmen how to use their battery; if they refused to pay him he
was to repossess the guns[5]. He had little success in either task and
despite his labours most of the guns lay rusting on the ground,
useless without carriages.

In 1579 Sir Robert Wingfield was ordered to go to Aldeburgh
to view the decrepit artillery and to try to get the Corporation to
carry out their responsibilities. Not all the guns were utterly
dismounted, for Robert Day, the town's gunner and "a man of
good skill and experience in such matters", had spent time and
money getting a few on to their carriages[6]. Yet another of
Wingfield's tasks was to try to get a salary for Day so that he could

*A drawing from the Cotton
Manuscript of the
proposed bulwarks at
Aldeburgh.*

go on looking after the guns[7]; but Wingfield met with little success in either of these endeavours and a year later the Privy Council ordered the Suffolk justices of the peace to use their authority to ensure that the cannon were mounted and the luckless Day paid[8]. They too failed, and in 1586 Sir Robert was once more charged with the thankless task of persuading the obstinate people of Aldeburgh to contribute "something towards the mounting and repairing of certain great ordnance belonging to Her Majesty

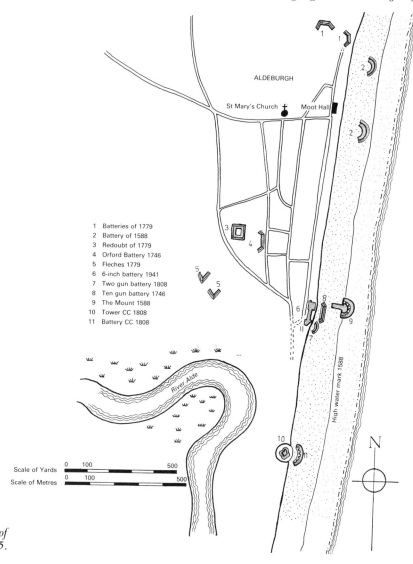

1 Batteries of 1779
2 Battery of 1588
3 Redoubt of 1779
4 Orford Battery 1746
5 Fleches 1779
6 6-inch battery 1941
7 Two gun battery 1808
8 Ten gun battery 1746
9 The Mount 1588
10 Tower CC 1808
11 Battery CC 1808

The fortifications of Aldeburgh, 1588–1945.

142

. . . which are said to be in great decay"[9]. Robert Day, still waiting "in hope of some allowance", was to take charge of the guns[10].

Such was the town's obdurate resolve to do nothing that this situation might have continued for years until the problem was solved by the guns rusting away completely had the threat of the Armada not finally alarmed the townspeople. They shamelessly petitioned the lords lieutenant to do something for them, demanding "that some meanes might be used to have their towne

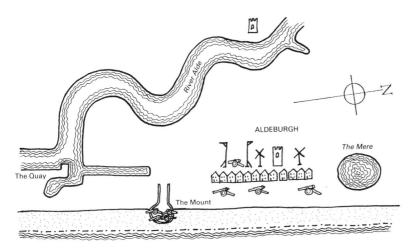

The defences of 1588 as shown in a map in the British Library Cotton Manuscript. Below is the "Mount" of 1588, based on Ananias Appleton's map.

fortyfied and made defencible in respect of the weakness thereof, being a fytt landing place and receipt for shipping"[11]. An experienced soldier, Captain Turner, was sent. He proposed building three emergency batteries made of gabions, one on "the shingle" and two "half-moons on the hill" armed with ten demiculverins[12]. The work was quickly completed, and by the summer of 1588 Aldeburgh was well protected by three bulwarks and twenty pieces of artillery[13].

The first and largest of the batteries stood at the south end of the town at the place still known as Fort Green. Called "The Mount", it was a large semi-circular battery with seven embrasures in the parapet and closed at the gorge with a wooden palisade. It stood at the end of a long causeway at the low water mark, so at high tide it must have been lapped round by the waves. A little way to the north, but set back at the top of the beach, were two semi-circular batteries mounting four cannon[14].

As the threat of invasion lessened, so did the efforts of the town in maintaining its defences. The guns rusted and their

platforms rotted, so that when the Dunkirkers began to prey upon the coast in the early seventeenth century Aldeburgh was in such a defenceless state again that the privateers impudently seized ships in sight of the shore, and even went so far as to fire upon the town[15]. In August, 1625, Sir John Coke examined the coastal defences of Suffolk and discovered only eleven guns at Aldeburgh. Eight of these, two sakers and six minions of iron, were all unusable, with badly pitted bores caused by the corrosive action of the salt-laden sea air. Only three brass pieces were deemed serviceable[16].

In January the next year the people of Aldeburgh, too impoverished by the pirates' depredations to afford their own defence, petitioned the Crown for ten or a dozen demi-culverins as they were afraid that the Dunkirkers might land and burn the place to the ground[17]. In October, 1627, the Privy Council ordered Sir John Pooley and Captain Gosnold of Landguard Fort to inspect and report on the defences; they confirmed Sir John Coke's observations and the truth of the town's petition[18]. The Council acted quickly and ordered the Master-General of the Ordnance to supply ten demi-culverins "of the best and largest sizes the store affordeth"[19]. The guns were to be loaned by the Crown; the powder was to be supplied and the cost of carriages paid by the town. Such were the demands on the Ordnance, with nearly every coastal town pleading for artillery, that the guns were not supplied until February, 1628; instead of the long guns originally specified, Aldeburgh received three full-length culverins and seven shorter ones[20].

During the next fifteen years the town acquired a further eight guns. When the Civil War broke out it had the largest battery of guns it ever possessed. Once again the earthwork batteries seemed to have been eroded by time, weather and neglect, and over two thousand pounds was spent on restoring them[21]; much to the annoyance of the town, Parliament offered a meagre one hundred pounds to defray their expenses[22]. To ensure that there was an adequate crew to man the guns, every townsman between sixteen and sixty was compelled to do duty on penalty of a fine[23]. The guns and their crews saw no service during the Civil War or the Commonwealth; the only attack came from the sea itself when in the winter of 1645 high tides swept away at least one of the batteries[24].

By the time of the Restoration in 1660 the enthusiasm of the townsmen had so waned that although there were twenty guns there were no men to work them, a state of affairs that lasted until the Second Dutch War. In the crisis year of 1667 the large Dutch fleet lying off the town despatched a longboat to burn down the lighthouse and to steal some sheep. When this foray was beaten off

the Dutch ships fired their guns all night to alarm the inhabitants, and then moved south to join the rest of their fleet in the attack on Harwich and Landguard Fort[25].

Most of the town's guns disappeared during the eighteenth century, either rusted away or carried off by the sea, which waged war on the town with far greater ferocity than either Dunkirkers or Dutch. Replacements arrived in 1746, when eight 18-pounders were sent to the town; a six-gun battery on the heights behind the town and a work for ten guns placed near the site of the "Mount" were built to receive them[26]. In 1779 these two batteries were augmented by new works defending the landward site of the town. A battalion of the West Norfolk Militia was camped on open ground behind the town and several field works were raised to convert Aldeburgh into an armed camp. Close to the militia lines a small square redoubt was constructed, supported by two breastworks or fleches on the slope above the marshes. Two small batteries, probably armed with field guns, were placed at the north end of the town facing up the beach towards Thorpeness[27].

All these works fell into ruin when the war ended in 1782, and twenty years later little remained. When Captain Reynolds arrived in 1798 to inspect the town's defences he found that only the two original batteries of 1746 remained. These were still armed with their elderly guns, six 12-pounders and two 18-pounders, but both guns and batteries were in such ruinous condition that they were quite unfit for service. The utility of the battery on the heights, known as the Orford Battery, was reduced even more by what Captain Reynolds called "a circumstance particularly absurd"[28]. Even if the rusty cannon could have been hauled on to their rotten carriages and fired, their shot would have struck the roof of a house built directly in front. This was especially galling as the Orford Battery was the town's major defence work, mounting six guns, while the remaining two guns were emplaced at Fort Green. Reynolds proposed replacing, or largely supplementing, the decayed works with a four-gun masonry tower to be placed near the Orford Battery to cover both beach and anchorage[29].

The tower was not built, and the fortifications were not remodelled until ten years later when the battery at Fort Green was reconstructed and armed with two 24-pounders[30]. A mile to the south of this, at Slaughden on the narrow spit between the River Alde and the sea, a large brick tower was built between 1808 and 1810. This had been authorised in 1806 as an eight-gun tower to cost an estimated £8,000, but it was completed as a four-gun tower, the very last in the long defensive chain that stretched along the south coast and up the east coast from the Colne northwards[31]. Designated CC, it was far larger than any of the other east coast towers; instead of being elliptical it was shaped like a four-leaved clover. It is probable that the design of Tower CC was originally formulated for the planned four-gun tower to guard the east end of Dymchurch Wall in Kent, which was never built[32]. It was surrounded by a wide dry moat with a brick counterscarp and was armed with four long 24-pounders on traversing carriages. Between the lip of the ditch and the sea was a simple barbette battery armed with five 24-pounders, which gave the town a total of eleven powerful and well-protected guns. To the north of Aldeburgh on a slight hill was built a semaphore and signal station connecting the town to the Admiralty in London, so that news of any impending attack could be sent to the capital in minutes[33].

The tower was the last started and the largest, and the danger of imminent invasion had long passed when work on it stopped, leaving the final coat of stucco to be applied. Its massive and sombre appearance failed to impress all the inhabitants, for when the war was over and the town was trying to promote itself as a genteel watering place with assembly rooms and subscription library one resident looked upon the tower and noted sadly: "It is truly lamentable to reflect on the prodigious sums that have been lavished on these useless erections"[34].

Tower and batteries were garrisoned and maintained by a

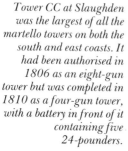

Tower CC at Slaughden was the largest of all the martello towers on both the south and east coasts. It had been authorised in 1806 as an eight-gun tower but was completed in 1810 as a four-gun tower, with a battery in front of it containing five 24-pounders.

Royal Artillery NCO and a Tower Master until the eighteen-sixties, but they were of little military use. The 24-pounders were replaced about 1870 by 32-pounder carronades for the use of the local Artillery Volunteers, and from time to time there were vague proposals to rearm the tower and its battery with modern guns[35]. These all came to nothing, and the two-gun battery was demolished about 1890. The battery in front of the tower was allowed to fall into ruin before being swallowed up by the sea in 1897[36]. Some time before disappearing it impressed itself on the imagination of M. R. James, who used it as the setting of a mysterious death in one of his ghost stories[37].

The First World War affected Aldeburgh very little, apart from the building of a Royal Naval Air Station nearby and the keeping of a constant watch on the sea and coast. After the war the Government examined the coast defences and found that Aldeburgh possessed many fortifications so completely obsolete that no possible use could be envisaged for them. One of these was the martello tower; it was sold in 1932 to be turned into a luxury residence with a modish flat-roofed concrete construction incongruously perched on top[38].

Its disposal seemed a little premature in the context of 1940; the tower's occupiers were evicted and the sun parlour on the roof became an observation post manned by the army. As in former times when threatened from the sea, Aldeburgh was found to be without guns or fortifications, but this time the defects were remedied with feverish speed. In June, 1940, an emergency coastal battery was hurriedly constructed as two six-inch naval guns were bolted to temporary platforms and protected by makeshift casemates improvised from steel girders heaped with sandbags[39]. Manned by sailors and under naval command, the battery guarded the coast during the summer and autumn of 1940, and the next year work began to replace it with a more permanent structure. The site adjoined the Brudenell Hotel, on the spot where the two-gun battery of 1808, one of the seventeenth-century batteries and the Elizabethan mount had stood.

The new battery, a typical brick and concrete structure, looked rather like an incongruous and futuristic new wing tacked on to the Victorian seaside hotel. The two guns, six-inch Mk XIIs dated 1914 and 1916, were emplaced in standard concrete casemates one hundred and seventy five feet apart, joined by the usual magazines and shelters. Number two gun, which adjoined the hotel, faced directly out to sea, while number one was turned to the south-east, giving the battery a wider field of fire than usual. Two searchlights were mounted on the sea front, with the engine house and generators behind the guns; an old windmill that had been converted into a seaside home was adapted to serve as the battery

The 6-inch battery at Aldeburgh was first formed in 1940 under naval command, and this permanent structure was built the following year by a local contractor.

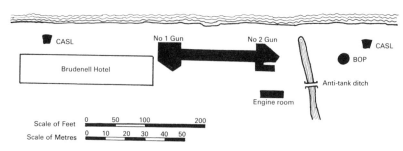

CASL

No 1 Gun   No 2 Gun

CASL

BOP

Brudenell Hotel

Anti-tank ditch

Engine room

Scale of Feet   0   50   100   200

Scale of Metres   0   10   20   30   40   50

observation post. A local contractor, W. C. Reade, built the battery, supervised by Royal Engineer officers, and it was ready for action by September, 1941.

This time the guns were manned by soldiers. After testing the guns they settled down to the routine required by an Examination Battery; all passing ships were questioned as to identity, cargo and destination, and any ship that approached nearer than three miles to the shore without having given a warning of its intention was fired upon[40]. Barbed wire and obstacles lined the sea front, long rows of concrete cubes ran north and south of the town and pillboxes defended both the coast and the roads leading inland. A wide and deep anti-tank ditch was dug from the sea to the Alde just to the south of the battery and a 75mm gun mounted to defend the beach[41]. Later in the war numbers of light AA guns were installed along the sea front to counter the threat of V1s flying in from Holland.

The sea proved a more dangerous enemy than the Germans; it undermined number one gun so badly that emergency repairs had to be made in December, 1942[42]. By February, 1943, the danger of invasion or bombardment had receded so much that the battery was relegated to Class E, one manned largely by Home Guard personnel. In May, 1944, it was reduced to a garrison of only one officer and seven other ranks, all regulars, and was put on to a care and maintenance basis. It was closed altogether in early 1945, although the guns were not removed until the next year[43]. Most of the pillboxes and obstacles were quickly demolished, leaving only one casemate of the battery to be converted into a seafront shelter and the martello tower, which has been recently restored and refortified against Aldeburgh's ever-present and implacable enemy—the sea.

Southwold 11

SOUTHWOLD's real strategic importance was not the town and its small harbour, hardly rich enough to warrant raiding on its own account, but the wide expanse of Sole Bay, which gave a reasonably secure anchorage for a whole fleet. In 1539, when the first surveys of the coast were made, Southwold had no defences at all, and the great bout of coastal fortifying initiated by Henry VIII resulted in nothing but plans. A contemporary chart shows a four-gun battery at the end of the town and a longer entrenchment armed with five cannon overlooking the harbour, but there is no evidence they were ever built[1].

Only in 1569 is it certain that the town had any guns at all, when it was presented with some artillery by the Earl of Warwick, Master of the Ordnance. The eight guns, demi-culverins, sakers and minions, were given on the strict condition that Southwold maintain them, provide the gunpowder and use them only in defence[2]. The town ignored these strictures and within a decade the cannon were lying rusting and dismounted; it was necessary in 1580 to send Sir Robert Wingfield, accompanied by a skilled gunner, to remind the townsfolk of their obligations and to persuade them to repair the guns[3]. In case Sir Robert's authority should not be sufficient to overawe the reluctant townsfolk, the local justices were ordered to support him[4]. Despite this massing of government forces, the guns remained in their neglected condition; six years later Sir Robert returned on the same fruitless mission[5].

The following year the prospect of the imminent arrival of the Spanish Armada galvanised the town into action as no mere knight armed with Royal warrants could. Once again Southwold was surveyed, this time by Captain Turner, who described it as a "weak town but strongly situated"[6]. He recommended placing eight guns at the north of the town, with further guns on what is now Gun Hill.

In 1588 there was a further survey and Captain Edmund Yorke drew a plan showing an elaborate trace running along the cliff top with two full bastions and a section of tenaille with two gates leading down to the beach. Yorke regarded Southwold as possessed of strong natural defences in the marshes and Buss Creek and planned no earthworks around Might's Bridge,

The proposed earthwork batteries seen on the right appear in a chart of 1540, but there is no evidence that they were ever built. The plan of further proposed fortifications below was drawn by Captain Edmund Yorke in July, 1588, but again the proposals were not put into full effect.

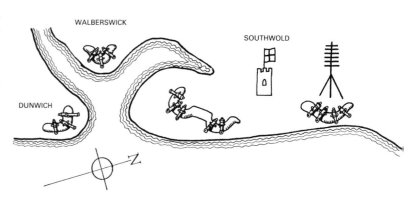

WALBERSWICK

DUNWICH

SOUTHWOLD

only a small guardroom to serve as a blockhouse[7]. July was far too late, however, to undertake such an elaborate and costly scheme and all that was done was to build a low parapet along the cliff edge, to scarp the face of the cliff and construct a bulwark at the north of the town to defend the narrow strip of beach that joined Southwold to the mainland[8]. A second map made in December,

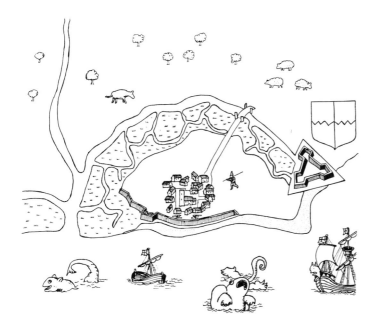

1588, shows the completed work with a two-gun battery on Gun Hill and the parapet along the cliff, but not the bulwark; its position is occupied by a symmetrical fort, triangular with a bastion at each angle, which was never built[9].

Once the danger was over the defences inevitably decayed until the attacks of privateers from Dunkirk seriously threatened local shipping and the coast towns. Southwold petitioned the Crown declaring its defenceless state; the artillery had been reduced to two iron culverins honeycombed with rust and dangerous to use, and Sir John Coke in 1625 recommended that four new guns be emplaced[10]. The pressing need for them was spectacularly demonstrated the following year when a privateer captured a ship in full view of the townspeople, drove the gun crews from their battery, and then, to demonstrate the feebleness of the defence, bombarded the town. That the gun crews were so easily beaten off suggests there was not an adequate parapet[11]. On 31st March, 1626, three weeks after this incident, Southwold asked for twelve demi-culverins[12], but it was not until the following year that the town was surveyed again; as a result the Earl of Totnes, Master of the Ordnance, was ordered to supply eight demi-culverins with carriages and shot[13]. The town was to pay for the powder at twelve shillings a pound and for the "planting of the ordnance"[14]. After a delay of several months, in March, 1628, five culverins and three sakers were delivered and placed on Gun Hill[15].

The Civil War and the First Dutch War passed without incident, but by the outbreak of the second war with Holland the guns had, with depressing inevitability, become almost useless. There were nine in 1666, but only four were mounted, and once again ships were snatched from beneath their impotent muzzles[16]. The continual presence of a Dutch fleet that sailed unmolested along the coast in 1667 had the town in "a distracted condition", with fears that it would suffer the same kind of visitation as Felixstowe[17]. A battery with a good parapet and a trench for shot was hurriedly constructed to emplace the guns, the work being carried out by volunteers who were rewarded by gifts of beer and tobacco[18]. This was the "antient fort" with platform and hollow way noted in 1754 by Gardner[19].

The guns were not called upon to defend the town throughout

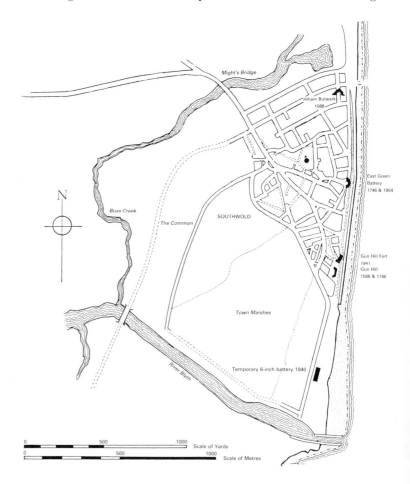

The defences of Southwold.

the early years of the eighteenth century, and yet again they began to fall victim to rust and decay. By 1745 the guns were pronounced more dangerous to those who attempted to fire them than to those at whom they were aimed. Nevertheless, the townspeople managed to put two of the least decrepit pieces on to carriages and then petitioned the Crown for more, claiming that they were "naked and exposed to the insults of the common enemies"[20]. In January, 1746, six 18-pounders with forty rounds apiece were delivered, with the usual provision that the town provide powder, platforms and a storehouse for the equipment[21]. A battery with a strong parapet was built on Gun Hill, close to the remains of the 1667 work, and to supplement them the two existing guns, ancient 9-pounders, were emplaced in a smaller battery nearby[22]. The eight guns remained in place throughout the American War but were virtually at the end of their active life. In 1798 a corps of volunteers was raised, but the guns were unserviceable, "having for many years lain unregarded on the grass"[23]. The Ordnance offered replacements if the town would maintain them and there was a plan to build a masonry tower behind the battery, but this never materialised and the old guns continued to serve[24].

In 1804 the two old 9-pounders were at last judged unserviceable, condemned, and replaced by two 24-pounders which were installed in a battery on the north cliff at the top of East Green Score[25]. These were manned by the sea fencibles, who had to borrow gunpowder, ladles and ramrods from the Corporation

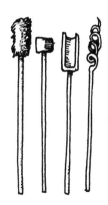

Three of the six 18-pounders sent to Southwold in 1746 seen in a photograph of Gun Hill taken towards the end of the nineteenth century.
Robert Malster

before they could use them[26]. In 1810, with the imminent danger of invasion past, Southwold's defensive priority had sunk so low that there was a proposal to remove all the guns to Yarmouth. The town refused to give them up, claiming that they were its own property and stressing their necessity for the defence of Sole Bay: "it has often already happened that these guns under the direction of the magistrates, before Sea Fencibles were embodied, have driven off privateers and saved many vessels from capture"[27].

This saved the 18-pounders, but the two 24-pounders were carried off, and the next year the north battery was dismantled[28]. In 1819, when the batteries were being disarmed all along the coast, another attempt to remove the 18-pounders was beaten off and they remained in position on Gun Hill[29]. They fired a loyal salvo in 1822 to greet George IV as he sailed past on his way to Scotland, although loyalty outran prudence on this occasion, for the guns were quite unsafe. The King did not appreciate the salute, despite the risk in firing it, and expressed his displeasure, but the town retorted that the guns belonged to Southwold and could be fired as and when thought fit[30]. In 1839 a survey of the coast defences pronounced the guns completely unserviceable and proposed replacing them with two small barbette batteries mounting four and two 24-pounders respectively; they were never built[31]. The old guns were last fired in 1842 in a salute to commemorate the birth of the Prince of Wales, but this ended in tragedy; a charge exploded in the bore of one of the guns, killing a member of the inexperienced crew, and from that date onwards the function of the guns was strictly ornamental[32].

The First World War affected Southwold little. Trenches were dug on the cliffs but the town, being of no military importance, was not fortified. The war slipped quietly by until the night of 25th January, 1917, when a flotilla of German destroyers appeared off the town and fired ninety-two shells into it. Only two houses and the police station were hit, and fortunately no-one was killed or injured[33]. In justification of what was then regarded as an evil and unsporting attack on a place of no military significance beyond the large number of retired army officers living there, the Germans pointed out that Southwold was fortified. The fact that the only guns at Southwold were far more dangerous to anybody who attempted to fire them than to any potential target was not a matter of great concern to the German Imperial Navy; the place had guns pointing out to sea and that made it a legitimate target, according to their interpretation of the rules of war. In case the guns should attract another more lethal visitation, they were removed from Gun Hill and buried for the duration of the war. To ensure some defence if the German navy should return, two field guns were sent and emplaced in the sandpit near the harbour[34].

At first the Second World War also meant little outward change, except for an influx of evacuees and a rampart of sandbags about the Town Hall. But with the end of the phoney war in 1940 and the abrupt translation of Southwold from safe backwater to front line town, matters changed. Most of the population was evacuated, along with those who had sought safety there in the first months of the war; eventually only eight hundred residents remained. In place of the evacuees came large numbers of troops who were billeted in the empty houses and hotels. The beach was festooned with scaffolding, barbed wire and various other obstacles, while the sand was carefully sown with hundreds of mines. A hole was blown in the pier, in case the Germans should decide to land on the end of it, and all the beach huts were collected from the seaside and strewn about the common to forestall the Germans if they changed their plans and decided to arrive in gliders or aeroplanes[35]. The remains of the eccentric Southwold Railway, closed in 1929, were ripped up and used in making beach obstacles; trenches and pillboxes were quickly built along the front and on the common. Roadsigns were taken down, sticky-tape criss-crossed the windows and Southwold was ready to face the enemy.

To defend the sea approaches two ex-naval 6-inch guns were installed in a hastily-constructed emergency battery on the low ground near the harbour's mouth[36]. The six old cannon were hurriedly buried to avoid giving the Germans any excuse to shell or bomb the town. Even out of sight they were not safe; there was a suggestion that they should be sacrificed along with railings, gateways and saucepans to the war's insatiable and indiscriminate appetite for scrap metal[37]. Fortunately they had their defenders and, despite suggestions that a token two be condemned, all the guns remained safely stored until 1945. This was a very sensible decision; the sacrifice of the cannon would have been in vain, as their metallurgical value, like that of the glittering mountains of kitchen utensils, was negligible.

The temporary guns were emplaced in June, 1940, but it was soon decided to replace them with another battery of a more permanent nature and on a better site. In March, 1941, senior officers arrived to choose a new location. They settled on a spot right in the centre of the sea front on the highest point between the pier and the harbour's mouth, and, in a nice touch of historical continuity, not a hundred yards from the old six-gun battery.

The new battery was built in the front garden of Marine Villa by a local firm of contractors. It was of standard design with two casemates, rather closer together than normal, connected by a war-shelter and magazines. A heavily disguised battery observation post stood a little way behind and two 90-centimetre searchlights at the foot of the cliff. The role of the battery was designated as close defence within a range of six thousand yards. The guns, two elderly Mk XI ex-naval 6-inch guns dating from 1906, facing slightly south-east to cover Sole Bay and not directly out to sea, were installed and proof fired by October, 1941[38].

As well as infantry weapons for close defence, the battery was equipped with two anti-aircraft rocket projectors. Gun Hill Fort, as it was officially known, was manned by 438 Battery of 544 Coast Regiment, RA, and was unusual in that it stood so close to buildings. Although these would have helped to break up the outline and contributed to its camouflage, the noise and shock of the guns firing would have been considerable to anybody still living in the nearby houses.

The most dangerous attacks Southwold suffered were from low-flying aircraft that swept in from the North Sea below radar cover; in all there were fifty-eight raids that killed thirteen civilians and severely damaged more than seventy houses[39]. During 1944 the danger most feared was that of flying bombs, with Southwold becoming an integral part of the "Diver Strip", a belt of anti-aircraft guns along the east coast to guard against V1s launched from over the North Sea. As part of this operation, a battery of 3.7-inch AA guns was placed on the common near the water tower[40].

In May, 1944, Gun Hill Fort was reduced to a state of care and maintenance with a token detachment remaining until January, 1945, when it was closed altogether. It was one of the first batteries to be considered for demolition as its presence was so obvious a blot on the sea front; the guns were removed and taken to Landguard Fort in November, 1945, and the battery was demolished shortly afterwards. The beach was cleared of its mines and jagged litter and, to mark the return of peace, the ancient guns were returned to their accustomed place upon Gun Hill.

Lowestoft 12

BEFORE Sir Morton Peto transformed it into a harbour and seaside resort, Lowestoft was little more than a fishing village with a reasonable anchorage; a convenient place for an invader to land but with no important interests of its own to defend. The Newcome and Holm sandbanks formed two roadsteads, one north and the other south of the town, with an entrance through the Stanford Channel. Neither anchorage was large enough to shelter vessels larger than coasters, but the Stanford Channel also formed an entrance to Corton and Yarmouth Roads, so its defence was not a matter of purely local concern[1]. Henry VIII first determined in 1539 that "two bulwarkes [be] set up at Lestoffe"[2]. These were duly built, armed and ready for action by February the next year, and a third battery was built shortly afterwards[3]. A gunner was appointed to the "blockhouse" and another to the "bulwark" to look after the guns and to train the locals in their use[4]. They were nothing more than simple earthwork batteries revetted with gabions and boards, armed with three or four guns each and sited at the south end of the town to cover the Stanford Channel, on the Ness to defend the anchorage, and the third a little way to the north[5].

When the Duke of Norfolk arrived in 1545, he was impressed neither by their location nor by their construction, as they were "but of earth as banks made of turves, and so far distant from the town, I think it should be no great adventure for a good puissance to land there and burn the said town"[6]. Two years later the defences were in need of repair, and in lieu of any money from the Crown the churchwardens of the parish were forced to sell some of the church plate to buy ammunition and mend the guns[7]. Kirkley and Pakefield also sold off ecclesiastical silverware to buy guns and ammunition; the former's accounts record mending a gun, which suggests that a cannon was mounted on the cliffs to command the South Roads[8].

The first attack on the new defences came not from the sea but from a completely unexpected quarter. In 1549 an armed band from Suffolk participating in Kett's Rebellion seized six guns from the batteries and dragged them off to provide the artillery for an abortive attack on Yarmouth, which was easily repulsed, both rebels and cannon being captured and taken into the town.

Yarmouth regarded the rebels' stolen artillery as legitimate spoils of war and refused to return them[9].

Over the next twenty years the defences went to ruin and the remaining cannon were left to rust until 1569, when Queen Elizabeth granted four cannons and two slings to the town on the usual conditions[10]. Nine years later it was obvious that the clauses concerning maintenance had not been complied with, for the guns were dismounted and needed repair. Sir Robert Wingfield was dispatched to try to persuade the town to contribute something to the guns' upkeep and to pay the salary of a gunner, but he appears to have been unsuccessful and in 1586 the Privy Council ordered him to try again[11].

Only fear of the Spanish Armada resulted in positive improvements to the defences. In 1587 only two of the town's guns were mounted and Lowestoft, in the report of one Captain Turner, "standeth open upon the sea". He recommended building a battery on the Ness and another so situated as to defend both the North and the South Roads, to be armed with a total of fourteen guns[12]. The next year eighty pounds was spent by the town on erecting bulwarks, sixteen pounds on mounting the guns and a further sixteen pounds on ammunition[13]. An extra six guns were sent from the Ordnance stores and these, combined with the cannon of Henry VIII and Elizabeth, made up the recommended fourteen pieces[14].

The new bulwarks were to be on the site of those of 1540, and to economise the town restored only two of the original three. This skimping was not to the Crown's liking and a warrant was sent by the lords lieutenant demanding another bulwark[15]. This was reluctantly built at a cost of sixty pounds, which Lowestoft

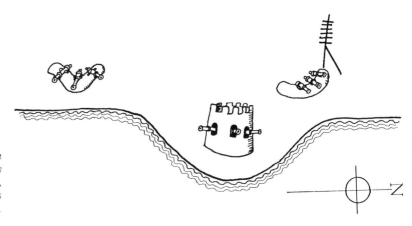

The blockhouse shown in this sixteenth-century manuscript was not built, but the earthwork batteries did exist.

deducted from its share of the cost of equipping a ship; Ipswich, their partners in this enforced contribution, complained and the legal wrangles went on long after the Armada had disappeared.

Nothing was done or even suggested in 1625 when so much was being built or repaired along the coast, implying that at least one battery was intact with some guns in working order. At the start of the Civil War, running against the trend of eastern England, Lowestoft declared for the King and prepared to resist Parliamentary forces. Two cannon were placed at the south end of the town, with another pair mounted at the head of Rant's Score pointing up the High Street. Oliver Cromwell arrived at the head of one thousand cavalry and in a brisk and almost bloodless action took the town. He carried off all the four cannons and two slings; later, with the growing threat of Royalist privateers, he was forced to return them and a new battery of four guns was built on the Denes[16].

In 1656, during the First Dutch War, five enemy men-of-war lay off the beach within musket shot, but no gun was fired at them as the cannon in the battery had no ammunition and no carriages[17]. Within a few years this battery was swallowed up by the sea during a violent storm; the townspeople rushed out with spades and ropes after the sea had subsided, dug the cannon from the shingle and dragged them unharmed into the town[18].

They were still there at the restoration of Charles II, but whether they were mounted and in a battery is doubtful. It was then that they were threatened from an unusual quarter. Sir Thomas Meadowes of Yarmouth decided that his town's need of guns was greater than Lowestoft's and tried to repeat the action of 1549 and take the cannon. Once again Lowestoft rallied to the rescue of its artillery, but this time with parchment rather than shovels; the townsfolk sent a petition to the Duke of Albemarle pleading that the guns should be allowed to remain. He quashed the designs of Sir Thomas and ordered that the guns should remain where they were[19]. A new platform and parapet was built, only to be devoured by the sea; the guns were rescued once again and a second battery built, although only after appeals to the lord lieutenant for assistance[20].

The form of this fortification was simple; it was probably only a timber platform with a low parapet revetted by timber or gabions, yet this meagre battery was the only one of Lowestoft's many fortifications to go into action, although without any great distinction. On 5th February, 1665, the alarm was sounded when a Dutch privateer arrived off the town and Major Wilde, at the head of a hastily gathered band of volunteer gunners, rushed down to the battery. As they gathered about the guns the privateer, seeing the activity, sailed closer and loosed a salvo that killed the major[21].

His disheartened troops could not manage to return a single round before the Dutchman sailed off unscathed.

The next year the town petitioned the Crown for artillery but stressed that there was no money to build a battery or to mount the guns[22]. Nothing seems to have come of this and for the next twenty years Lowestoft was apparently defenceless, a report of 1681 noting briefly "here is no castle for defence"[23]. In 1702 the town joined with the other Suffolk coastal towns in petitioning the Crown for guns, and as a result a battery was built on the Ness armed with either new guns or the old ones repaired and remounted[24]. In 1715 there was what was described as a "block-house on the Ness well furnished with ordnance", but this too was destroyed by the sea and the guns lay abandoned and half buried until the seventeen-forties[25].

In 1744 six new 18-pounders were sent by the Ordnance and emplaced in a new earthwork fort at the south end of the town where they could defend both the Stanford Channel and the South Roads[26]. Twelve years later another battery was built near the Ness and armed with two of the 18-pounders taken from the south fort and some of the older guns as well[27]. Although the Ordnance owned the land on which the south fort was built it provided nothing else, apart from the guns. The ammunition to fire them and the men to work them were the responsibility of the town.

The inevitable fate of all Lowestoft's defences soon overtook the two batteries, and they slowly fell into ruin, without anyone showing much concern. One local chronicler noted "these batteries were never of any great service to the town, for vessels belonging to the enemy seldom approach so near to the coast as to come within reach of the guns", apparently never wondering how close the enemy might have come had the guns not been there[28]. When the American War broke out and Lord Amherst arrived to inspect the batteries, they were entirely ruined[29]. The engineer, Captain Thomas Hyde Page, noted "Lowestoft should be attended to, as

The South Fort in 1782, a much bigger work than its predecessor. This fort stood on what is now known as Battery Green.

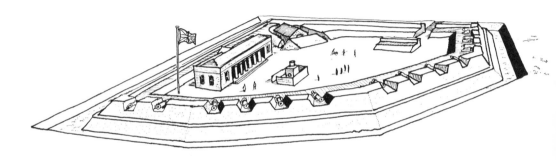

ships are obliged to come very near to the shore in order to get into Yarmouth Roads. There are some guns and the remains of two batteries well placed to take ships ahead in coming between the sands"[30].

Nothing was done until 1781 when Lord Amherst returned and the batteries were surveyed once more[31]. Both were described as ruined; the cannon were all dismounted and most had been buried for years. There were two 24-pounders, six 18-pounders and a 9-pounder lying in the south battery and two 24-pounders and three 12-pounders in the north, with six carriages for all these guns kept in the church. Pakefield had two 18-pounders, dating from 1744, to command the South Roads, but these had no platforms[32].

A few weeks after Lord Amherst's visit Lowestoft was thrown into a panic when a mysterious and unexpected fleet appeared sailing directly towards the town. To oppose what most thought was the Dutch navy were fourteen rusty guns lying useless amidst the ruins of their emplacements. To the heartfelt relief of all, the ships were eventually revealed as British, but the scare vividly emphasised the state of the town's defences[33].

The next month, September, 1781, General Tryon, the newly appointed Commander of the Eastern District, ordered the guns to be tested as some had been lying buried in the sand since the middle of the century. A detachment of artillery, accompanied by a curious crowd, went to the south battery and loaded the cannon with proof charges: sixteen pounds of powder and an 18-pounder shot. Three guns were fired safely but the fourth burst, throwing fragments over hundreds of yards; one fragment struck a small boy. The next month the older guns at the Ness battery were gingerly loaded and fired with extreme caution; three promptly blew up[34].

On being informed that Lowestoft was defended by two ruined forts and a rusty collection of cannon that were more likely to destroy themselves than their enemies, the Ordnance ordered the building of three new forts. The South Fort was to be much larger than its predecessor, and before work could begin an extra piece of land had to be bought[35]. The forts were designed by Colonel Debbieg, although the actual construction was supervised by Captain Fisher of the Royal Engineers; the work was carried out by a force of three hundred labourers[36]. Sited where all the previous batteries had stood, the South Fort was on what is now Battery Green, in front of the old coastguard cottages; the Beach Battery stood on the Ness, while the third, the North Battery, occupied a site in what is now Belle Vue Park where the Royal Naval Patrol Service memorial stands. The two forts on the beach were very substantial fortifications with strong ramparts on all

A plan of the Ness Battery, which was armed with four 32-pounders and two 9-pounders.

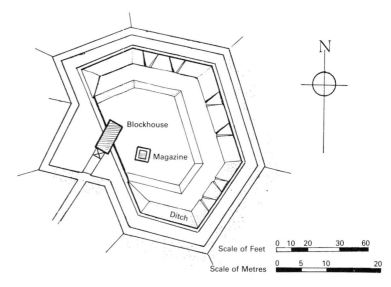

N

Blockhouse

Magazine

Ditch

Scale of Feet   0 10 20   30   60

Scale of Metres   0   5   10   20

sides, designed to resist not only the fire of enemy ships but also the attacks of landing parties intent on storming them. Vulnerable to attack from the cliffs behind, they were not intended to hold out against a prolonged siege; they were essentially self-defensible coastal batteries whose main task was to command the roads.

The South Fort was the largest. It was an irregular hexagon surrounded by a ditch eighteen feet deep and fifteen wide, made even more formidable with *cheveaux-de-frize*. On the ramparts, firing through embrasures, were thirteen heavy cannon: ten 32-pounders and three 18-pounders. At the north-west angle was the magazine, a sunken bomb-proof chamber thirty feet long with room for three hundred barrels of powder. A touch of permanence and elegance was given to the fort by the guard house, a single-storey brick building with long sash windows and a small colonnade. The final detail was given by a giant flagpole sited in the south-west angle of the fort from which, over fifty feet above the parade ground, fluttered an English Jack[37].

The Ness Battery was slightly smaller and a more regular hexagon. Although the ditch of the fort surrounded it on all sides, the rampart alone faced the sea, leaving the gorge to be closed by a simple palisade and a small blockhouse covering the gate. The battery was armed with six cannon, four 32-pounders and two 9-pounders[38]. The North Battery was the smallest and least substantial; standing high on a cliff and well back from the sea, it did not need such massive earthworks as the others. It was a four-sided work with no ditch, only a palisade and a parapet behind which sheltered four 18-pounders. To complete the command of the anchorage four 32-pounders were mounted at Pakefield in a small stockaded battery[39].

Once the guns were in place and all three forts completed, the problem arose of who should garrison them. Regular troops were out of the question, but there were not enough able-bodied men in the town to man the guns as so many were serving in the navy. Fears and rumours of invasion hastened the completion of the forts, and they were all ready to fire the five celebratory salvos to greet the peace signed in January, 1783[40]. Lowestoft's historian Edmund Gillingwater, writing in 1790, assumed that the batteries would follow the traditional pattern when he noted "the fortifications which had been so lately erected at this town, at a great expense, will probably soon fall into utter decay"[41]. Events were to prove him completely wrong.

In 1793 war broke out again between Great Britain and France and the forts were regarrisoned. Fortunately they had deteriorated very little; the South Fort had a damp magazine and was overlooked by a house, and the North Battery needed enclosing

The South Fort of 1781 was the last of four built on the same site to command the entry to Lowestoft Roads through the Stanford Channel. It was armed with thirteen heavy cannon.

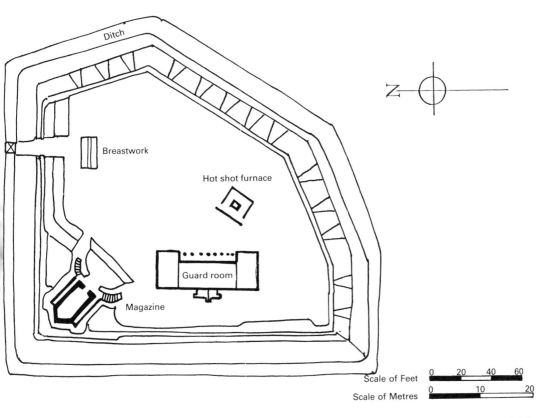

Ditch

Breastwork

Hot shot furnace

Guard room

Magazine

Scale of Feet

0   20   40   60

Scale of Metres

0   10   20

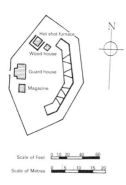

Scale of Feet

Scale of Metres

The North Battery, which stood high on a cliff and did not need so substantial a system of earthworks as the other Lowestoft fortifications. The site of the battery can be seen on the right of this photograph, taken about 1860.

with a palisade, but apart from this they were soon ready for action[42]. In 1798 the Ness Battery was enlarged slightly to mount eight 32-pounders, while the armament of the South Fort was reduced to ten 32-pounders, with a furnace for heating shot[43]. In the same year it was proposed to build two masonry towers in support of the batteries, one behind the Ness Battery and the other on the cliff by the North Battery[44]. In 1803 three towers were planned, but they were still not built five years later when there was yet another proposal for two martello towers and a four-gun battery[45]. These were not built either, and Lowestoft ended the Napoleonic Wars with the same defences with which it had begun them.

After 1815 the fate predicted for the forts by Gillingwater began to overtake them; the Ness Battery was abandoned, leased to a tenant who appeared to engage in stealing pigs, and the guns were removed and distributed to the remaining two batteries; the South Fort had twelve 32-pounders and the North Battery three[46]. It was proposed to rebuild the Ness Battery and to repair the South Fort in the eighteen-thirties, but as usual nothing was done[47].

From 1845 the harbour of Lowestoft was gradually developed and with it the importance of the town as a commercial and fishing port grew, but no new fortifications were built or even seriously proposed. With typical bureaucratic caution, the War Office kept its options open by insisting on the insertion of a clause in the

Improvement Act of 1854 that read: "Nothing shall be built in front of the Fort that shall or may in any way interfere with the efficiency of the said fort"[48]. The War Office refused to relinquish the land on which the fort stood and even went so far as to sue the lord of the manor, in a case vaguely reminiscent of Tomline and Landguard Fort, and to erect stones to testify to its continued ownership and control. These the town council threw down; and no more was heard of the matter.

Various plans for the new fortifications were proposed and discussed during the last half of the nineteenth century, including a scheme to build a large casemated battery to replace the completely ruined South Fort, but none came to anything. By 1870 the North Battery had been sold, the Ness Battery had been washed away, and there was another more realistic plan to replace all three works with a defensible battery armed with two heavy and four medium RMLs sited to the north of the harbour[49]. Legal disputes continued over the ownership of the remains of the South Fort, and the council petitioned to turn it into a park[50]. In 1880 the War Office handed the site over to the Admiralty, who built a coastguard station behind it and obliterated the remains of the ramparts; whatever remained of the North Battery was removed

The Suffolk Volunteer Corps being reviewed on the North Denes at Lowestoft in 1865. The day of the review was a public holiday in the town, and large numbers of the townspeople watched the events from the Denes and from the cliffs above.

Robert Malster

165

A decorative detail on the Artillery Volunteers' drill hall in Arnold Street, Lowestoft.

when Belle Vue Park was laid out in 1886[51]. For the remainder of the nineteenth century and well into the next the only guns in Lowestoft were some old 32-pounders for the use of the local Artillery Volunteers. These were kept in a small practice battery outside the armoury on the North Denes[52].

In 1914 Lowestoft faced the German Ocean and the German High Seas Fleet with nothing more in the way of defence than the old muzzle-loaders from the practice battery ornamenting the promenade. Troops were stationed in the town and surrounding villages but no efforts were made to fortify the coast or to mount guns. Desultory attacks on the town began the next year when a Zeppelin dropped bombs on two occasions and a single incendiary rocket whistled in from the sea to land ineffectually in a field[53]. In February, 1916, the town was bombed for the first time by aeroplanes, but although there were mobile anti-aircraft guns stationed locally they had no success against the raiders.

A far more spectacular attack was made by the German fleet on 25th April. At 4.30 am a squadron of battle-cruisers appeared off the town and for twenty minutes hurled heavy shells into the houses and harbour installations before rapidly steaming back across the North Sea, leaving forty houses destroyed and two hundred damaged and four people killed[54]. This attack was reported with quite extraordinary composure, the *Norwich Mercury* remarking that "Lowestoft had a very trying experience on Tuesday morning, the bombardment of the town by a powerful German cruiser squadron"[55]. The damage would have been much greater had the Germans fired high explosive instead of armour-piercing shells; one of these passed through the length of a terrace of houses without exploding.

Although the material damage was slight the effect on morale was tremendous; people poured out of the town in terror and

A gunboat of the Aphis *class similar to HMS* Glowworm. *Built under the Emergency War Programme, they were designed for service on the Danube but were employed on a multitude of other duties.*

many did not stop until they reached Bungay, fifteen miles inland. A month later there was still a nightly exodus into the country, and every shed and barn was full of those who dared not sleep at home in case the Germans returned[56]. In response to the public outcry and vociferous demands for protection two warships, the monitor HMS *Havelock* and the little gunboat HMS *Glowworm*, were sent. At over 6,000 tons displacement the *Havelock* was probably the largest vessel ever to enter the harbour. She was armed with two 14-inch, two 6-inch and two 12-pounders, and these, combined with the *Glowworm's* two 6-inch and two 12-pounders, gave Lowestoft a powerful defensive armament—but not for long. After the initial scare had subsided the two ships were removed and sent where they could do more damage to the enemy.

This bombardment and an increasing fear of a German invasion resulted in the digging of miles of trenches along the clifftops north and south of the town and the stationing of a battery of six 4.7-inch field guns at Pakefield, although these would have been of little use against shipping[57]. There were no further visits from the High Seas Fleet; two more Zeppelin raids and an odd shell fired from a U-boat were the remaining German attacks. Anti-invasion measures continued right up to the armistice, and as well as the trench lines several concrete pillboxes were built on Corton Cliffs and at Carlton Colville[58].

When the Second World War broke out Lowestoft was at once transformed from a depressed and moribund seaport into a naval base of vital importance. The Sparrow's Nest Theatre and gardens became HMS *Europa*, headquarters of the Royal Naval Patrol Service, and the harbour filled with minesweepers, MTBs and armed trawlers. No fixed defences were installed to protect these extensive facilities; instead the old cannon were taken from their ornamental positions on the seafront and buried in the corporation depot[59].

This relaxed attitude to defence changed in 1940, and the provision of coastal artillery and other fortifications became a matter of frenetic urgency. Two problems presented themselves immediately. The first was to defend the town from being captured by a force that had landed elsewhere and then struck at Lowestoft in an attempt to capture a port through which to receive supplies and reinforcements; the second was to protect town and harbour installations from direct assault and bombardment from the sea.

In order to guard against the first possibility Lowestoft was given an all-round defensive perimeter of trenches, pillboxes and dense belts of barbed wire. The strongest defences were on the north side of the town; trenches were dug along the top of Corton cliffs and on the slopes below a line of seven pillboxes was built. The defences then swung due west, running along the crest of the shallow valley in which lies the lake before Gunton Hall. Between Corton Road and Yarmouth Road there were nine pillboxes, some separated by no more than fifty yards, and fronted by lines of concrete anti-tank obstacles. This line continued round the south-west to Oulton village, with more pillboxes and anti-tank obstacles; it ended on Oulton Broad. Around the south of the town a deep anti-tank ditch with wire entanglements and numerous strongpoints ran from Oulton Broad to the sea at Pakefield, following the line of Elm Tree Road and Bloodmoor Lane[60].

To guard against attack from the sea an array of beach obstacles was constructed; long lines of scaffolding ran along the water's edge, concrete blocks and metal rails disfigured the sand, which was planted with mines, and the Claremont Pier was blown in two. The first guns emplaced to defend the sea approaches symbolised the defenceless state of Britain in 1940; two elderly field guns of 1916 vintage, hardly adequate for engaging any target other than a stationary rowing boat, were emplaced within low rings of sandbags on the North Pier extension and on the Esplanade. Heavier weapons arrived in June, 1940, when a detachment of Royal Marines brought three 6-inch guns to the town and mounted them on Gunton Cliff. The emplacement, called Kent Battery, was of a very hasty and makeshift construction. The guns, old naval pieces, were fixed on slabs of quick-setting concrete with gunhouses of sandbags laid on a steel framework. Kent Battery was operational for only a few weeks before work started on a new and more permanent successor[61].

The new battery was built directly on Gunton Cliff Esplanade, and despite the urgency and danger of the moment the Borough Council objected to the road being closed. The town clerk wrote to the army with a proper sense of real priorities: "As you are aware, Gunton Cliff Esplanade is in a high class residential district and it would be a considerable inconvenience to the residents there to have a portion of this road closed"[62]. His objections were equally strong to the closing of the north sea wall on which the battery searchlights and several pillboxes and anti-tank emplacements were built. "I think that the military authorities will appreciate that while the civil population must be put to a certain amount of inconvenience in wartime, there should be as little interference with civil life as possible"[63]. The army answered this request not to restrict the access of the residents by evicting them from their homes and turning the houses into offices and quarters for the battery[64].

The new battery had two guns, army pattern Mk VII 6-inch on conventional central pivot mounts, the same as installed in permanent coast batteries, which gave fifteen degrees of elevation and a better range than the ex-naval guns that were normally

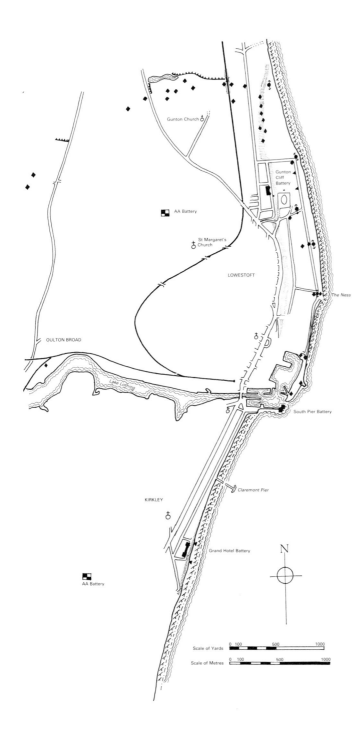

The defences of Lowestoft, 1940–45.

Gunton Church

Gunton Cliff Battery

AA Battery

St Margaret's Church

LOWESTOFT

The Ness

OULTON BROAD

Lake Lothing

South Pier Battery

Claremont Pier

KIRKLEY

Grand Hotel Battery

N

AA Battery

Scale of Yards 0 100   500   1000

Scale of Metres 0 100   500   1000

installed in emergency batteries. The steel-framed gunhouses were first walled with corrugated iron and later encased in brick and concrete[65]. The casemate for number two gun stood at the corner of Gunton Esplanade and Heather Road, with number one gun two hundred feet nearer Belle Vue Park. The magazines and war shelters ran between the two guns in the gardens behind, and two thatch-roofed summerhouses were adapted with the provision of reinforced concrete ceilings to act as shell stores[66]. The battery observation post stood on the cliff top opposite Briarcliff Lodge while the engine room for the searchlight generators was built on the denes below by the Oval cricket ground. The two searchlight emplacements were on the sea wall, one perched on top of a reinforced public lavatory. The battery was finished in the remarkably short time of three months; when it was ready the Royal Marines and their guns from Kent Battery moved elsewhere, and from then to the end of the war the new battery was manned by regular troops of 235 Bty, RA[67].

To provide close defence for the harbour mouth a battery armed with two 12-pounders was built on the end of the South Pier, where two brick gunhouses and associated shelters clustered around the lighthouse. The guns were old Mk I 12-pounders, one dating from 1898 and the other from 1900, which had once formed part of a battleship's secondary armament. They had a maximum range of eight thousand yards during the day, restricted at night to no more than 1,400 yards, the furthest extent of the illumination provided by the two fixed-beam searchlights[68].

While the guns on Gunton Cliff and the South Pier were being installed a third battery was built at Pakefield. The holiday camp

A 6-inch Mk XI gun of the kind installed in many of the emergency batteries of 1940. This example was mounted in HMAS Brisbane *and is now preserved in Australia.*
Ivan Kent

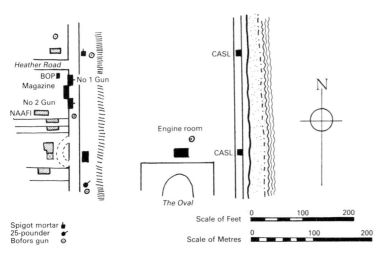

The Gunton Cliff Battery, which had two Mk VII 6-inch on central pivot mounts instead of the ex-naval guns more usually mounted in the emergency batteries.

Heather Road
BOP
Magazine
No 1 Gun
No 2 Gun
NAAFI
Engine room
CASL
The Oval
CASL
N

Spigot mortar
25-pounder
Bofors gun

Scale of Feet

0   100   200

Scale of Metres

0   100   200

there was commandeered by the Royal Navy, who quickly emplaced two naval 6-inch guns in a battery at the cliff's edge. This was taken over by the Royal Artillery as 326 Bty in July, and the emplacements were gradually built up as the standard brick and concrete shelters and casemates with a battery observation post and two searchlights[69].

Although this armament seemed adequate, Lowestoft had one serious gap in its defences; the guns at Gunton Cliff and Pakefield could not cover the harbour entrance or the South Roads[70]. To remedy this another 6-inch battery was planned for the south of the town. A site was selected in Kensington Gardens by the Grand Hotel and work began in the summer of 1941. Two 6-inch Mk XIII guns on naval mounts were installed in casemates cunningly disguised as clifftop shelters with chestnut shingles and masses of foliage. The underground magazines and shelters were dug into the formal walks of the gardens and the two searchlights were emplaced on the promenade at the foot of the cliff. There was nothing unusual about the design, except that the roof of the casemates was made up of plastic armour slabs[71]. The battery was protected from the assault of any Germans who might be so suicidally inclined as to land on the beach directly beneath by barbed wire, machine-gun posts and "flammer fougasses" buried in the face of the cliff. These latter were an example of the imaginative but impractical lethal devices used to compensate for the lack of duller but more efficient weapons of orthodox design; the fougasses were pots filled with explosives and inflammable materials that were intended to shoot a belch of fire like a bessemer converter over the enemy[72].

Lowestoft was one of three locations on the east coast

171

designated as a permanent gun-defended area for anti-aircraft defence[73]. To cover the town two heavy AA batteries armed with 3.7-inch guns were emplaced on Pakefield Golf Course and at College Farm near St Margaret's Church. As the danger of low-flying hit-and-run raiders grew, more light automatic weapons were installed along the seafront and about the harbour[74].

In 1942 there was a proposal to rationalise the defences by combining the coastal and AA guns in one battery of three 5.25-inch dual purpose guns at Pakefield, but this was never implemented[75]. The coastal guns never saw action; the nearest contact with the enemy was when a Heinkel 111 dropped two bombs behind the Gunton Cliff battery and another Luftwaffe plane bounced a 250-kilogram bomb off the South Pier battery[76]. This bomb did little damage; far more was caused when the battery was hit by a ship that missed the harbour entrance in the dark[77].

As the seaborne threat became ever more remote and the coastal batteries became less essential the Grand Hotel battery was handed over to the Home Guard in 1944 on a reduced state of readiness, and the following January all the batteries were closed down[78]. The guns were removed in November, 1945, and taken off to Landguard Fort to be scrapped. The concrete emplacements were all broken up, most of the fragments going to form rockeries in gardens throughout the town. The beach was cleared, the mines lifted and the anti-invasion scaffolding converted to peaceful purposes in the shape of market stalls. All that remains now of all these fortifications, apart from a number of pillboxes along Corton cliffs, is the casemate for the number two gun of the Grand Hotel battery which has been fitted out with seats to serve as a seafront shelter. Few, if any, of those who rest there and seek to escape the biting wind realise that it was originally built to protect its occupants against a far more deadly onslaught.

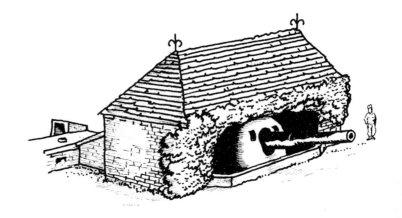

The casemates of the Grand Hotel Battery at Lowestoft were disguised with a false roof of shingles and much foliage.

Norfolk   13

'**N**ORFOLK is a maritime county and liable to descent from the sea," a simple fact that has determined the shape and siting of Norfolk's fortifications over the last four hundred years. More than one hundred miles of deserted coastline, with long flat beaches and gentle cliffs, have rendered the county vulnerable both to raids and to full-scale invasion. Fortunately, natural defences in the form of steeper cliffs and marshes have reduced those areas in need of the engineer's art, making a good proportion of the coast impracticable as a landing place for an invading force. Most of the Wash coastline is protected by shoals and mudflats; salt marshes and winding channels make the stretch between Thornham and Blakeney difficult, while high cliffs render the whole coast between Sheringham and Happisburgh impossible of access to all but the smallest of landing parties.

Although most of Norfolk's fortifications have been concentrated about the ports and along those stretches of the coast not protected by nature, the first specific defences designed to mount the primitive artillery of the fourteenth century were built inland. It was not until the late fifteenth century that any cannon of a suitable size to play a useful role in coast defences existed. The cannon of the previous century were mainly primitive handguns requiring only the simplest of adaptations of existing fortifications.

The earliest of these modifications in the county were carried out in Norwich; Castle Rising may have had guns earlier, for two handguns dating from the thirteen-forties were found there, but if any gunports were made they have not survived[1]. As early as 1385 the City of Norwich possessed a good store of artillery, bought in London[2]. The thirty-nine towers and twelve gates of the city walls were maintained by the wealthier citizens, who were also assessed to provide artillery; altogether more than forty guns were placed on the fortification[3].

More important was the rebuilding of the Cow Tower with loopholes specifically designed for guns[4]. The tower, standing alone on the bend of the River Wensum at the north-east corner of the city, replaced the original which had been built by the Cathedral Priory as a post to collect tolls and as a prison for those who had fallen foul of ecclesiastical jurisdiction. That passed to the City, which reconstructed it in brick in 1390[5]. The bricks alone

A medieval handgun, from a contemporary manuscript.

173

Above: *This composite
loophole in the Cow Tower
at Norwich could be used
either for guns or for
crossbows.*
Below: *The Cow Tower.*
Robert Malster

would have made it architecturally important, but it was also
provided with gunports, making it the first artillery blockhouse in
the country[6]. The upper two of its three floors were provided with
loopholes which, given the size of the openings, could only have
been for handguns.

Elsewhere in the county there were no great fortresses, apart
from Castle Rising and Castle Acre, but some of the lesser county
magnates were beginning to purchase guns and to make alterations
to accommodate them. Oxborough Hall in the west of the county,
begun by Edmund Bedingfeld in 1482, is hardly more than a
moated house with a stupendous gate tower that owes more to a
desire for martial display than to an attempt at serious and efficient
defence. The tower does, however, contain provision for handguns. Flanking the gate are some rather unusual gunports which
consist of a cross-slit running down to a stirrup-shaped aperture, a
type common in Germany; perhaps their presence here is due to
Oxborough's proximity to King's Lynn, with its Hanseatic
connections[7].

Roughly contemporary with Oxborough was Baconsthorpe
Castle in North Norfolk, several miles from the coast, built by the
dubious and shifty Sir Henry Heydon, a lawyer and Recorder of
Norwich. Despite his legal profession, he omitted to obtain a

licence to crenellate the existing manor house, which he transformed into a fortress of some strength. Surrounded by a moat widening to a lake on the east side, with towers, a curtain wall and a strong gatehouse, Baconsthorpe was a little less than a castle and rather more than a normal manor house. It was also equipped with artillery. In the south-west corner tower there is a single keyhole gunport flanking the curtain wall, and in the south wall beside the gatehouse there is a row of vertical slots for handguns[8]. These are unusual, as they are divided at the internal face so that two men could use the one embrasure; there are horizontal slots for a timber support for the guns.

More important than either Baconsthorpe or Oxborough, although no more original in its defensive arrangements, was the castle built by Sir John Fastolf at Caister-by-Yarmouth. Caister Castle has two main claims to distinction, the first being that it is the only English example of a *Wasserburg*, the water-ringed castles of Flanders and the lower Rhineland, the second that it is one of the first major brick buildings in England[9]. Fastolf was an unusual man of enormous wealth, increasing an initial income of £50 a year to £20,000 by careful marriage and the astute exploitation of the opportunities offered by soldiering in France. He began to build his castle in 1432, a time of internal disorder made worse by external threat, and although a private residence Caister Castle played an important role in coast defence. Norfolk was particularly vulnerable to continental pirates who landed without any opposition and "played them on Caister sands, as homely as if they were Englishmen"[10]. Caister Castle countered this threat by acting as a hub of local defence and by covering the main road leading inland.

The castle is built on a large moated platform divided by a cross moat, around the edge of which runs a low curtain wall with a slim, elegant tower rising ninety feet sheer from the moat in the south-west corner, quite unlike anything else in England. Fastolf possessed an unusual amount of artillery; an inventory of 1470 listed twenty guns, and gunports were built into the castle to accommodate them. The curtain wall has simple loops consisting of a slit with a central oeillet, but those in the great tower are circular, implying the use of heavier guns. The castle proved its strength in 1469 when it endured a six-week siege before yielding to the Duke of Norfolk, who had sent a force of three thousand men and many guns against it.

With the reassertion of Royal authority in the sixteenth century the private castle became less important and the emphasis passed to defending the coast; Henry VIII's first nationwide scheme did not ignore Norfolk. In February, 1539, the King ordered "expert persons to be sent to view the coasts of Norfolk, Suffolk and Essex and the dangerous places to be fortified"[11]. The

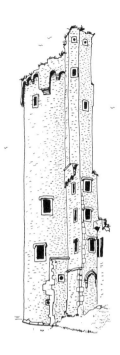

Caister Castle had several circular gunports flanking the curtain wall, but it is hard to see what use those high in the tower could have been.

175

"expert persons" given the task of tramping the shores of Norfolk were a group of local gentry, including Sir John Heydon, Sir William Paston and Sir Thomas Bedingfeld, led by the Earl of Surrey, the younger son of the Duke of Norfolk, whose position was due more to his aristocratic than his "expert" qualities. Whatever their recommendations, nothing of any significance was built, all the Crown's efforts being concentrated on the major ports.

Later small-scale local efforts provided defences intermittently along the coast, including a primitive battery and a single cannon at the Old Hythe[12], a landing place between Sheringham and Cley, and guns at Waxham, Bacton and Winterton[13]. The coast was inspected again in 1568 and 1577, and probably as a result of one of these scrutinies a small earthwork fort or sconce was built to cover the entrance to Blakeney Harbour.

Kett's Rebellion in 1549 graphically demonstrated how obsolete and useless the existing inland fortifications were. The rebels, without artillery and armed only with makeshift weapons, easily broke into Norwich by swimming the River Wensum, outflanking the Bishopbridge Gate and seizing it from behind. Later the government forces of the Marquis of Northampton and the Earl of Warwick found no difficulty in scaling the decayed walls without any sort of preliminary bombardment. This feat owed something to the incompetence of the defending rebels, but more to the derelict state of the fortifications, which Blomefield later described as the burst bindings of a great volume[14]. When Kett's men obtained some artillery and emplaced it on Mousehold Heath, the complete vulnerability of the city was evident to all.

The prospect of the Spanish Armada and imminent invasion prompted yet another survey of the coast in 1587, certificates of dangerous places and measures necessary for their defence being supplied to the Government. Norfolk was judged to have only twelve places where the enemy could easily come ashore, compared with Suffolk's twenty-nine, but this did not prevent a great burst of defensive construction, most of it planned too late to be completed—or even started—before the danger had passed[15].

The scale of the crisis was so great that efforts were not concentrated solely on defending the coast; lines of defence necessary to delay the Spaniards long enough for a field army to be collected were also planned. The Privy Council ordered that defences be concentrated at the crossings of the Little Ouse at Thetford and Brandon and at the crossing of the Lark at Barton Mills, in case the Spanish forces landed at Weybourne and set out for London, bypassing Norwich to the west[16]. Such defences, had they been built, would have been no more than uncomplicated breastworks or at the most a simple sconce; there was no time for anything more elaborate.

The cannon guarding the Old Hythe between Sheringham and Weybourne, from a 1588 map of Weybourne and its entrenchments.

Bishop's Gate was the only defence of Norwich on the east. It was easily outflanked and captured by Kett's rebels in 1549. The gate, which stood on the still-existing medieval bridge, was demolished in 1790.

If the invaders landed between Yarmouth and Bacton and marched on Norwich, they were to be resisted at the crossings of the Broadland rivers which formed successive lines of defence. There were only four bridges; the Way Bridge over the Ant near Stalham, Acle and Wroxham bridges over the Bure, and Potter Heigham bridge across the Thurne. These vital strategic points were to be defended by earthworks and barricades; if they could not be held, the bridges were to be demolished[17].

Norwich was the hub of Norfolk's defences; for the first time the security of the city was seen as a national concern and not as a purely civic one. The defence of Norwich had two distinct purposes; the first to prevent the capture and sack of one of England's richest cities, and the second to prevent the enemy from penetrating further inland. The instructions to the lords lieutenant commanded that "Norwich, which is a place imparting greatly the honour of Her Majesty, is to be preserved from their spoils," and the castle and walls were to be repaired[18]. The Privy Council sent plans for an entrenched camp on Mousehold, where it was determined that "the assembled army of the county" should gather and hold out until relieved[19].

177

Three vulnerable spots where the Armada might attempt to land troops were noted at Weybourne, Winterton and Yarmouth, all of which had the dangerous combination of a sheltered anchorage and deep water close inshore[20]. Of the three, Weybourne was regarded as the most likely. There the shore shelved so steeply that a large ship could lie within a hundred yards of the beach; circumstances so favourable to an invader that they occasioned the old adage:

> "He who would old England win,
> Must at Weybourne Hoop begin."

The plan by Captain Edmund Yorke of the proposed fortifications to guard a vulnerable stretch of coast between Weybourne and Cley. The flanking arrangements of the bastions and the design of Black Joy Fort were extremely sophisticated, in spite of the haste with which the plan was produced.

Between the end of the cliffs at Weybourne and the entrance to Cley Haven lay nearly two miles of open flat coast backed by a salt marsh. To defend this a line of continuous rampart was planned, with three bastions and a fort to secure either end[21].

The plans, drawn by Edmund Yorke, showed a considerable knowledge of theory as well as an original and pragmatic mind and were far in advance of anything prevously seen in East Anglia,

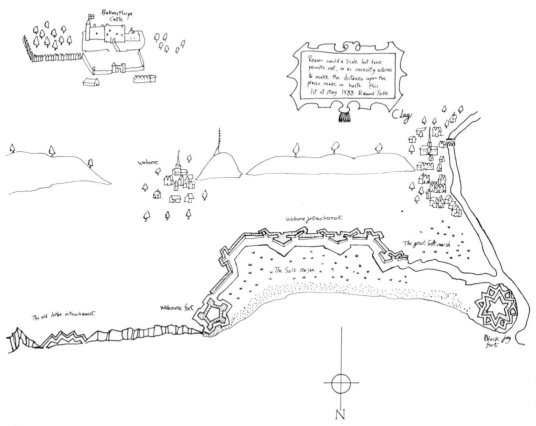

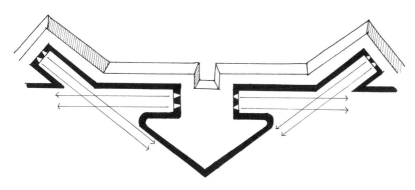

Left: *A detail of Yorke's plan showing the proposed method of flanking the faces of the bastions with flankers recessed in the adjoining curtain. This ensured that all parts of the ditch could be swept by defensive fire.*

Below: *Yorke's design for Black Joy Fort was an extraordinarily elaborate one, with truncated bastions fronted by ravelins, and with more ravelins in the ditch before the angled curtains. It seems more an exercise in theoretical geometry than an emergency defence work required to be built quickly in a grave national crisis.*

comparing well with contemporary continental practice. The fort at Weybourne was a conventional pentagon with small, acute-angled bastions; interesting innovations were reserved for the connecting rampart and second fort. The rampart was an odd mixture of tenaille trace and large, obtuse-angled bastions with orillons; the most remarkable features were the recessed chambers in the adjoining curtain whose purpose was to flank the faces of the adjoining bastion, an ingenious and sophisticated solution to the vexing problem of dead ground. The plans show Black Joy Fort at Cley as a six-pointed star with ravelins placed in the angles between the adjoining faces, the first representation of such a feature to be seen in England[22]. It was probably Yorke's astute solution of the problem of quickly rebuilding an unbastioned sconce. Some part of the fortifications already existed, as orders were given to enlarge "the sconce at Weybourne Hoop"[23].

It is doubtful that these works were ever built in anything like their intended form. There has been so much erosion since the sixteenth century that there are no clues to be seen on the ground, and the documentary evidence is almost as scanty. An entry in Holt parish records notes "In this year [1588] was the town of Weybourne fortified with both a continual garrison of men both of horse and foot with sconces, ordinance and all manner of warlike appointment to defend the Spaniards landing there . . ."[24]. Some work was certainly under way in 1588, as the Privy Council reprimanded the lords lieutenant for stopping it and ordered that "those workes begonn . . . be hastened and perfected"[25]. However, there is a contradictory entry in the Calendar of State Papers that seems to suggest that no works were built at all. "No new fortifications are made except those begun last year [1588] at Harwich, Yarmouth and Tilbury"[26]. The most likely explanation is that the elaborate plan remained largely on parchment and that all that was done at Weybourne was to renovate the existing fort guarding Cley Haven and to build a few trenches and breastworks along the edge of the beach and at the Old Hythe.

For the rest of the coast extensive defences were neither practical nor necessary, but some minor defences were ordered. The cliffs at Sheringham and Cromer were ordered to be cut sheer or scarped like the walls of a fortress, all the paths down to the beach were to be barricaded with ramparts and the landing place at Sheringham was to have extra entrenchments[27]. Elsewhere reliance was to be placed on "certain bands of footmen and some horsemen to be in readiness to repel the enemy"[28]. Beacons were built on the highest points along the coast and trusty men were appointed to watch beside them[29]. Throughout the rest of the county, as well as the beacon building, scouring of old armour and rustic manoeuvres, there was some mending of manor walls and

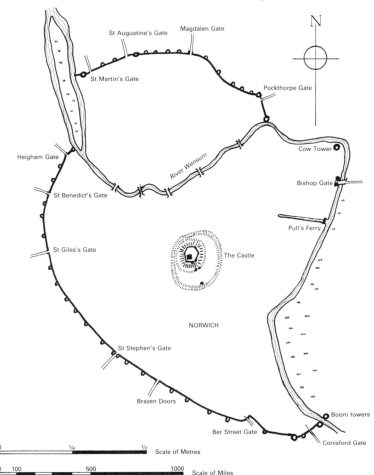

The city walls of Norwich were put into a state of defence for the last time during the Civil War, though it is unlikely that they would have been able to resist any serious assault.

180

gates and digging of trenches. Baconsthorpe Castle, the seat of Sir Christopher Heydon and the headquarters of the north coast of the county, was put into a state of defence for the last time.

Pirates attacked coastal shipping in the first half of the seventeenth century, but nothing was done beyond the Crown's exhorting the coastal villages to be more active in their own defence.

On the outbreak of the Civil War Norfolk joined the defensive alliance known as the Eastern Association. The county needed little in the way of frontier fortifications, lying behind the defensive barrier of Cambridgeshire and Huntingdonshire, but the nervous anxiety that war engenders found its expression in the fortification of Norwich. Not that it made any real strategic sense, for if the King could capture Cambridge and so defeat the army of the Eastern Association as to be in a position to threaten Norwich, then the war was as good as lost. Nevertheless, the work on the defences reassured the citizens, for in war activity, however misdirected, is always reassuring.

Almost as soon as hostilities had opened Norwich sent its mayor, suspected of a lack of enthusiasm for the Parliamentarian cause, to Cambridge and invited a Mr Christian from Lynn to advise on the best means of fortification, for which he was paid five pounds[30]. In November, 1642, two hundred pounds was voted towards repairing the walls and making minor alterations[31]. The booms defending the river were reinstated and there was enough surplus material left to send a massive chain to Yarmouth. The twelve gates were reduced to nine as St Augustine's, Conesford and Bishop's Gates were all locked, barred and then backed with earth and rubble. These repairs might have restored the effectiveness of the old walls as a simple barrier, but they did nothing to enable them to resist artillery or a formal siege; to make Norwich into even the barest approximation of a modern fortress would have been a very expensive operation indeed.

These emergency measures taken, a more elaborate and expensive scheme was proposed which involved building seven earthwork "bulwarks" at points along the wall and a breastwork running along the bank of the Wensum from the boom towers to the Cow Tower[32]. What form the bulwarks were to have taken is uncertain. They might have been regular bastions attached to the medieval wall or detached ravelins, but whatever the shape they were expensive; this scheme was to have cost £1,500, and a further more extensive scheme with twelve bulwarks was estimated to cost £750 more[33]. Oddly enough there was no plan for a fort or citadel to command the city from Mousehold Heath. These defences remained mere proposals, for there is no further mention of them, nor is there any indication of any earthworks on later maps.

By 1643 the citizens felt secure enough to unblock the gates; their permanent closure had proved most inconvenient. In August of that year the castle, which up to then had been left out of any plans, was ordered to be refortified and brought back into use[34]. The citizens were persuaded to undertake voluntary war work by clearing out the castle ditches while significant alterations were made to the castle itself; the old decayed curtain wall around the rim of the mound was demolished and an earth rampart substituted[35]. A battery was built on the north-east side of the castle mound and all the city's artillery was placed there[36]. One feels there was a touch of irony in these alterations, for the castle was still a Royal one, albeit turned into a stronghold of the King's enemies.

The Civil War brought no real threat to the coast of Norfolk, for the navy had gone over to Parliament almost to the last small boat and attack from the sea in the form of a landing of troops was as unlikely a possibility as could be imagined; nor was there any danger during the First Dutch War, which began in 1652 during the Protectorate. The Second Dutch War in 1665 was a rather more serious affair; the decayed warning beacons were renewed, watchers were appointed and regiments of militia marched in to guard the sensitive points about Weybourne and the beaches north of Yarmouth[37].

Little more was done in the third war of 1672. The militia was called out but no defences were built, although panic and alarm spread along the coast. The people of Sheringham looked out to sea dreading the appearance of the Dutch and sent a hasty petition to the lord lieutenant in which they stated that they were "afraid every night the enemy should come ashore and fire our town when we be in our beds for we have nothing to resist them but one gun with a broken carriage and four muskets which we bought at our own cost and charges"[38]. They were granted six muskets with fifty pounds of powder and a similar weight of lead and sternly warned to keep them safe and to use them only against the Dutch.

Nothing was heard of the coastal defences throughout the eighteenth century. The odd cannon guarded some of the smaller ports; Cromer had two small 6-pounders on home-made carriages and Mundesley four 2-pounder swivel guns, but these were the result of local rather than county or national efforts[39]. During the war with the American colonies a small battery armed with four 18-pounders was built at Cromer on the cliffs to the west of the town to protect shipping from privateers[40].

It was not until the wars with revolutionary France began in 1793 that serious concern was once again felt for the security of the whole coast rather than specific harbours. Volunteer corps mustered and beacons were piled all along the coast, but very few batteries were built. Weybourne was still regarded "as the most dangerous place and most open to an enemy, of any on the Norfolk coast; the shore is the boldest of any and the transport ships may approach it so very near as almost to land an army without the assistance of flat-bottomed boats. It is an object worthy of consideration when an invasion from France is so much threatened whether it would be proper to renew the fortifications, and erect a fort of modern construction, with batteries and heavy cannon to defend it. It still remains unnoticed, and its defenceless situation seems to invite an enemy, and to court attack"[41]. In case the enemy should get ashore and press inland, interior lines of defence were planned to block their advance. A line of redoubts was proposed to run between Aldeby and Haddiscoe, with field works at Reedham, Acle Bridge and Wroxham[42].

The most acute fear of invasion was experienced in 1803; although it was unlikely that the French would actually land in Norfolk there was always the possibility of diversionary raids which could be countered by batteries at all the likely landing places. As usual Weybourne was first on the list, but because of the continual erosion it was planned to build the batteries on the west end of

Norfolk's medieval castles were all sited inland, largely because they were intended to subjugate an indigenous population. Since the sixteenth century most defences have been located on the coast to guard against invasion.

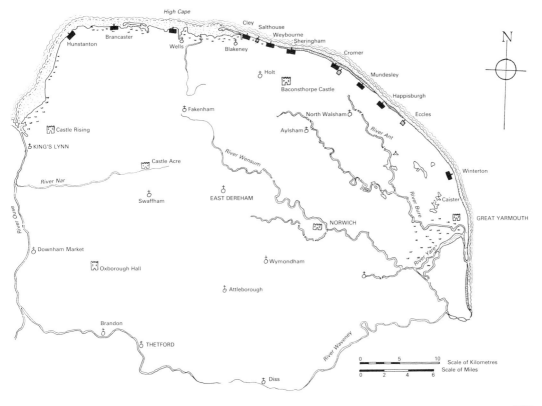

183

Sheringham cliffs and on "Flat Eye", a broadening of the gravel bank in front of Salthouse[43]. Batteries were proposed for Blakeney Point and High Cape at Wells but rejected because of their remoteness and the difficulty of getting reinforcements to them in an emergency. Three batteries were proposed to defend Holkham Bay, but doubts were expressed whether their amateur garrisons of sea fencibles would stand an attack in such isolated positions[44]. Brancaster Bay, "the most secure anchorage on this part of the coast", had only one possible site for a battery, on the sea wall between Brancaster and Titchwell[45]. The natural obstacles of the Wash were thought defence enough for the coast between Hunstanton and King's Lynn; after some consideration, the official view taken of the sector between Hunstanton and Sheringham was that it was best to rely on flooding the saltmarshes behind the beaches and to defend the few roads leading inland[46]. General Money, Commander of the Eastern District, proposed mounting cannons on wagons and moving these about the coast wherever they were needed, but it is not recorded if any of these mobile guns were ever built[47].

Of all the proposed works only those at Cromer and Mundesley and one, or possibly two, on Holkham beach ever materialised[48]. Cromer had three batteries. The original battery was replaced with one armed with four 24-pounders, but as its guns could not enfilade the beach two parapets, one above the pier and the other to the east of the town, were raised. In each was a pair of 24-pounder carronades[49]. Another similar battery, with similar armament, was built at Mundesley for the sea fencibles; but it was more for training than for defence.

Although these guns never fired at the French they did claim one victim. On one occasion when the Cromer sea fencibles were demonstrating their skills by firing with grape and canister at a target on the beach below a large crowd gathered to watch the show. The guns were loaded and the order was given to fire. A wayward ball struck the commander on the foot then passed on to shatter the leg of John Smith, a popular local surgeon. The injured limb was amputated as soon as possible and the people of Cromer, shocked by the demonstration of the power of their guns, contributed five hundred pounds to their maimed surgeon[50].

Just in case the French could not be prevented from landing, all the paths leading down to the beach at Cromer were demolished. Gaps in the cliffs which gave access to the shore were blocked with palisades of wood, formidable obstacles of uprooted thorn bushes and a barricade of fishermen's boats[51]. These arrangements did not meet with wholehearted approval and gratitude from the residents and visitors. Some unpatriotic, subversive or apathetic people objected to the unaccustomed hedge placed across their path to the beach, preferring the possibility of the Imperial Guard appearing upon the top of the cliff to the certainty of thorns in the bottoms of their feet[52]. The batteries were closed and the Volunteers disbanded in 1813[53].

It was not until the sense of insecurity caused by the development of steam warships had become acute that the coastal defences were examined once more. In 1839 an extensive scheme of coastal fortifications was proposed. Small batteries, each armed with two 18-pounders, were planned for Caister, Winterton, Waxham, Happisburgh, Mundesley, Weybourne and Hunstanton, with two larger works at Cromer. The only masonry fort was a large martello tower planned for the shoals at the mouth of Blakeney harbour[54]. Although the total cost was no more than seven thousand pounds nothing was built. What a pity; such a tower, standing lonely in the ruffled waters beneath the wide sky, would be a famous landmark now, a rival with Cley mill for the watercolourists' attention.

In 1870 the coast was surveyed again, but by this time the railways and accumulated silt had removed whatever commercial importance the north Norfolk ports had once possessed. "These little harbours are so unimportant and their access so difficult that we do not consider important interests sufficiently concerned in their defence to justify recommendations of any expenditure upon work for that object"[55]. Only Wells was considered in any way worth plundering. To guard against the very remote possibility of a raid a few mobile batteries of Volunteer Field Artillery were suggested, but no permanent works at all[56].

Towards the end of the nineteenth century interest in coastal defence revived slightly. The War Office did not foresee a full-scale invasion and defined the most likely threat as a raid of two thousand men and some light guns. A realistic appraisal of the coast resulted in a report that most of it was quite impossible for an enemy force to land on, apart from the traditional danger spots of Weybourne and the stretch from Happisburgh to Hemsby. Instead of fixed defences, a mobile column based in Norwich was allocated to oppose the invaders once they had been located by the bands of military cyclists who would roam the coast in time of war[57].

When the First World War broke out Norfolk faced the enemy across what was then called the German Ocean, and as soon as war was declared the usual fears of invasion arose and the coast was patrolled and guarded. Weybourne was soon fortified with trenches, and troops quickly established a camp there. By December, 1914, elaborate networks of trenches appeared on Shering-ham golf links and further lines were dug between Hunworth and Briston to back up the defences on the coast[58]. Two heavy batteries of Royal Field Artillery, each with six 60-pounders, were stationed

Circular pillboxes such as this well-preserved example at Bradfield, near North Walsham, were built during the First World War to form a defence line in north Norfolk based largely on the River Ant. As late in the war as 1917 there were fears of a German invasion which produced a multiplicity of defences in the eastern counties.

at Weybourne and Mundesley for most of the war and a few extra guns were installed along the coast in semi-permanent emplacements[59]. Cromer had two 4.7-inch guns, but these were on travelling carriages, not on fortress or naval mountings, which reduced their range and their ability to engage moving targets. Salthouse had two 15-pounders and Newport, Eccles and Caister one each, but it is hard to see what use they could have been[60].

A more interesting addition to the defences was an armoured train employed to give an element of mobility. Its use was rather more reassuring than practical, for although an armoured train combined all the mystique of the railway with the panoply of warfare it was not really an effective weapon. "Nothing looks more formidable and impressive than an armoured train; but nothing is in fact more vulnerable and helpless,"as Sir Winston Churchill wrote[61]. Norfolk's train was stationed at North Walsham; made up of four armoured wagons and an engine and armed with two machine-guns and two 12-pounders, it clanked impressively up and down the Mundesley branch line and as far afield as Yarmouth until it was withdrawn at the end of the war, without ever firing a shot in anger[62].

Later in the war the coast defences were strengthened by a line of pillboxes running from Weybourne through North Walsham and along the line of the River Ant to near Sea Palling. Small and circular and made of concrete blocks with steel-throated loopholes and steel doors, they were among the first to be built in the country.

The only attack that Norfolk suffered was the novel and terrifying experience of being bombed from the air. The stretch of coast between Happisburgh and Hunstanton was regularly crossed by Zeppelins on the way inland and on 19th January, 1915, the first bomb to be dropped on England burst in Whitehall Yard, Sheringham. It did little damage, but there were to be many more airship raids and many bombs were to fall on Norfolk with unhappier results. Mobile anti-aircraft guns and searchlights were installed in increasing numbers in the county as the war progressed, although their effect was more deterrent than actual. A Royal Navy mobile anti-aircraft brigade was stationed in the county throughout most of 1916. Armed with lorry-mounted 75mm guns and 3-pounders, they were based on the coast about Bacton, where a double emplacement for two 75mm was built[63]. When they were withdrawn they were replaced by three mobile batteries, each with one 3-pounder and three 12-pounders, who moved about the county as needed. Three 3-inch AA guns were permanently emplaced around the airship base at Pulham St Mary[64].

With the armistice all these defences were abandoned. The guns were returned to ordnance stores, the barbed wire rolled up and the trenches filled. All except the most pessimistic planners in the War Office thought that coast defence was an activity that they would never need to think of again.

The first intimations of the coming Second World War were the plans to establish two anti-aircraft practice camps at Stiffkey and Weybourne. Local resistance to the invasion was outspoken and General Sir Edmund Ironside, Commander-in-Chief of the Eastern District, had to appear before the irate villagers to persuade them of the nation's need for such facilities[65]. Despite the protests, the shore was disfigured by huge sprawling camps and the villagers' ancient quiet shattered, by day with the boom of heavy anti-aircraft guns as they fired out to sea at towed targets, and by night with the singing of soldiers in the streets.

At the same time as the camps were built a vital radar station was built at West Beckham. With its three-hundred-feet-high masts, it was the modern successor of the old beacons and their trusty watchers on the heights about the coast. The station was something of a fortress in its own right, for it was surrounded by a heavy metal fence and all its installations were protected by concrete bunkers and blast walls. Another of these "chain home" radar stations was built at Stoke Holy Cross, south of Norwich.

The outbreak of war in September, 1939, brought no anxiety about the county's defences. There was a plan to deal with the unlikely event of an invasion, given the suitably bellicose title of

Julius Caesar; its main provision was to maintain troops within easy reach of the east coast. Eastern Command was allotted two divisions, of which one, the 18th, was based in Norfolk around Thetford[66].

These low-key arrangements disintegrated with the fall of France in June, 1940, and a German landing becoming a frightening possibility. Work had begun on coastal defences at the end of May, even as the remains of the British Expeditionary Force were being evacuated from the beaches of Dunkirk. The plan of defence was simple; a crust of fortifications was to hold the enemy on the shore and further lines of defence were designed to stop them penetrating inland, with extra defences at vital points like important junctions and airfields. Every available building contractor was enlisted in the race to build defences before the Germans arrived.

The coast was the first and most urgent priority. Trenches were dug, pillboxes built, barbed wire strung across the sand dunes, miles of scaffolding set up on the beaches, hundreds of concrete blocks cast and thousands of mines buried. Equal

attention was not given to every mile of coast; only those regarded as vulnerable received extensive defences, among these being Snettisham beach, Weybourne and the stretch between Happisburgh and Yarmouth[67]. General Ironside, now Commander-in-Chief, Home Forces, was one of the first of a horde of distinguished visitors who stumbled their way through the trenches to view the work in progress. He confided to his diary his feelings about the immensity of the task: "... have been looking at troops and their work. They are working and the guns and wire are being put up at all the likely points. Work will never end. It ought to have been begun months ago"[68].

The most formidable component of the defences, the emergency gun-batteries, were then added. The first of these were installed in June, 1940. Each had two ex-naval guns and two searchlights; at first they were manned mainly by sailors and Royal Marines in the absence of suitable army personnel[69]. Twin 6-inch batteries were sited at Hunstanton, High Cape, covering Wells harbour and Holkham Bay, Cley Eye, Sheringham, Cromer and Happisburgh, with a solitary 4-inch battery at Winterton. In addi-

An emergency battery armed with two 6-inch guns was built at Brancaster in 1941. On the opposite page is one of the casemates, now masked by dunes which have grown up since the war. On the right is a searchlight emplacement, with the remains of scaffolding erected as an obstacle to invading forces in front. Each of the batteries had two lights with 90 cm reflectors mounted in small shelters like this. They were protected by steel shutters and each was powered by its own diesel-engined generator.

tion to these heavy coastal guns, the anti-aircraft artillery at Weybourne and Stiffkey could be used in an emergency to fire on enemy shipping. In December, 1940, Weybourne had only two 3.7-inch guns in place, but ten months later there were six, with a further ten 40mm guns at Stiffkey[70]. The makeshift emergency batteries were soon replaced by more permanent structures which retained the original 6-inch guns in all cases, except Happisburgh, where they were replaced by two 4.7-inch[71]. A new battery was built at Brancaster and another at Mundesley. Plans to fill the gap between Happisburgh and Winterton were abandoned when the ground at Waxham proved too unstable to take a heavy structure.

The guns were elderly and long past their best; most were half worn out and had a barrel life of less than one hundred and fifty rounds. Those at Cromer were made in 1906, and first served aboard the battleship HMS *Africa* (1905) and then the cruiser HMS *Dublin* (1912) before going into store[72]. The 4-inch guns at Winterton were slightly more youthful, having emerged from the factory in 1909[73]. Each battery was surrounded by infantry defences, wire, weapon pits and several pillboxes. There was usually a secondary armament for local defence consisting of a field or anti-tank gun and several Blacker Bombards or Spigot Mortars. Anti-aircraft defence was provided by light machine-guns and 40mm Bofors.

Between the batteries were strings of pillboxes, the main infantry strongpoints. Even now, after coastal erosion and demolition gangs have taken their toll, there are still more than seventy left. The greatest concentrations were at Weybourne, where there are still eighteen left, and from Walcott to Horsey, where twenty can still be seen. The most common type is the hexagonal, but several square ones can be found at Weybourne as well as two round ones, several anti-tank gun emplacements and two small steel turrets for light machine-guns. Allowing for demolition and erosion, it is likely that about two hundred pillboxes of various sorts were built along the coast.

After the coastal crust there were three successive stop lines based on the rivers. The first line, some six miles from the coast, was based on the River Ant. From Bradfield, above North Walsham, to Ludham Bridge every crossing of the river was covered by one or more pillboxes; a total of twenty. This line was continued by the Bure to Acle, where a heavy concentration of defences barred both routes from across the Bure and from Yarmouth, before running along the edge of the marshes to Reedham, where it joined the defence lines formed by the Yare and Waveney.

The second line ran along the Bure from Acle to beyond Aylsham, with every river crossing defended either by a pillbox or by a road block and sometimes by both. Behind this came a third, resting on the course of the Wensum, but this contained very few pillboxes, most bridges obstructed by anti-tank blocks. In the south of the county the crossings of the River Little Ouse were fortified at Thetford and Brandon, and so was the crossing of the Lark at Barton Mills. Any invading force landing on the stretch of coast about Happisburgh would have to force its way through five lines of defences before reaching the GHQ line. As an illustration of the continuity of defensive strategy, all those places recommended for fortification during the Armada were fortified in 1940.

Most of the towns in the county were defended to some extent as virtually all of them were situated at road junctions and so were vital in delaying an advancing enemy. The region's airfields, probably the most vital component in the nation's defences, were fortified by trenches, wire and pillboxes. Coltishall, the most vulnerable, was surrounded by a ring of pillboxes, of which six remain. Marham, West Raynham, Bircham Newton, Oulton, Horsham St Faiths and Ludham all gained one or more pillboxes

A drawing of a typical emergency battery, with two 6-inch guns in brick and concrete casemates with sunken magazine and shelters between them. On the extreme right is one of the searchlight emplacements and rising above the nearer casemate is the battery observation post. The battery is surrounded by barbed wire and protected by pillboxes and sandbagged machine-gun emplacements.

A reinforced concrete basement and loopholes were inserted in the ruins of Bromholm Priory at Bacton to provide a well-disguised strongpoint. Elsewhere all kinds of buildings were adapted similarly to serve as makeshift defence positions.

of varying design. The general design of pillboxes was standard-ised, but there were local variations caused by particular conditions or by the availability of materials; the commonest type was the medium-sized hexagonal. Where possible, in the interests of concealment and deception, existing buildings were adapted. Simple loopholes were cut in walls; garden sheds and lean-tos were lined with concrete or sandbags. At Ludham Bridge a windpump had embrasures cut in the walls to make a highly original strongpoint, and at Thetford the pillbox covering the bridge on the London road was faced with knapped flints to blend with the

ancient wall to which it was joined; an elegant and effective piece of camouflage.

Norwich was not only important in its own right but, as the hub of communications for the county, it was a city whose defence was tactically essential. During June, July and August a defensive perimeter was constructed stretching round the north side of the city, a mixture of concrete block anti-tank obstacles and an anti-tank ditch, with every road leading into the city blocked by sturdy obstacles[74]. The defences began on the River Yare at Griffin Lane, Thorpe, ran north up Pound Lane to Plumstead Road, then to Salhouse Road, swinging round to Sprowston, through Catton and past Reepham Road to reach the Wensum at Hellesdon Bridge. A short stretch ran beside Larkman Lane between the Wensum and the Yare, to end at Earlham Bridge. To the south of the city from Cringleford to Trowse there was no extensive chain of defences, but every bridge over the Yare was blocked and there were some trenches on either side of Hall Road covering the approach from Harford Bridges[75]. There were pillboxes covering most of the entrances to the city; one at the junction of Pound Lane and Thorpe Road was ingeniously disguised as a war memorial. Norwich also had to be defended from air attack, but it was not until September, 1940, that any anti-aircraft guns were installed[76]. Eventually four 3.7-inch guns were emplaced at the top of Mousehold Heath at the corner of Salhouse Road. At first the guns were mobile 3.7-inch, later converted to static pieces and supplemented with 2-inch anti-aircraft rockets.

At the end of 1940 Norfolk's defences were largely completed. As well as the Home Guard there were an independent infantry brigade and the 18th division to garrison the county[77]. The guns along the coast were ready, and to supplement them heavy weapons were provided by rail-mounted artillery located on the line about Burnham Market. To add another mobile element, a small armoured train with a 6-pounder pottered along the line between Heacham and Wells. Apart from the defending troops the coast had never been so deserted. The whole area ten miles deep from the shore was declared a probibited area, and those civilians who remained were as hedged about with restrictions as the coast was with steel and concrete. Their binoculars, telescopes and cameras were confiscated; no visitors were allowed; ugly crops of nissen huts grew behind the barbed wire, mines lay concealed and jagged obstacles sprouted in the sand. At the end of 1941 there was a reappraisal of the coast defences, for even at this early stage in the war the danger of invasion had receded. The trained troops were withdrawn and the coastal areas garrisoned by three county divisions of lower category troops, with one mobile field division held in reserve[78].

From 1943, when the coast defences had reached the peak of their extent and efficiency, there was a gradual reduction; about a quarter of the existing batteries were declared redundant[79]. In Norfolk only Hunstanton was closed, mainly because erosion had threatened its stability[80]. The rest of the batteries were stripped of regular troops, who were replaced by the Home Guard[81].

Early in 1944 further reductions took place. Sheringham was closed completely, Brancaster, High Cape, Happisburgh and Cley Eye were all put into care and maintenance, and only Winterton, Cromer and Mundesley remained operational. At the end of the year they too were closed and plans made to dismantle them[82]. Minor items and electrical equipment were removed, but the guns remained until the end of 1945, when they were withdrawn and scrapped. The beach obstacles and mines were lifted, although many areas of beach were still closed several years after the war, and the pillboxes and batteries were either demolished or left to succumb to the drifting sands and battering waves.

The two anti-aircraft camps continued in operation after the war, much to the annoyance of the inhabitants of nearby Sheringham. Weybourne had 3.7-inch guns on static and mobile mountings, and shortly after the war three emplacements for 5.25-inch guns were built on the west of the site. Firing was heavy throughout the nineteen-fifties, especially in the summer when there might be several regiments of territorials on their annual shoots, but advances in missile development made anti-aircraft artillery obsolete and the camp was closed, the last of one and a half million rounds being fired by 459 (Essex) HAA Regiment, TA, on 2nd October, 1958[83].

Great Yarmouth 14

A T THE beginning of the sixteenth century Yarmouth was a prosperous port surrounded on three sides by a high battlemented wall with sixteen towers. Only to the west was the town open, looking across the river Yare and the waste of Breydon Water to the marshes beyond.

From a distance the town looked impressive, but this appearance of strength was deceptive. To any European military engineer Yarmouth's defences would have seemed dangerously obsolete; its walls and towers were too thin to resist cannon and too lightly built to mount them. There had been slight modifications to accommodate guns in the fifteenth century; the south-east tower and a short adjoining stretch of town wall had several small loops for handguns similar to those at nearby Caister Castle, but there was no provision for anything heavier[1].

The town did not ignore developments in artillery and by 1509 was the owner of several cannon, some breech loaders made of iron and some brass pieces[2]. Three years later Henry VIII remitted a portion of the town's taxes on condition that they provided four large iron guns. These were to be breech-loaders, over nine feet long, of 3.5-inch bore with a range of over a mile[3]. They would have been too large to install on the walls or in the towers, and the insistence on a long range implies that their intended role was to defend Yarmouth Roads, an anchorage of great strategic importance. It is probable that a small bulwark was built on the beach to receive them.

As a result of the commission on coastal defence appointed by Henry VIII, several "bulwarkes of earth" were built along the beach in 1539. One stood near the mouth of the haven covering the channel known as St Nicholas's Gat and was armed with three guns "new cast and not yet trimmed"[4]. Another work was planned for the heights at Gorleston to cover the river mouth; but although this is shown on a contemporary chart as two semi-circular parapets armed with five guns it is unlikely that it was ever built[5].

The Duke of Norfolk arrived in 1545 to report on the condition of the town's defences and found the moat choked with sand and rubbish, huge wind-blown sand dunes looming over the walls, at the foot of which huddled a ramshackle collection of sheds, shanties and lean-tos. Yarmouth was, he reported, "the weakest walled town he ever saw", its defences so feeble that a few

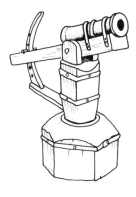

Small primitive cannon like this would have been installed on town walls and in castles. Inaccurate and with a slow rate of fire, they were hardly more effective than crossbows.

shots would batter a breach, the towers too small and the walls
"evil", with neither "bulwarks outside nor rampart within"[6]. The
bulwarks on the beach, which had been recently repaired, he
condemned as badly sited; they were too far from the town and
might easily be captured by a landing party; he ordered new ones
built nearer the town. The Duke, unmoved by the quaintness of the

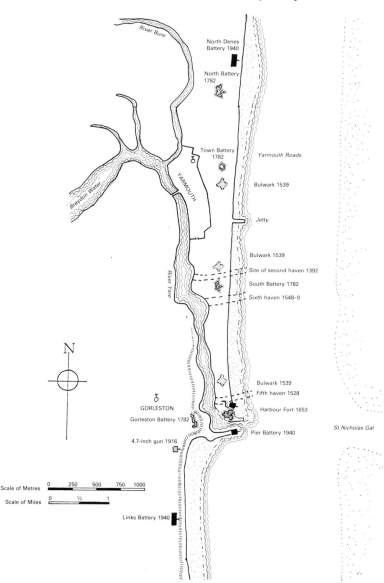

*The defences of Yarmouth
had two functions, to
protect the harbour mouth
and to cover the anchorage
in Yarmouth Roads. This
is as true of the batteries of
1940–45 as of the
bulwarks of 1539.*

tumbledown architecture, then ordered the wall to be cleared of all obstructions.

The townsfolk were summoned, and with bucket, basket and spade they levelled the sand dunes, dug out the moat and heaped up earth and sand behind the wall. They worked with such energy that half a mile of rampart wide enough to drive a cart along was completed within six weeks. This feat so impressed the Duke that when he left, satisfied that the town was in a fit state of defence, he asked the Privy Council that an official letter of commendation be sent to Yarmouth to thank the inhabitants for the work they had done[7].

The following year the bulwark near the haven entrance proved to be useless, possibly because it had no guns, when three French privateers entered the roads and captured an English merchant ship. It was only after the townsmen had dragged four guns down to the shore and sent an armed pinnace out that the captive was liberated[8]. After this there were no further references to the bulwarks, which fell into decay. In 1557, the townsfolk again turned out to work three days a week to extend the earth backing of the walls[9].

The first substantial modification to the town walls to enable them to mount artillery was not made until 1569; until then all emplacements for cannon had been in exposed positions outside the walls. In that year eight guns were sent by the Crown in answer to the urgent request of the Town Assembly[10]. The guns, three demi-culverins, two sakers and three minions, were too heavy to fit upon the towers and too valuable to leave in isolated batteries, so a suitable emplacement on the town walls had to be built. In December, 1569, work began on a huge mound of earth, a cavalier, sited where St George's Church now stands. The New Mount,

The walls of Yarmouth in 1545, with a collection of ramshackle sheds and shanties built against them. The Duke of Norfolk ordered the clearance of all such obstructions.

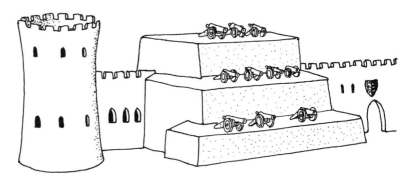

The Mount, as portrayed in a manuscript plan of about 1570.

designed by Captain Jennins, took nearly nine months to build. The townsfolk provided the labour, or rather the poorer ones did, while the wealthy sent substitutes[11].

The mount was nearly complete when the town wall, unable to resist the enormous pressure of the mountain of soil behind it, bulged outwards and tumbled into the moat. It was quickly repaired and the rubble cleared; the mount was finished in August, 1570. It measured over two hundred feet long, projected thirty feet beyond the face of the wall, was about fifty feet high and appears to have mounted ten guns on three tiers[12]. Another two guns were emplaced on a small mound behind the wall between the South Gate and the river, where they could bar the passage of the river to any ships[13].

In 1587 when England was alarmed by rumours of the impending Spanish Armada Yarmouth, along with Weybourne, was regarded as the most vulnerable point along the east coast and a place of national importance, for the Roads provided a convenient and safe anchorage within striking distance of London. As usual in times of crisis the town was found to be almost incapable of defence. As a start, before building more elaborate works, the rampart behind the wall was completed by ramming in more earth until it was forty foot thick at the base. Brick tunnels were constructed behind the gates so the broad roadway could continue without interruption and the delighted townsfolk found they had a promenade around the town, with extensive views over beach and sea[14].

The following year, as the Armada prepared to sail, the Privy Council renewed its concern for the security of the town. They realised that Yarmouth itself could not reasonably be expected to bear the whole cost of extra fortifications, especially as it was impoverished by the heavy expense of the newly-constructed haven and the decay of its trade, and they suggested that the counties of Norfolk and Suffolk should contribute something to the overall cost[15]. The town also wrote to the lords lieutenants of Norfolk pleading their poverty and asking for advice and help. They stressed that the town was in an "undefencible state" and "subject they were to the invasion of the enemy"[16]. Sir Robert Southwell, the town's MP, saw Sir William Heydon, the deputy lieutenant, and gained an agreement that money should be collected for the fortifications. The lord lieutenant hoped that purses would be freely opened, but hinted at compulsion if the county did not respond with sufficient generosity, for such was the narrow nature of local patriotism that being asked to pay for the defences of Yarmouth seemed as irrelevant as contributing to a fund for the walls of Jerusalem[17]. The justices of the peace met,

The South-east Tower, showing the early gunports. These were sufficient for early hand guns, but until the building of the Mount there was no proper provision for mounting anything heavier.

199

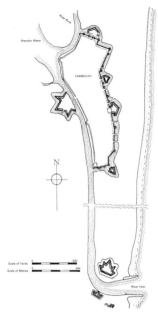

were informed of the probable cost, and decided who should bear it. Yarmouth itself was assessed at £23 6s 8d, Norwich at £333 6s 8d, and Lynn at £26 13s 4d; the rest of the shire was required to find £971 18s 1d—a total of £1,355 4s 9d.[18]. All this, bar four hundred pounds or so for Weybourne, was for the new works at Yarmouth.

To supervise the defences, Sir Thomas Leighton arrived in the town with a large and hungry retinue of knights and captains to be lavishly entertained at the town's expense. After the feasting a committee was appointed to confer with him about fortifying the town[19]. Sir Thomas quickly made a comprehensive survey and saw that the circuit of walls was particularly weak in two places. The New Mount on the east side spread over the wall, forming an easy bank that could be scaled without difficulty; it failed to provide adequate flanking fire to cover the adjoining stretches of wall. To the south, regarded as the most likely point of attack, there were no defences beyond the medieval walls; these, despite the earth backing, were vulnerable to artillery fire and difficult to flank. In addition, the haven entrance was completely unprotected.

To remedy these grave defects, Sir Thomas had a complex set of additional fortifications in the very latest bastioned style designed by Edmund Yorke[20]. The surviving plans show four large triangular ravelins built out from the medieval wall to give flanking fire and to advance the line of defence. Two detached forts guarded the haven entrance; a star-shaped fort with palisades in the ditch stood on the Yarmouth side of the river faced by a smaller but similar battery built at the foot of Gorleston cliffs. The bridgehead at Southtown was defended by an extensive outwork formed by a tenaille trace, and a parapet with three batteries

Above: *The proposed fortifications of 1588. If they had been constructed Yarmouth would have been one of the strongest fortresses in the kingdom.*

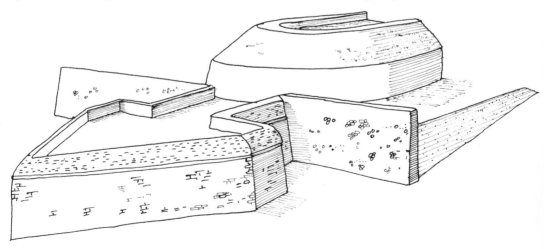

covered the river and Breydon Water. It was a modern, extensive and elaborate scheme, far too complex to execute given the shortage of time and money; it was near the end of June before authorisation was given, and one thousand pounds could not have paid for such an ambitious undertaking.

Instead the new defences were concentrated where the town was weakest. The New Mount was judged to be the most vulnerable spot, and here the largest, strongest and most permanent of the 1588 works was built. This was not a ravelin but a large brick

Opposite page: *The Mount was encased in brick in 1588 and turned into a large bastion with recessed flanks to cover the adjoining stretches of medieval town wall. The following year the rest of the mount was further revetted in brick to form a cavalier giving command of the ground outside the walls.*

The salient of the 1588 bastion seen from St Peter's Plain. The curved brick parapet and the stone cordon can be seen above the modern boundary wall.

201

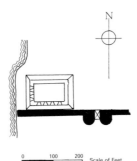

0 100 200 Scale of Feet
0   50   Scale of Metres

*The South Mount, from
Sir Bernard de Gomme's
plan of Yarmouth drawn
in 1688.*

bastion with a scarp fifteen feet high and with recessed flanks; most of this still survives, having been buried under the foundations of the old General Hospital where the salient with its original rounded parapet can still be seen jutting out into St Peter's Plain. The mount behind was enclosed with a wall to form a cavalier overlooking the bastion and adjoining walls, a common enough contemporary arrangement[21].

The work on the mount cost over half the amount allotted for the town's defence, £682 13s 4d, the rest being spent on what was loosely described as ravelins, ditches and exterior bulwarks to the east of Blackfriars Tower[22]. This terminology was vague, for what was built, according to de Gomme's map of 1688, was a line of earth rampart running from the river by the South Gate and following the wall round to the Blackfriars' Gate. The map shows this line to be formed by three bastions and an irregular demi-bastion, but they might well have been remodelled during the Civil War[23]. Before the rampart and extending around the complete circuit of the walls was a ditch one hundred and eighty feet wide filled with water; until it silted up, a small boat could be sailed along its length from Bure to Yare[24]. The defences were completed by slinging a boom across the river at the south end of the walls[25].

Throughout the summer of 1588 the town was heavily garrisoned by its own men and by levies from the county. Four men watched continually from the steeple of the parish church.

Activity did not stop with the defeat of the Armada. The bastion and cavalier could not have been completed in time and work on them must have gone on until the end of the year. Even when they were finished there was still work to be done; in 1590 the river approach was strengthened by raising a large mound between the South Gate and the river bank and planting seven guns on its summit[26]. Part of the function of the new South Mount was to cover the boom, which was renewed at a cost of over one hundred pounds. The castle, a square tower with four turrets, was repaired, and two extra brass guns which had been taken from the Spaniards at Cadiz were acquired[27]. This done, the town's fortifications were complete.

In the seventeenth century the town's defences were allowed to revert to their natural state of partial dereliction. Houses began to nestle once more about the foot of the walls, towers were converted into dwellings, the moat filled with sand and one of the citizens, with little care for civic duty, carted away the rampart at Blackfriars to make a garden. The castle was demolished in 1621, and the artillery was so neglected that most of the guns lay rusting and useless on the ground[28].

A new threat to the town and its shipping arose in the

Right: *The South Gate, one of the ten gates that once gave admission to the town, showing the Admiralty shutter telegraph installed in 1808 as part of a line communicating with London. Yarmouth was at that time an important naval anchorage.*
        Robert Malster

Below: *The South Gate from the inside, showing the extension to the gate built in 1587 when the rampart behind the town walls was completed. The wide rampart was thus made continuous, being carried across the back of the gate.*   Robert Malster

sixteen-twenties; in common with most eastern ports and coastal districts Yarmouth began to suffer from the depredations of pirates from Dunkirk. Its ships were seized and plundered, and there was a continual fear that the Dunkirkers might land and loot the town. In 1626 the town sent urgent warnings and appeals to all who would listen; both the Privy Council and the lords lieutenant received demands for help, in response to which a committee led by Sir John Corbet and Francis Mapes set off on a tour of inspection of the walls to note the numerous defects[29].

The list of recommendations they drew up was long and expensive: the boom was rotten and needed replacing, the towers needed their battlements cut down and they had to be filled with

The North-west Tower, close to the end of the town wall where it meets the River Bure. This view is from an etching by John Sell Cotman which was published in 1818.
Robert Malster

earth to make solid gun platforms. To cover the river more effectively the committee planned a short stretch of wall alongside the river by the South Mount to be armed with two sakers, with three guns on the mount itself. Three more "good guns" were ordered for the New Mount, plus another five for the bastion; a further thirteen pieces were ordered to be placed on the gates and towers. This made a total of twenty-four guns, although there were only five brass and eight iron guns in the town[30].

All this artillery needed men to work it, and as there was no possibility of regular troops being supplied, the gunners would have to be volunteers from the town. The committee recommended that permission be obtained from the Crown for the building of an artillery yard where the men could be trained; the seventeenth-century equivalent of the territorial army drill hall. In answer to a petition of the Yarmouth magistrates the Privy Council authorised setting up an artillery yard and urged the townsmen to "learn the true use of all sorts of arms, as well offensive as defensive . . . and also to keep watch day and night with shot and otherwise, for the safety and defence of their town, against any invasion or attempt"[31].

The artillery yard or Main Guard was established the following year between the market place and the wall[32]. Roughly triangular in shape, with two faces and two flanks like a bastion projecting into the town, it appeared "to have been built there as a small citadel to keep the inhabitants in awe"[33], for there were platforms for artillery on both sides, and a cavalier overtopping the walls beside the Market Gate[34].

The town was reluctant to spend all its own money on the defences and tried to use its undoubted strategic importance as an argument for making everybody else pay. This ploy failed; little money was collected from the rest of the county, and because of this shortfall not all the planned renovations were carried out. The towers were not modified and the extension to the south wall remained unbuilt, although the town's artillery was increased by the arrival of twelve demi-culverins sent by the Ordnance[35].

Sixteen years later when the Civil War began Yarmouth, without hesitation, declared for Parliament. The majority of the few Royalists fled to Holland or kept their allegiance hidden; those who did neither were locked up in the towers[36]. For the next eighteen years Yarmouth was a stronghold of Parliament, the home of Miles Corbet the regicide, and a bulwark of the English revolution. As the King's navy had mainly gone over to Parliament there was little danger of attack from the sea, and the main requirement was to defend the town from a landward assault. The existing works were first put in order; a body of artillerymen was raised and a town gunner appointed to supervise them[37]. To mount the town's artillery, nine new batteries were built, some on the walls, some fronting the sea, and two others covering the open river side of the town, sited halfway down the South Quay by the town crane and beside the bridge[38].

The most elaborate works were built around the north of the town, where a line of powerful bastioned earthworks was constructed fifty yards in advance of the medieval wall running from the Bure to the Pudding Gate. When the earthworks to the south were repaired and the moat dug out, Yarmouth possessed a modern bastioned enceinte and was as strong a fortress as any in England. Further works were undertaken in 1645, when breastworks and gun platforms were built near the sea to cover the roads[39]. The next four years passed in armed vigilance while the war raged elsewhere, the royalists were defeated, the King tried and executed and the Protectorate established.

At the end of the Civil War the town's fortifications shifted from the defence against a land attack to the protection of the roads and the haven entrance. Ninety-five miles due east lay Holland, full of royalist refugees who, unable to fight in England,

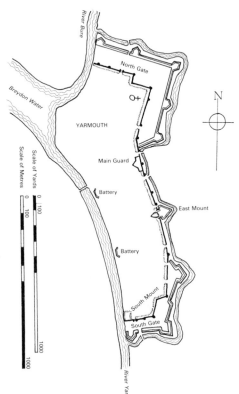

The Civil War fortifications of Yarmouth incorporated the remains of the earthworks dug about the south of the town in 1588, with the bastion. A new ditch and rampart were added about the north of the town to form a complete bastioned enceinte.

carried on the struggle at sea, preying on Parliament's ships with a mixture of piracy and principle. Prince Rupert exchanged saddle for ship and proved to be more successful as a seaman than as a cavalry commander.

To counter this new threat the Town Assembly agreed in 1648 to build a fort to protect the river mouth and the roads[40]. Nothing was done until the First Dutch War goaded Parliament into action, and it was only in 1653 that the fort was completed[41]. It stood a little behind the North Pier and, unlike Landguard Fort or Erith Bulwark, was not a conventional bastioned work but something of a hybrid. Two semi-circular bastions built of red brick fronted the sea in a style reminiscent of one of Henry VIII's castles, with an oblong enclosure behind flanked by a small angle bastion. Armed with eight cannon, the new fort made a debut of remarkable ineffectiveness when from beneath the muzzles of its guns a privateer took four Hamburg ships without it being able to interfere at all[42].

When Charles II returned to England in 1660 the Royal Arms were restored throughout the town, Miles Corbet was hanged and the fort passed into the possession of the Crown. Almost at once over five hundred pounds had to be found for repairs to the fort

The harbour fort with its two semi-circular bastions of red brick. Built in the sixteen-fifties, the fort survived until 1832 when it was undermined by a powerful tidal scour.

The two rounded bastions of the harbour fort were designed so that the guns could bear on as wide an area of sea as possible. Its high profile and lack of adequate flanking fire made it unable to resist anything more than a landing party from enemy ships. In any case it was overlooked from the heights of Gorleston.

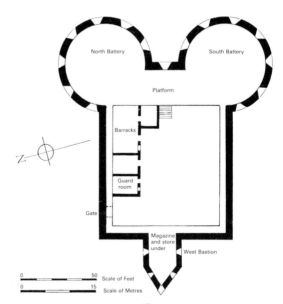

and the wages of the garrison[43]. The rest of the town's fortifications, the walls and earthworks were allowed to fall into decay.

When the Second Dutch War broke out in 1666 Yarmouth prepared to resist raids and possible bombardment. The fort was repaired, the guns mounted and militia regiments marched in until there were more than two thousand infantry and five troops of cavalry in the town[44]. The boom had long since vanished, but three ships were prepared to be sunk in the river at a moment's notice; for once Yarmouth was facing the enemy well prepared, with its guns in good order and a strong garrison. Morale was good and it was reported to the King that "the guns are fixed, hearts are up and many officers and soldiers wish the Dutch were in the road"[45]. But the Dutch chose to attack Harwich instead, and by October the militia had all been sent home and the garrison of the fort had been disbanded.

During the Third Dutch War the fort's role was uneventful. Instead of trying to keep the Dutch out it was used mainly to keep them in; it served as a prison for those captured at the Battle of Sole Bay—several Dutch captains escaped from the fort although they had given their parole[46]. In 1681 it was described as a "strong fort well planted with guns", but it still needed to be repaired by Sir Thomas Medowes. His repairs were not very effective, for by 1683 a shed as high as the fort's walls had been erected alongside and Sir Thomas was summoned to attend a meeting of the Privy Council. At that meeting he was reprimanded and ordered to clear the area around the fort of all obstructions for a distance of one hundred feet, "by which means His Majesty's fort will be secured and made useful for the purpose for which it was intended"[47].

Five years later the fort was stormed for the only time in its career; as a result of the political excitements of 1688 a mob from the town marched on the fort and broke in, perhaps in search of weapons, but they were quickly expelled by Lieutenant-General Bellasis' Regiment of Royal Fusiliers[48]. In 1695 the danger of privateers from Dunkirk became apparent once more, and to remedy the lack of guns covering the roads it was suggested that some might be placed on the jetty[49].

During most of the eighteenth century no additions were made to the defences and the main strength of Yarmouth lay in the fort. Nevertheless, a useful role for the medieval walls was still envisaged as their circuit remained complete. The earthworks and South Mount were much worn down, but the East or New Mount was described as a "modern well-built spacious bastion with platforms for great guns to flank the town walls and to defend the country"[50]. All the gateways were in reasonable repair, although the doors were greatly battered, and there were still a dozen 12-pounders on the New Mount[51]. It was not imagined that the walls could hold out for long, but they could protect the town from a raiding party.

In 1734 the fort was surveyed by a military engineer who reported that only a great deal of remedial work would make it efficient. The barracks were derelict, the gate decayed and the parapet ruinous[52]. Thirty years later it was still in need of repair, though armed with fifteen guns; and in that condition it remained until the outbreak of the American War.

When the Dutch and French joined the American colonies Yarmouth remembered that Holland was only ninety-five miles away; an alarum of Armada proportions swept town and county. Bands of volunteers with vainglorious names and impractical uniforms mustered themselves and declared their readiness to die for their country, while the Town Assembly looked to the defences. Apart from the fort and the old town wall they did not exist; the civil war ramparts were mere humps and folds in the ground. An official survey on behalf of the Board of Ordnance reported the fort as "small and badly situated being commanded by the ground behind on the opposite side of the river"[53].

In 1781 the Town Assembly wrote to General Tryon, Commander of the Eastern District, complaining of their defence-less state. They asked whether it was possible for an old fifty-gun ship-of-the-line crewed by invalids from Greenwich Hospital to be moored off the town[54]. Their odd preference for a floating battery crammed with nautical geriatrics was inspired by the fear that land batteries manned by regulars would mean troops quartered in the

*The North and South
Batteries on Yarmouth
Denes as originally built.*

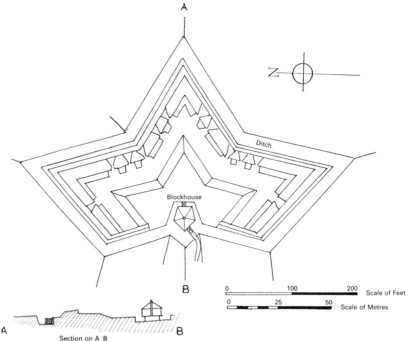

Section on A B

town—a fate considered, in terms of looting and rapine, to be little better than being sacked by the Dutch—but the Assembly eventually agreed to vote one hundred pounds for the building of batteries on the Denes[55]. Colonel Bramham, after inspecting the town, recommended four batteries armed with eighteen 24-pounders and left plans with the Mayor[56]. The town began to build a battery in the centre of the beach, but ran out of money and left it unfinished; the Government then assumed responsibility and completed it, as well as building two more batteries to north and south so that the whole anchorage was protected[57].

The North and South Batteries were well-built solid earthwork forts with a tenaille trace and surrounded by a wide ditch revetted with wood. The gorge was defended by a ditch, palisade and a small wooden blockhouse rather like those built in North America. The central or Beach Battery, showing its municipal origin, was of a different design from the others, with no facility to flank its ditch and no blockhouse. The old fort was rearmed with eight 24-pounders and four 6-pounders, but its main strength lay in an earthwork battery outside which was armed with five 32-pounders and ten 24-pounders. Across the river on the heights of Gorleston was built a small stockaded battery armed with six 24-pounders[58]. The American War ended in 1783, but the defences were

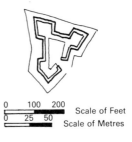

maintained in reasonable condition, to be reactivated when war broke out with revolutionary France in 1793.

By this time a blockhouse had been added to the town battery, and all three batteries were equipped with furnaces to heat shot to red heat[59]. The major problem of the batteries was that their ditches were filled with drifting sand, but there were other deficiencies in both siting and design, the harbour battery attracting the most severe criticism. It was "totally insignificant by command of the heights of Gorleston on which it should have been originally placed"[60]. Instead of the small battery at Gorleston there should have been a regular fort for a thousand men which, secure from assault from the land, would have denied both harbour and anchorage to an enemy force. The same critical eye also fell on the three batteries along the beach. With their embrasures pointing seaward they were vulnerable to the fire of enemy men-o'-war, and it was proposed to rebuild them with a solid parapet facing the sea and all the guns mounted in the flanks to enfilade the beach[61].

For probably the last time the walls were seriously considered in the general scheme of defence. Yarmouth and the adjoining "isle" of Lothingland would have made a strong base for the enemy, from which they could have launched attacks on the interior, using it as a giant *place d'armes*. Anything that helped strengthen the position was welcomed. The town "might be rendered remarkably strong" with the gates blocked by heavy carts and wagons chained together and men posted along the walls[62].

The invasion scare died down after 1798, to be revived with even greater anxiety in 1803. The existing batteries were once more examined with a critical eye that found them difficult to maintain and of doubtful utility. "One thing is certain, the batteries now in existence do not in the slightest degree tend to give any security to the place"[63], it was reported. General J. H. Craig recommended replacing them with permanent works, and four

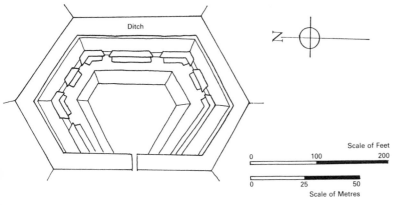

Scale of Feet
0 — 100 — 200

0 — 25 — 50
Scale of Metres

Above: *A fort on the heights at Gorleston overlooking the harbour mouth would have been far more effective than those below, but apart from one small open battery the Gorleston site was never fully utilised. This bastioned fort was planned for the site in 1779.*

Left: *The Town Battery had no facility to flank its ditch and lacked the blockhouse provided at the North and South Batteries.*

211

martello towers were proposed[64], reviving an idea of Captain Reynolds's; in 1798 the captain had recommended constructing five towers between a point midway between the fort and the South Battery and the rising ground at Caister[65]. As the threat of invasion receded after 1805 the forts were allowed to deteriorate.

By 1808 they were virtually derelict, with choked moats and rotten blockhouses. Three years later their condition was even worse, and it was recommended that they either be rebuilt with permanent brick revetments, as the constantly drifting sand and the sea air had destroyed the original sod work, or be completely replaced with martello towers[66].

After Napoleon had been finally banished to Saint Helena the volunteer artillerymen were disbanded and the forts virtually abandoned. The Gorleston battery was the first to be demolished, the harbour battery was next, and by the mid-eighteen-twenties only the three beach batteries and the old fort remained[67]. The fort was the next to be reduced to ruin, although the cause of its destruction was natural rather than man's neglect. Despite the fact

The bastions of the harbour fort can be seen in this print of the harbour mouth from a painting by James Stark about 1830. Within a few years it had been undermined by the tide and demolished.

that it was well maintained—it was described in 1819 as unused for some years but "kept up in proper repair and in neat order"[68]—alterations to the North Pier produced a fierce and powerful tidal scour that undermined the fort's south bastion as effectively as a band of enemy sappers. In April, 1832, half the semi-circular bastion fell into the river and part of the wall was demolished to form a breakwater to protect what remained[69]. It was obvious, however, that the remnant of the fort was irreparable and indefensible, and the following year what remained was demolished and the materials sold[70]. The gate alone survived and was incorporated into a folly at the Gorleston home of the antiquarian F. D. Palmer[71]. The three remaining batteries lost several guns, but those that remained were remounted on traversing carriages to make them more effective. All three were armed with 24-pounders, the South Battery with nine, the North Battery with eight and the Town Battery with four[72].

In 1839 there was a tentative proposal to replace the demolished fort with a large martello tower armed with three 24-pounders and a 32-pounder carronade[73]. A rather archaic addition to the river defence would have been an iron chain to act as a boom; this was to be fixed to the Gorleston shore and winched taut to close the passage by a windlass in the basement of the tower. At five thousand pounds this was an expensive replacement for a work that had never been in the right place. A much cheaper and far more effective alternative would have been to rebuild the battery on the heights at Gorleston.

By the eighteen-fifties the town had burst from the corset of its medieval walls and had begun to spread over the denes towards the sea. The Town Battery stood in the middle of what an estate agent would call land ripe for development, and at the conclusion of the Crimean War in 1855 it was abandoned. Four years later it was sold for eighty-four pounds and demolished[74]. It was somewhat ironic that in the same year that the Town Battery was sold a Royal Commission was proposing to spend twelve million pounds on coastal fortifications. Although the money was destined for the major ports, the Government had plans to build a replacement for the long-demolished harbour fort.

In 1859 the War Office had announced its intention to install five heavy guns on the cliffs at Gorleston, but it abandoned the idea in favour of building a battery at the haven's mouth[75]. The town sold four acres of land, and a public house, *The Jacob's Boat*, was demolished, much to the annoyance of those who made it the object of a long walk from the town and of local fishermen who claimed an ancient right to lay out their nets to dry on the denes[76]. Their sense of grievance was increased when they learnt that the sacrifice was unnecessary, for the new fort never materialised.

The Town Battery was demolished in 1858 and the remaining two were rebuilt to a totally different trace the following year, as shown here. The armament consisted of 68-pounder smooth-bores and 10-inch smooth-bores.

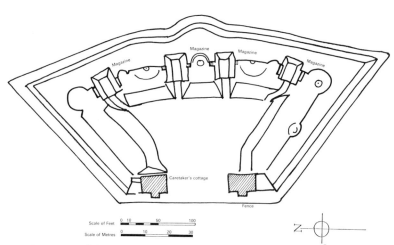

One tangible result of the invasion scare of 1859 was the formation of the volunteers. Yarmouth was not immune to the craze for amateur soldiering, and an artillery company was raised to man the guns in the two remaining batteries, which had been rearmed in 1859 with 68-pounder SB and 10-inch SB "in lieu of the pop-guns hitherto in position"[77]. The batteries themselves were reconstructed with brick revetments, bomb-proof expense magazines and a pair of cottages for the caretakers. The town continued to press the War Office to build a fort at the haven mouth and to replace the Town Battery, but by 1863 the Government had lost interest and the project was postponed indefinitely[78].

The rebuilt batteries and their guns had been almost obsolete in 1860, and by the end of the decade their ineffectiveness could no longer be disguised. "The existing works are neither in construction nor armament adequate for the defence of the harbour and roads"[79], said a report of 1870. The proposal for a modern fort was renewed and the rearming of the existing batteries urged[80]. There was no new fort, but the guns in the batteries were replaced in 1872 with the first rifled guns to be emplaced in Yarmouth. Both North and South Batteries had three 80-pounders and two 64-pounders each, all mounted on traversing carriages fitted with graduated arcs[81].

During the eighteen-eighties a fresh wave of anxiety about the nation's coastal defences was felt. Most coastal towns, Yarmouth among them, realised that their guns were useless, unable to fire far enough or fast enough to prevent an enemy ship from bombarding them. A public meeting was held in 1886 and a resolution was sent to the War Office demanding modern guns for the defence of town and anchorage[82]. Those who knew about such things talked knowledgeably about breech-loaders, quick-firers and hydro-pneumatic mountings. Maps were studied, possible sites canvassed, and eventually a proposal emerged that suggested rebuilding the North Battery and rearming it with 5-inch BL, but only if the town met most of the cost[83]. This quelled the agitation; nothing was done, and as if to dissociate itself from the defence of Yarmouth, the War Office sold the land it had acquired in 1860.

The rest of the century proved uneventful for the two batteries. The true purpose of the guns seemed to be to give the volunteers something to do at the weekends and an excuse to spend a summer fortnight by the sea. They built themselves a sumptuous mess, amassed quantities of ornate silver tableware, gorged themselves at annual banquets and occasionally fired a few rounds before an audience of small boys and elderly gentlemen in bathchairs. In 1895 the firing was watched by the Prince of Wales; on this occasion, as if to mark its importance, the South Battery fired at a moving target for the first time[84]. After this, firing at towed targets became more general and tugs were regularly hired for the purpose[85].

As the town expanded both batteries were regarded as something of a nuisance; the site of the North Battery was coveted

The Norfolk Artillery Volunteers at practice in the South Battery. The gun being fired is a 64-pounder RML, a Palliser converted 32-pounder smooth-bore. By 1898, when this photograph was taken, the effectiveness of these guns was negligible.

by the town council for housing, and the noise of the firing, although never prolonged—each battery fired about two hundred rounds a year—annoyed both residents and visitors[86]. In 1896 the South Battery became the sole fortification in the town when the North Battery was declared surplus. Its guns were transferred to the South Battery and for two years it lay empty while various bodies wrangled about its fate. The town council wanted the land for building, but Trinity House wanted the battery and the small RNR battery beside it to store explosives[87]. Eventually the council had its way, the site of just under five acres was purchased, and in 1898 the North Battery was demolished. In the same year the South Battery was reconstructed and armed with four 64-pounders, six 80-pounders, two 9-pounder field guns and a single 9-inch RML, the largest gun ever to be emplaced at Yarmouth[88].

The presence of the guns in the battery was increasingly irrelevant, for there was no unit to operate them. In 1890 the volunteer batteries had been armed with 16-pounder field guns. One battery was retained as a garrison unit to man the coastal guns, but this was abolished in 1892[89]. In 1902 the volunteers were re-equipped with four 4.7-inch field guns[90]. These carried out annual firings from the South Denes, but the guns in the battery were rarely fired.

In response to the threat of German naval power, in 1905 the War Office proposed building a new battery on the South Denes armed with 6-inch and 4.7-inch guns[91]. To counter objections that might be raised it was pointed out that the town would gain great economic advantage from the hundreds of troops who would come to Yarmouth for their annual training. Vague fears of damage to property were discounted by the explanation that no windows would be broken by the concussion of the guns if they were left open. What finally sank the project was the demand that Yarmouth contribute one thousand pounds[92]. The council declined, and the new battery was never built.

At the outbreak of the First World War, the South Battery with its obsolete artillery was Yarmouth's only defence. The harbour was used by light naval craft and there was a Royal Naval Air Station on the South Denes, but it was not thought necessary to mount any modern guns to protect these installations. Even after the first ineffectual bombardment of the town by the German fleet in November, 1914, the War Office resisted demands that heavy guns be installed. After the second bombardment in April, 1916, as a concession to public alarm, a solitary 4.7-inch was installed on Gorleston Cliffs. Sited on the upper esplanade midway between Clarence Road and Park Road, the battery consisted of two dugouts, a magazine and the gun-pit, all surrounded by an enclosure of barbed wire[93].

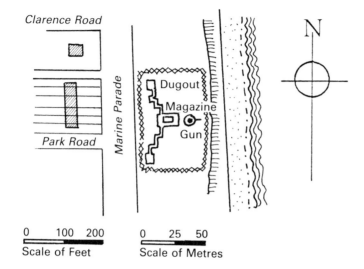

Clarence Road

Marine Parade

Dugout

Magazine

Gun

Park Road

N

0   100   200
Scale of Feet

0   25   50
Scale of Metres

The 4.7-inch gun installed on Gorleston Cliff in 1916 to cover the harbour entrance. It was replaced by a 15-pounder in 1918.

Yarmouth was first attacked from the air on the night of 19th/20th January, 1915, when the German airship L-3 drifted silently over the town and dropped seven bombs, which fell around the area of St Peter's Plain and killed two people[94]. This prompted the War Office to send some anti-aircraft guns. Two 18-pounders were placed on the South Denes, one by Nelson's column and the other a little nearer the haven mouth[95]. Some pillboxes were built towards the end of the war, facing inland to protect the town from an invading force that had landed elsewhere and needed to capture the port and its facilities. There was a third German bombardment in January, 1918, but this resulted in no new defences; instead the 4.7-inch gun was replaced by a smaller 15-pounder.

After the Armistice the modern guns were withdrawn, and in 1924 the South Battery was finally sold and demolished. An estate of council housing was built on the site; only the name Battery Road now pays tribute to its existence of over a hundred and forty years.

At first the outbreak of the Second World War affected Yarmouth very little. Large numbers of evacuees arrived, some naval ships and personnel were busy in the harbour, but there were few other visible signs of hostilities. Almost a year later, with the Germans making preparations to invade, the same air of calm gentility prevailed. In July the tennis courts along the front were still thronged in the summer evenings; strollers passed by bowling greens and gardens as well kept as ever. The only indication that there was such a thing as a war was the reappearance of ice-cream salesmen in new and martial guise as air raid wardens[96]. But while

217

flannelled figures gambolled in the twilight work was proceeding on erecting defences for the port.

As early as 21st May, 1940, guns were installed in the first of three emergency batteries. The North Denes Battery, which stood at the junction of Jellicoe Road and North Drive, was a standard work armed with two 6-inch ex-naval guns, two searchlights and various light weapons for close defence[97]. The second battery was at the haven mouth. By 25th June, two 12-pounders were installed on the end of the South Pier as an anti-torpedo-boat defence. This arrangement lasted until mid-1941 when one of the guns was shifted to the Yarmouth side to give a wider field of fire. The battery had three searchlights, one at Gorleston on the pier and the others on the Yarmouth bank. Underground shelters were built behind the cafe by the North Pier and a 40mm Bofors was

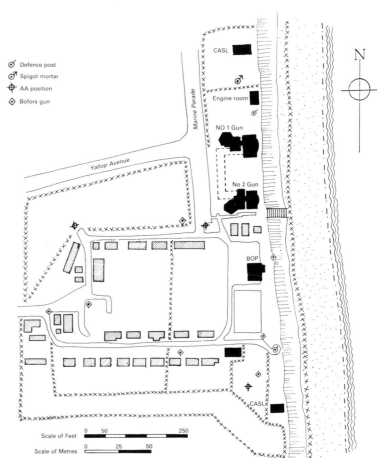

The Links Battery at Gorleston occupied a position at the southern end of Marine Parade amidst a colony of bungalows, some of which provided quarters for the personnel.

emplaced on the pier. The greatest damage the battery sustained was when the violent explosion of a rogue British torpedo destroyed the magazine and most of the battery buildings on the South Pier[98].

The third battery stood on Gorleston cliffs a mile south of the river mouth, astride the borough boundary at the very end of Marine Parade. The guns were in Norfolk while the battery observation post and one of the searchlights were in Suffolk. This battery occupied a rather incongruous position close to the golf links amidst a colony of bungalows and villas between the railway line and the sea. They were the sort of seaside houses that provide the settings for Agatha Christie novels, peopled with men in flannels and girls in white with golf-bags who drive about in small, jolly open cars and sip cocktails to the thin scratchings of a horned

The original casemates of the Links Battery consisted of a steel framework covered with sandbags. They were later rebuilt in brick and concrete.

219

gramophone. All were requisitioned and surrounded by barbed wire and defence posts built of sandbags and armed with Bren guns and spigot mortars.

Some of the bungalows became living quarters, others stores, and one the officers' mess, but there remained something of the carefree pre-war spirit about the place. Preserved among the generator rooms, searchlights and gun emplacements was the tennis court, in the shadow of the observation tower overlooking a beach tangled with jagged obstacles and liberally sown with mines. The guns were two 6-inch Mk VII guns that were equipped, unusually for an emergency battery, with land service mountings capable of 15 degrees elevation[99]. They had an appreciably greater range than those on ex-naval pedestal mountings. Underground shelters and magazines joined the two gun emplacements, while the rear approaches were covered by two adjoining pillboxes. The two searchlights stood on the cliff edge at either side of the guns. Later the armament was increased by two 40mm Bofors and a 25-pounder field gun[100].

At first all three batteries were manned by regular troops, but as the dangers decreased so did the necessity to keep every battery at a high state of readiness. In April, 1944, 325 Battery, RA, turned the guns at the North Denes over to the Home Guard, and the battery closed down in the following November[101]. The Links Battery with its longer-range guns was manned until January, 1945, when it was closed and put on a care and maintenance basis. Only the Pier Battery remained fully manned by regular troops until the end of the war[102].

The guns had lost most of their functions very early in the war when the danger of invasion receded. They were unable to fire at the range needed to break up concentrations of E-boats operating in the North Sea against coastal shipping, and as early as 1942 it was proposed to install three 5.25-inch guns at the North Denes[103]. These were dual-purpose coast artillery and anti-aircraft guns with a much greater range than the antiquated ex-naval guns already installed. Despite prolonged investigations and much discussion, the new guns were never emplaced and the North Denes Battery saw out the war with its old 6-inch pieces.

Two batteries of heavy anti-aircraft guns were installed; one with four emplacements for 4.5-inch AA guns at Ashby near Gorleston and the other, similarly armed, at Warren Farm in the middle of Gorleston golf links. The guns were not allowed to spoil the amenities and it was noted with approval that "great care has been taken to avoid disturbing the golf course more than necessary"[104].

As well as the major batteries large numbers of other fortifications were built. The deserted sea front was disfigured by

A detail of one of the pillboxes built on the Acle New Road just outside Yarmouth to defend the landward side of the town. They faced towards the town and were sited to prevent an enemy force breaking out after a landing at Yarmouth.

concrete blockhouses of varied shapes, sizes and functions. The beach was mined and covered with barbed wire and obstructions made of scaffolding. More than two dozen pillboxes were sited along the sea front from the North Denes Battery to the harbour mouth, interspersed with a dozen spigot mortar emplacements and two 75mm guns. Later in the war the main danger came from strikes by low-flying fighter-bombers, and to counter these numbers of Bofors and other light AA guns were installed until the whole front was un unbroken line of gunpits and blockhouses bristling with weapons of all calibres[105].

On the cliffs at Gorleston the defences were equally dense, with pillboxes, trenches and emplacements for a 75mm, two light AA guns and two Bofors[106]. Almost as much attention was devoted to the landward side of the town with the aim of creating a fortress with an extensive perimeter. This line, running from Caister Road to the Acle New Road and then roughly following the line of the Yarmouth to Lowestoft railway, consisted of about twenty pill-boxes, roadblocks and associated trenches. An inner redoubt was created by utilising the Yare as a moat and heavily fortifying all the approaches from the Haven Bridge and siting a pillbox to cover the junction of the Bure and Yare.

When the war ended most of these defences were removed almost as quickly as they had been built. The guns in the major batteries were withdrawn in early 1946 and the casemates and magazines demolished. To prepare the town for its first summer season most of that year was spent clearing the seaward defences. The mines were lifted and the pillboxes and emplacements reduced to rubble in what proved to be a lengthy and expensive process, the total cost to the council being £115,000[107]. Each pillbox cost the ratepayers about two hundred and fifty pounds to demolish, about half the cost of building, and each acre of beach cost one hundred pounds to clear of all the various obstacles and bits of lethal ironwork[108]. The mines were lifted by the army, but it was well into the nineteen-fifties before all the beach was regarded as completely safe. Once the process of demolition was complete and the crowds had returned to the beach, the last chapter in Yarmouth's long history as a fortress was closed.

King's Lynn   15

A T ONE TIME in its long history Lynn was the fourth port in
the Kingdom. Over its quays and wharves passed a rich and
extensive trade, and ships from the Baltic, Germany and the Low
Countries crowded the river. The great German trade confeder-
ation, the Hanseatic League, established a depot or steelyard in the
town as early as 1271, but the town's greatest period of prosperity
came in the fifteenth century when cargoes of English wool flowed
down the rivers from the hinterland and across the North Sea to
foreign markets[1].

From that high point to the nineteenth century the fortunes of
the port declined as the silt in the river channel increased. As the
passage to the sea grew more tortuous and difficult to navigate,
trade began to desert the town. What was a hindrance to commerce
was an aid to Lynn's defence, however, and formed a partial
substitute for seaward fortifications. This, combined with the
circumstances of Lynn's commercial decline coinciding with the
introduction of artillery, meant that the port never had any large
or particularly interesting harbour defences. It was the land
fortifications that were always of greater size, complexity and
significance, and Lynn was one of only three towns in East Anglia
to have a bastioned enceinte and the only place where there are any
surviving remains.

Lynn was first fortified in the thirteenth century, when the
town was surrounded by an earthwork and ditch[2]. The natural
advantages of the site made the task very easy. The River Ouse
defended the west, the River Nar protected the south and the
Fisher Fleet barred entry from the north, making artificial
defences necessary only on the east. From the Fisher Fleet there
ran a distance of four hundred yards to the south a stone wall with
a single tower, but the rest of the circuit round to the Nar consisted
of an earth bank and ditch topped by a palisade. The two principal
entrances to the town, from south and east, were defended by
stone gatehouses, and there were three smaller postern gates. Of
these fortifications the most impressive and technically advanced
was the South Gate, built in 1437–40, through which the London
road entered the town[3]. In the towers, flanking the entrance on the
first and second floors, are small circular gunports about ten inches
in diameter, the commonest variety from the fifteenth century[4].

The East Gate was the second principal entrance to King's Lynn. It was demolished in 1800.

Below: *Saint Anne's Fort, redrawn from a manuscript map of 1589.*

The alarms and scares of the early sixteenth century were not unnoticed in Lynn. Henry VIII, who gave his name to the town, changing it from Bishop's to King's Lynn, resolved that it should be fortified with up-to-date artillery works to defend the harbour, and in 1539 Lynn was included in the list of fortified places that formed Thomas Cromwell's Remembrance[5]. In the same year Cromwell's protégé Richard Morison enthusiastically enumerated the King's fortification projects, noting that among them "Lynne also shall be made strong"[6]. As it turned out Lynn remained weak, for no defences were built; at least, none significant enough to figure in the list of the King's bulwarks made in 1540 and 1541[7].

In 1570 a fresh invasion scare prompted the town to build a small fort at the north-east corner of the quay where the Fisher Fleet joined the Ouse[8]. This was not a large or ambitious work, consisting of a platform for the guns, some buildings and a section of wall and gate giving access to the Fisher Fleet. This is clearly shown on a manuscript map[9] of 1589 in the form of a gate flanked by two towers and could well have incorporated part of Saint Anne's or Saint Agnes's gate mentioned by Hillen[10].

Eighteen years later Lynn, like the rest of England, looked to its defences. Sir John Paynton was appointed commander of the local forces and directed to put the fortifications in order[11]. The moats were scoured and repairs were made to the walls. Further preparations were made to cut the causeway before the East Gate and to wall up the posterns if the enemy approached.

Sir Thomas Leighton then decided it would be wise to advance Lynn's defences seawards. He recommended that a small fort or sconce be located at a point called the Crutch a mile north of the town where the channel divided into two. Despite the fact that the town was regarded as of some strategic importance, Sir Thomas insisted that its citizens provided the money, labour, guns and ammunition[12]. The fort was not a bastioned work as might have been expected but a rectangular earthwork enclosure about three hundred feet by four hundred and fifty, which seems rather large for what was only a coastal battery[13].

It is also somewhat odd that there were no arrangements for flanking fire, but the need was urgent and knowledge of the new bastioned trace was still largely confined to professional military engineers, who were employed elsewhere. One advantage was that it was certainly cheap, for no records of any relevant payments exist in the Chamberlain's Accounts of Lynn[14]. Once the Armada had been defeated no-one paid much attention to the fortifications and the battery at the Crutch was allowed to decay.

There were no effective defences in the early seventeenth century when the Dunkirkers began to pay their unwelcome attentions to Lynn and its shipping. In 1625 several of the port's vessels were snapped up by privateers and for many weeks the rest lay idle in harbour, too scared to poke their bowsprits out into the open sea. At one time the danger was so great that the fishing fleet could only sail and shoot its nets packed together in armed convoy[15]. If this was not threat enough, the town feared that a daring pirate might sail up the river and attack the shipping at the quays and even Lynn itself. The fort at the Crutch had virtually disappeared by this time and was too far from the town to be kept in a state of readiness without a resident garrison, so Saint Anne's Fort was repaired.

This done, the Crown was asked, not unreasonably, for some ordnance to arm it with. Twelve guns were humbly requested and the answer that no suitable artillery existed in the ordnance stores came as a surprise. The town, however, was informed that the King's gun founder did have some suitable pieces that he had cast for the royal forts and, if Lynn cared to pay the sum of £1,109, they could be delivered[16]. The town protested, believing, not without good reason, that the Crown had some responsibility for defending them or at the very least for providing the weapons for them to do so themselves. This protest was successful; the Privy Council overruled the Master-General of the Ordnance and granted Lynn ten cannons, culverins and sakers[17]. The Master-General protested that this would set an expensive and inconvenient precedent if the Crown admitted that it was obliged to defend those subjects who lived near the coast.

The guns were delivered in 1626 and installed in Saint Anne's Fort, which explains why all of Lynn's historians assert that it was actually built in that year; a further four guns were obtained shortly afterwards[18]. It is, however, probable that the town did after all have to pay for its artillery. In 1627 Lynn begged to be

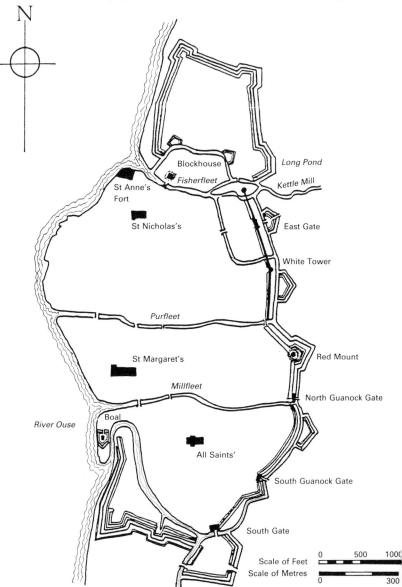

The Civil War fortifications of Lynn at their greatest extent in 1645.

226

relieved of taxes as it had expended £1,200 on fortifications, a sum that almost exactly matched that demanded in payment for the guns[19].

The guns that the King had sent to Lynn were shortly to be turned against him; when the Civil War broke out in 1642 Lynn, with some reluctance, declared for Parliament. At once the fortifications were put in order, the drawbridges were renewed and the gates guarded day and night. In September additional fortifications were begun, designed by a local engineer called Christian[20], and in December the town petitioned the Eastern Association for five hundred pounds to complete them, as well as demanding an extra ten cannon[21]. These first works probably went no further than strengthening the existing ramparts and building additional earthworks to the north of the Fisher Fleet.

The artificial channel known as the Loke could well have been dug at this time, for the northern side of the town had no ramparts to speak of and only the Duce Hill Gate to defend the crossing of the Fisher Fleet. A blockhouse might also have been built in advance of the gate, although it is possible that this was constructed in 1626 as part of the defensive programme undertaken then[22]. The Red Mount Chapel was turned to secular use and became a gunpowder store and strongpoint dignified with the title of the Mount Fort. These new defences were hardly completed before Lynn abruptly changed its allegiance.

Lynn had never been firm in its support of Parliament and emphasised this by appointing a known Royalist, Sir Hamon L'Estrange of Hunstanton, as governor. He had secretly agreed with Charles I that if the town were to declare for the Crown the King would send troops to its aid. Strategically Lynn was very important, as it was the only port on the east coast in the King's hands through which munitions might be imported, as well as being a gateway into Norfolk from the North, where there was a strong Royal army under the command of the Marquis of Newcastle.

In August, 1643, the town closed its gates to Parliament and prepared to fight. There were enough provisions and large quantities of munitions, including five hundred barrels of gunpowder[23]. Approximately forty guns were mounted on the ramparts; fourteen were from Saint Anne's Fort, another ten may have been sent by the Eastern Association and the rest were commandeered from ships in the harbour. The garrison numbered about one thousand five hundred.

Parliamentary forces gathered rapidly to reduce the town. A squadron of warships commanded by the Earl of Warwick appeared in the Wash to prevent relief by sea while a force of three thousand cavalry and fifteen hundred infantry under the Earl of

Manchester threw a cordon about the town; levies were gathered from Cambridgeshire and Norfolk.

The defenders lost the initiative early when the Parliamentary forces seized the blockhouse and dominated the northern defences. Siege batteries were thrown up and a train of artillery collected, to which Norwich contributed four guns, two heavy old culverins and two smaller falconets[24]. For weeks the bombardment went on. Shot poured into the town from all sides, doing much damage to the houses and forcing the inhabitants to keep shelter. Even the church proved insufficient sanctuary; as the congregation sat in Saint Margaret's, the sermon was enlivened by a shot fired from across the river that crashed through the west window, shattered a pillar and showered them with fragments of multi-coloured glass and stone[25]. More earthworks were raised by the besiegers to the east of the town and, had the siege lasted long enough, Lynn would have been surrounded by lines of circum-vallation as at Colchester and Newark[26].

An assault was planned for mid-September to forestall any attempt at relief from the north. The plan was simultaneously to assault the walls from east and south, while more troops crossed the river in boats to attack the unprotected quayside. Suitable craft were collected, carts and scaling ladders were gathered in the besiegers' camp, while the cannonade went on and the garrison, no doubt aware of what was about to happen, continued to try to strengthen their defences. Some of them felled trees to make obstacles while others tried to break the dykes near the South Gate to flood the ground over which the attack would have to pass. Most of the defenders gradually lost heart, however, until, weakened by lack of food and with no hope of relief, they were so impressed by the besiegers parading in full strength before the walls that Sir Hamon was forced to ask for terms. On September 16th the gates were opened and the Earl of Manchester's army marched into Lynn. The casualties during the six weeks of siege were extremely light; some sources indicate that, despite the apparent fury of the bombardment, nobody at all was killed[27].

As soon as Lynn was secure, elaborate measures were undertaken to ensure that it remained so. Captain Valentine Wauden was appointed governor and a garrison of loyal troops installed[28]. Wauden's first action was to inspect the circuit of fortifications and to repair any damage or obvious weak spots. When this was done an almost completely new set of fortifications was built, surrounding Lynn with a bastioned enceinte of modern design and making it the strongest fortress in East Anglia. These new defences were probably designed by the same engineer, Christian, who had begun the defences the previous year[29].

Huge amounts of timber were needed for revetting the

Opposite page: *The Red Mount Chapel at King's Lynn with its surrounding earthworks, seen in Samuel and Nathaniel Buck's "prospect" of 1744.*
L. W. Malster

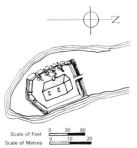

Scale of Feet
Scale of Metres

Above: *The* World's
End *on the Boal converted
into a small fort covering
the southern river
approach to Lynn.*

Opposite page: *The
East Gate and parts of the
King's Lynn walls, as
portrayed by the brothers
Buck in 1744.*
L. W. Malster

Below: *The profile of the
most elaborate stretch of
defences south of the River
Nar. These were the only
completely new
construction involved in
the defences installed
following the fall of Lynn
in 1643.*

parapets and building platforms and palisades. Most of this was
provided as an involuntary contribution by the Earl of Surrey,
Thomas Arundel, whose woods at North Wootton, just outside
Lynn, and at Kenninghall, over thirty miles away, were felled on
the pretext of fortifying Lynn[30].

The new fortifications closely followed the medieval defences
except in the north and south, where outworks were raised beyond
the Loke and the River Nar. Most of the additional bastions were of
a very slight profile, hardly more than a simple bank and ditch,
except those south of the Nar. These works were the only
completely new constructions and thus, being free from the
constraints of adaptation and extension of existing defences, were
the most symmetrical and technically correct. They adopted the
Dutch device of a fausse-braye or parapet at the foot of the scarp
and had all the regular textbook components, including a covered
way and even a second ditch at the foot of the glacis. On the Boal
peninsula between the two rivers Ouse and Nar a small earthwork
with embrasures for seven guns was thrown up around the *World's
End* public house.

In 1652, with the Civil War over, Parliament felt that Lynn
could safely be demilitarised. The blockhouse, having been made
redundant after the building of the northern fortifications and
being in a near-derelict state, was ordered to be demolished[31].
Later in the same year the townspeople heard to their dismay that
they were to lose all their artillery. They pleaded that the guns of
the fort be left for the protection of the harbour, but to no effect,
and the next year all the cannon in the town were collected and
prepared for loading aboard a ship for transport to London[32]. At
this point the need for the artillery was made clear when the master
of the ship refused to sail until a warship arrived to escort him
safely down the coast[33].

The guns returned with Charles II, but they were removed
again in 1688 and taken to Hull following the flight of James II.

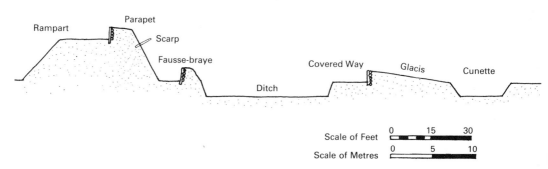

Scale of Feet
Scale of Metres

230

The government obviously wished for no repetition of the events of 1643. With the new regime safely established, however, Saint Anne's Fort was rearmed with twelve 9-pounders[34].

These guns were returned to the Ordnance in 1716 and the earthworks were allowed to decay, but Lynn was still a potentially viable fortress, as Daniel Defoe found when he visited the town in 1724: "The situation of the town renders it capable of being very strong, and in the late wars it was so; a line of fortification being drawn round it at a distance from the walls, the ruins or remains of which works appear very fair to this day, nor would it be a hard matter to restore the bastions with the ravelins and the counterscarp upon any sudden emergency to a good state of defence, and that in a little time"[35].

That sudden emergency occurred twenty years later. In 1744 the fort was rearmed with ten 18-pounders, and the following year the news arrived of the Jacobite rebellion and Prince Charles's march southwards[36]. When it was known that the rebels were at Derby, the people of Lynn were transfixed with fear; bands of volunteers scoured the fens seeking Scotsmen, and even the clergy walked to church armed with pistol and sword. The fortifications were hurriedly surveyed and the Corporation resolved to repair them.

The first priority was to strengthen the South Gate, for the Civil War outwork had long disappeared. The Mayor and Corporation, with all the gentry of the town, set out for the main entry to the town bearing shovels. There they began to dig a trench and to build a parapet, setting an example to the humbler citizens by their exertions. They were unused to digging, and a large crowd gathered to wonder at the sight of sweat glistening on such noble brows. The Mayor publicly regretted that there was more than one entrance to the town, for if there had been a single bridge he could have held it alone against the advancing tartan horde like Horatius. This new fortification was unfinished when the diggers received news of the rebels' retreat; they abandoned their labours with relief[37].

The outbreak of war between Britain and France in 1778 led to a fresh inspection of the defences. The ten guns in Saint Anne's Fort were quite unserviceable, and they were replaced by ten newer 18-pounders sent from London[38]. One hundred and seventy-one volunteer artillerymen were enrolled to man them. In smart new uniforms with orange facings, they were full of patriotic enthusiasm and dreadful poetry.

> Watch round the land with Britain's eye
> Your wealth defend or bravely die.
> Feast on roast beef—plum pudding too,
> Then with good cheer the foe subdue[39].

The South Gate of King's Lynn as it stands today. Circular gunports can be seen in the face of the gate and in the turrets.

Die they surely would have done had the fort ever been attacked, as it had no parapet, a deficiency that remained unremedied throughout the Napoleonic Wars. The guns were the pride of their crews and were all given pet names, so the town could rightly be said to have been defended by "Queen Boadicea" and the "Lynn Independent"[40]. No efforts were made to restore the landward fortifications, although the War Office thought in 1798 that the French might land at Lynn[41].

Three years later this inactivity was justified by the pronouncement that "a predatory incursion is all that is to be looked for at Lynn"[42]. Such an attack could easily be dealt with by Saint Anne's Fort, although there were those in the town who had never been convinced "that it proved of any material use to the town in that time of danger, nor does it appear to have been ever calculated for the defence and protection of the place, or for any other purpose

233

but to please little or full grown children, who are naturally fond of ribands and rattles"[43]. Such was the lack of concern about any attack from the land that the East Gate was demolished along with the South Guanock Gate and a long section of the stone wall, while the heightening of the earth bank on the south was merely a scheme to provide work for the unemployed[44].

More efficient guardians of the town were the tortuous shoals

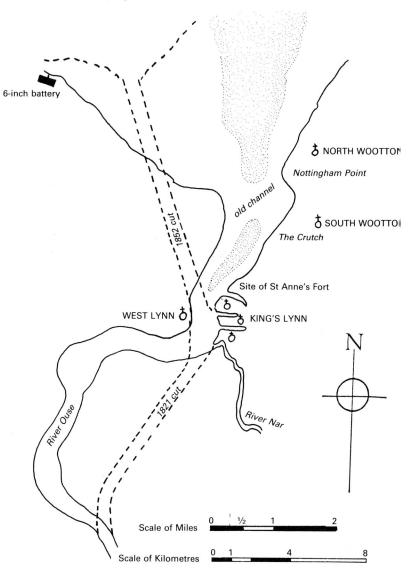

The course of the River Ouse was radically changed in the nineteenth century, leaving the sites of sixteenth-century fortifications well inland.

of the approach channel, likely to prove a far greater hazard to an enemy ship than the fort's artillery and its amateur garrison. A further inspection of the area during the invasion scare of 1803 confirmed this, but nonetheless those responsible recommended the building of a small battery north of the town near the site of the old Crutch fort to guard against light, shallow-draught vessels running in across the sandbanks[45].

After the peace in 1815 the volunteers were disbanded, but the guns remained. In 1822 they were still in place and Lynn was described as still being "encompassed by a deep ditch and an ancient wall which was formerly defended by nine bastions and might now be made a place of considerable strength"[46]. But with every year this potential strength grew less as natural and deliberate depredations took their toll; although the northern ramparts maintained their outline they were gradually levelled by the allotment holders until only the ditch remained[47].

The guns of Saint Anne's Fort were removed some time before 1839, when a report of the east coast defences made no mention of any armament at Lynn[48]. It did, however, propose to remedy this by building two new batteries downstream. One was to stand on Nottingham Point and to be armed with eight 32-pounders and

Saint Anne's Fort in the eighteenth century, with the cupola of the Pilot House rising above it.

two of the new 10-inch shell guns. The other, smaller fort on the west bank was to mount six 32-pounders[49]. Simple but powerful earthworks, these forts were never built. Saint Anne's Fort still stood in 1853 when the new estuary cut, which realigned the River Ouse, left it stranded more than a hundred yards inland.

In 1870 another survey was made on behalf of the War Office and the possibility of any serious attack was dismissed, but a small work mounting a few light guns was still recommended[50]. The main purpose of this was to provide a practice battery for the local volunteer artillery rather than to protect the port; but as Lynn had no volunteers the battery was never built.

Lynn's status as a minor port meant that no defences were planned or constructed for the rest of the century, apart from a small battery attached to the Coast Guard station built in 1883[51]. At that time the Coast Guard was a department of the Admiralty and had a far more militant role than it does today. Both the coastguards themselves and their cutters were armed, and the service was considered as a naval reserve. The new station at Lynn, which stood just north of the new outlet of the Fisher Fleet, included an armoury and magazine. The battery was probably for

The battery observation post of the emergency battery at Clenchwarton and one of the casemates, now buried under the sea bank. The sea is now more than five hundred yards away.

a couple of small 3-pounders whose purpose was solely training.

During the First World War there was little danger from either sea or land attack. It was from the air that the only bombardment came. On the night of 19th January, 1915, the Zeppelin L-4 dropped eight bombs into the town, killing two people and injuring thirteen[52]. Over the next three years Lynn was to suffer several more raids, but no permanent installations were built to counter this novel threat.

When war broke out again in 1939 the only installations remotely resembling fortifications were the shelters being assembled in back gardens and the slit trenches dug in the parks. This changed in 1940 when the fear of invasion thrust Lynn into the front line and initiated a bout of fortification such as had not been seen since the Civil War. Anti-tank obstacles and roadblocks ringed the town and pillboxes covered many roads. To defend the seaward approaches and to hamper any attempt to land enemy forces an emergency battery armed with two ex-naval 6-inch guns was hurriedly built in the summer of 1940 on the bleak marshes on the west bank of the Ouse. It was solidly if hurriedly constructed of stock brick with roofs made of concrete poured direct on to corrugated steel shuttering. The two guns were mounted in casemates two hundred feet apart, standing on the sea bank and connected by magazines and shelters. Behind these stood a three-storey battery observation post and engine rooms for the searchlight generators.

Like most projects undertaken hastily it had its faults, the most glaring of these being that it was in the wrong place. Only six months after its completion it was critically examined by a coastal defence committee who realised that when the tide went out the water receded so far into the Wash that the guns would have nothing floatable to shoot at[53]. Even at high water the maximum depth of water, except in the extremely narrow ship channel, was only seven feet, which meant that nothing large enough to warrant a 6-inch shell could approach near enough to be hit. The heavy guns were completely superfluous and their role could be much more efficiently filled by lighter field guns quite capable of dealing with those landing craft that were thought to be the only likely form of attack. Accordingly the battery was moved in September, 1941, to Druridge Bay, Northumberland[54]. As the serious threat of invasion receded most of the other defences were allowed to lapse. Lynn suffered several air raids, the most serious in September, 1942, but damage was relatively slight and no permanent anti-aircraft batteries wre installed[55].

After 1945 most of the wartime defences were cleared away, leaving the South Gate as the oldest and most impressive reminder that King's Lynn was once a strong and powerful fortress.

Cambridgeshire, Huntingdonshire and Lincolnshire 16

ALMOST all fortifications built since the introduction of artillery have been on the coast, leaving Cambridgeshire and Huntingdonshire virtually bereft of modern works; Lincolnshire, too, has little to show because its mudflat coast is so difficult to land on and fixed defences are unnecessary.

The inland medieval strongholds of the three counties must have had some small modifications to accommodate hand guns, but the only evidence that survives are stirrup-shaped gunloops, similar to those at Oxborough Hall, in the Bishop's Palace at Buckden, Cambridgeshire[1]. The only ports of any consequence, Boston and Grimsby, might have had one or two guns and perhaps a small bulwark at the beginning of the sixteenth century but little of importance after. Grimsby was mentioned in Richard Morison's list of those places that were to be fortified by Henry VIII, but no works seem to have resulted from this[2].

The coast was surveyed at the time of the Armada and again in 1598, but no fortifications were proposed nor any existing ones mentioned[3]. In 1626 the coast was examined again, but ships were thought to be the best defence[4]. Only when the Civil War began did all previous conditions and requirements of defence completely change, resulting in an extensive programme of inland fortification. Cambridgeshire and Huntingdonshire both supported Parliament and joined the Eastern Association, while Lincolnshire reflected the nation's general turmoil as rival factions fought for control of the county. The five counties of the Eastern Association resembled an independent state, with Cambridgeshire and Huntingdonshire the frontier zone on the edge of enemy territory open to attack. Not since the days of separate Anglo-Saxon kingdoms and the building of the Devil's Dyke had border fortifications against an enemy advancing from the west been necessary.

The Fens, then largely undrained, formed a natural barrier, with rivers and meres providing formidable water defences that forced any invader to take well defined and thus easily defended

Earith Bulwark.

routes; about three thousand pounds was raised by the Eastern Association in 1642 for fortifying the bridges across the Ouse[5]. All the fords from Earith to Eynesbury were made impassable and the earthworks at the latter place, known as Castle Hills, probably date from this time. Drawbridges were made at St Ives, Huntingdon and St Neots, while the artillery of Ely was taken to Wisbech to defend the passage across the Nene[6]. In 1642, or the following year, two large earthwork forts were built at Earith and Horsey Hill near Peterborough, while a small redoubt and other earthworks were thrown up at Huntingdon[7]. Another two small batteries were built at Sawtry and Leverington to command the Great North Road, and an isolated redoubt was thrown up at Stretham in Cambridgeshire as well as an irregular three-bastioned sconce near March[8].

The fort at Earith, known as the Bulwark, still stands in low marshy ground about one hundred and fifty yards north of Earith bridge. Although the topography has been greatly changed by the digging of the New Bedford River, one can still see how the fort guarded the original crossing of the Ouse and the causeway leading to Ely. The work is undocumented and its designer unknown, but whoever he was he was an accomplished and sophisticated military engineer. The fort is a large square-bastioned earthwork, clearly visible today although somewhat eroded, covering an area of just under five acres, each side about eighty yards long. The rampart, with a total length of over a thousand feet, was provided with a fausse braye and an outer ditch at the foot of the glacis, and there was a covered way with a *place d'armes* at the re-entering angles on the north and east faces and a large wing battery to the north-west[9].

The fort at Horsey Hill, even larger than the Bulwark, was sited to cover the crossing of the River Nene; it still remains as a large pentangle enclosing an area of about five acres. It too is a very sophisticated and professional design, with a berm or possibly a fausse braye in the ditch and a covered way. The entrance in the south curtain was covered by a slight salient which acted rather like a ravelin in defending the gate. Unlike Earith it does not appear to have been provided with a *place d'armes*[10].

Horsey Hill.

Cambridge, the headquarters of the Eastern Association, was not fortified until March, 1643, nearly eight months after the outbreak of war[11]. The existing defences of the city were a castle, standing on a hill to the north overlooking the main river crossing, and a ditch and earth rampart known as the King's Ditch that ran to the south and east, completing the natural moat of the River Cam.

The castle, consisting of a large motte, some ruinous curtain wall and a tumbledown gatehouse, was virtually derelict, fifty years previously having been described as "completely decayed"[12]. It was quickly rebuilt as a bastioned fort, "for preventing the enemy's inroad and the better to maintain the peace of this county"[13]. The modifications meant that fifteen houses and much of the crumbling stonework of the castle were demolished. On the east of the castle enclosure massive earth ramparts replaced the earlier fortifications, the resulting irregular trace following the natural contours of the site. Only on the west was the masonry wall left, as well as the gatehouse, the remainder of the perimeter being newly built with four large earthwork bastions. There was no ditch to the south and east as the ground fell away so steeply, although to the north and west there must have been a moat. Inside the castle bailey, which was over four acres in extent, a brick barracks for the garrison was built on the site of the old Guildhall[14].

The city itself was fortified by clearing out the King's Ditch and destroying all the bridges over the Cam except for the Magdalen and Silver Street bridges. A single cannon stood on Magdalen Bridge, a breastwork was built in Jesus Lane, and ten other guns were planted around the defensive circuit. At the end of the summer of 1643 it could be reported "Our town and castle are now very strongly fortified being encompassed with breastworks and bulwarks"[15].

Huntingdon was formed into one of the small barrier fortresses of the Eastern Association; its position on the route from Stamford and the North and its control of the crossing of the Ouse

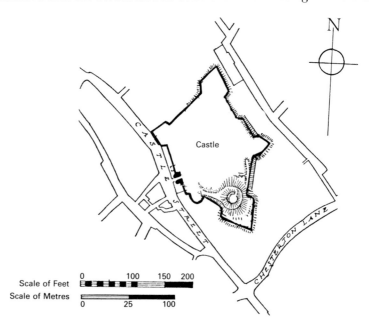

A plan of Cambridge Castle, from a map of 1688.

Scale of Feet

Scale of Metres

gave it strategic importance. On the outbreak of the Civil War the town, solidly Parliamentary in sympathy and with Oliver Cromwell as its MP, set about defending itself. A drawbridge was installed in the medieval bridge across the Ouse connecting Huntingdon with Godmanchester, light earthworks were constructed about the town, and to the east a tiny fort with rudimentary bastions was built[16]. Then the tide of war ebbed until the next year, when it surged back as the King's army advanced rapidly from Newark to retake Stamford and continue to Huntingdon.

The garrison had been warned, but all they could do was to clean out the ditch around the town and hastily pile up a breastwork before the gate[17]. When the Royalists appeared the Parliamentary garrison fired a single wild volley and fled. Charles I remained in Huntingdon for several days; his tactless collection of long-overdue taxes and the attentions of his troops to the townsfolk left him with substantially fewer supporters every day that he prolonged his visit. After a few days the King retreated to Stamford, and the fortifications of Huntingdon were never called upon to redeem themselves after their ignominious failure. If Huntingdon had been defended by stronger fortifications and stouter soldiers it would never have fallen; and if the King had been more vigorous in his campaign he might have thrust deep into the heartland of his enemies. As it was the cowardice and negligence of Parliament was balanced by the ineptitude of the King.

Lincolnshire was a model of the realm's political divisions; in 1642 neither party had overall control of the county. The rival factions each had its own administration. Boston, as a town full of merchants and puritans and "eminent in disloyalty", was the local Parliamentary stronghold, unfortified at first except for barricades with cannon in the principal streets[18]. Lincoln, the Royalist headquarters, needed only to put its castle and circuit of medieval walls into a state of defence and possibly build some breastworks about the gates. At Sleaford, Sir Robert Carr turned his house into a defence post against the Cavaliers while Torksey, Hougham, Belton, Gainsborough, Grantham and Bolingbroke Castle were all fortified for the two factions, although the amount of new work was negligible[19].

In the far south of the county Croyland, surrounded by water and clustering round the remains of its ancient abbey, unlike its neighbours declared for the King and began to build earthworks to supplement its water defences. Mr Ram, the rector of nearby and politically opposed Spalding, bombarded the town with letters full of earnest pleadings, pointing out to the townspeople the error of their ways, and in answer a group of armed Croyland men raided Spalding and carried its rector back to Croyland. When Parliamen-

*The fortifications of the
counties of
Cambridgeshire,
Huntingdonshire and
Lincolnshire.*

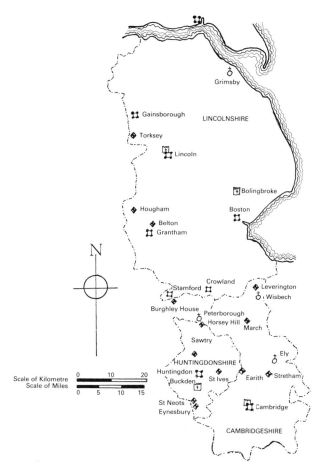

tary forces arrived to subdue the Royalist fortress Mr Ram was
pinioned to the north bulwark[21]. The besiegers, many of whom
came from Spalding, both failed to recognise their pastor and to
consider why anyone other than a prisoner would have been staked
out as a target. Perhaps they did recognise him and remembered
his sermons, as they fired numerous bullets at the recumbent
rector; it says little for their skill as marksmen and much for Mr
Ram's luck that they all missed. Croyland itself was not so fortunate
and was forced to surrender.

The main Royalist stronghold in the region at the start of the
war was Stamford, which the Cavaliers fortified by repairing the
old medieval walls. The ornate pile of Burghley House on the
outskirts of the town was also held until it was stormed by Cromwell
in 1643; at the same time Stamford was captured[22].

With the end of the war none of the region's fortifications served any useful purpose whatsoever, and they were all abandoned. The Jacobite rebellion of 1745 caused a brief flurry of alarm and several of the local gentry raised defences, but the only Jacobites to appear in Lincolnshire were prisoners on their way south[23].

The only response to the Napoleonic threat was the building of two batteries in 1804, one mounting ten 24-pounders at Goxhill Ferry opposite Hull and the other at Jenny Hill near Stallingborough armed with six 24-pounders[24]. They were built despite a report the previous year ruling out the coast of Lincolnshire as a point of invasion, and were dismantled when peace returned without ever having been in action. Nothing was built again until the twentieth century.

Immingham docks and the Admiralty oil stores at Killingholme were built in the early nineteen-hundreds, prompting the Committee of Imperial Defence to consider upgrading the defences of the Humber[25]. It proposed installing four 6-inch Mk VII on both banks of the river below Immingham, and in 1913

The casemates of the battery at Frieston Shore, with one of the searchlight positions in the distance.   Terry Ransome

work began on a two-gun battery at Stallingborough[26]. During the First World War two 4-inch were installed at New Clee and two 12-pounders at Killingholme. To add extra weight to the defences a 9.2-inch rail gun was stationed on the railway line at New Clee in 1915 and later in the war field defences and some pillboxes were constructed at Gibraltar Point[27]. After the Armistice the guns were withdrawn from the batteries, and they were not restored until the Second World War.

The invasion scare of 1940 resulted in the reinstatement of the battery at Stallingborough, rearmed with two smaller 4.7-inch ex-naval guns, and the building of four emergency batteries each equipped with two 6-inch ex-naval guns. One was at Grimsby, one at Mablethorpe and a third at Jackson's Corner north of Skegness[28]; the fourth, built at Frieston Shore to defend Boston, was a typical work with two concrete gunhouses and connecting shelters and magazines. The Frieston Shore battery's active life was short since it was badly placed; in 1942 it was closed and the guns transferred to a replacement battery with a wider arc of fire at Gibraltar Point[29]. Two beach batteries each armed with a' single 12-pounder, later replaced by a 4-inch, were built at Saltfleet and Northcoates. In addition to these there were in 1940 eleven 4-inch guns mounted on the backs of lorries, eight 6-pounders, two 3-pounders and twenty 2-pounders dug in along the shore[30]. In between the guns was a line of pillboxes, armed with standard infantry weapons, trenches and lines of anti-tank obstacles backed up by field artillery, a super-heavy battery of two rail-mounted 12-inch howitzers and an armoured train[31].

The GHQ Line ran through Cambridgeshire, following the course of the River Cam north of the city to Ely and Littleport, from where it ran north-westwards to Ramsey, Bourne and Newark-on-Trent. This section followed the line of the fenland drains and rivers, which were deepened where necessary to improve their capability as anti-tank obstacles. Most of the batteries were handed over to the Home Guard early in the war and all were closed by 1945.

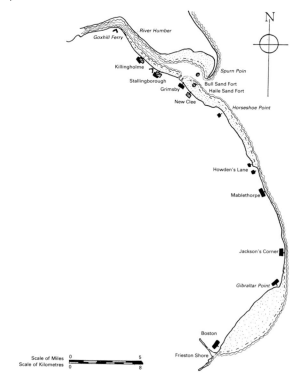

The batteries on the Humber, 1800–1945.

Scale of Miles 0   5
Scale of Kilometres 0   8

Notes and References

Chapter one

1 Uncle Toby, who dug fortifications in his bowling green, was the hero of Lawrence Sterne's *Tristram Shandy*. Prince Albert had built a small "wendy fort" for the Royal children in the grounds of Osborne House.
2 *L & P*, XIV (1), 398.
3 Ibid., 655.
4 Colvin, H. M., *The History of the King's Works* (London: Her Majesty's Stationery Office, 1982), iv (part 2), p. 371.
5 Ibid., pp. 373–374.
6 PRO SP 12.206(28).
7 BL Lansdowne MSS 58, no 66.
8 Kingston, A., *East Anglia in the Civil War* (London, 1902), p. 98.
9 Palmer, C. J., *The History of Great Yarmouth Designed as a Continuation of Manship's History* (Great Yarmouth, 1858), iii, p. 219.
10 Strang, Lord, *Britain in World Affairs* (London, 1961), p. 79.
11 Ibid.
12 BL Add. MSS 15,533.
13 PRO WO/55/1548/1.
14 Callender, G., *The Naval Side of British History* (London, 1924), pp. 194–197.
15 PRO WO 78/923.
16 Glover, R., *Britain at Bay* (London, 1973), p. 29.
17 Bartlett, C. J., *Great Britain and Sea Power: 1815–1853* (Oxford, 1963), p. 143.
18 Ibid., p. 192.
19 PRO WO/55/1548/19.
20 PRO WO/55/1548/4.
21 *Report of the Commissioners Appointed to Investigate the Defences of the United Kingdom* (London, 1860).
22 PRO WO/33/25.
23 Marder, A. J., *The Anatomy of British Sea Power; A History of British Naval Policy in the Pre-Dreadnought Era: 1880–1905* (London, 1964), p. 71.
24 Ibid.
25 Ibid., p. 81.
26 Hankey, Lord, *The Supreme Command* (London, 1961), ii, p. 215.
27 Woodward, Sir Llewellyn, *G. B. & the Great War of 1914–18* (London, 1967).
28 PRO WO/33/872.
29 Ibid.
30 Collier, B., *The Defence of the United Kingdom* (London: Her Majesty's Stationery Office, 1957), p. 51.
31 Ibid., p. 61.
32 Ibid.
33 Ibid., p. 85.
34 Ibid., p. 83.
35 Churchill, W. S., *The Second World War* (London, 1965), ii, p. 258.
36 PRO WO/199/99.
37 Ironside, W. E. 1st Baron Ironside, Kelly, D. and Macleod, Col. R., eds., *The Ironside Diaries, 1937–1940* (London, 1962), p. 344.

38 Ibid., pp. 368–369.
39 Ibid., p. 368.
40 Ibid.
41 Collier, pp. 299–300.
42 Hogg, I. V., *Anti-Aircraft: A History of Air Defence* (London, 1978), p. 130.

Chapter two

1 Kenyon, J. R., "Early artillery fortification in England and Wales", *Fort*, 1 (1976), pp. 22–25.
2 Colvin, *The History of the King's Works*, iv (2), p. 381.
3 Ibid., p. 567.
4 Ibid., p. 410.
5 *Victoria County History, Suffolk*, ii, p. 225.
6 Historic Monuments Commission, *Huntingdonshire*, pp. 20–21.
7 Sutcliffe, S., *Martello Towers* (Newton Abbot, 1972), p. 20.
8 PRO WO/55/1548/3.
9 Sutcliffe, p. 64.
10 Lewis, J. F., *Textbook of Fortification and Military Engineering* (War Office, 1893), p. 140.
11 *Report of the Commission Appointed to Enquire into the Construction, Condition and Cost of the Fortifications* (London: Stationery Office, 1869), p. xcix.
12 Clarke, G. S., *Fortification; its Past Achievements, Recent Developments and Future Progress*, 2nd ed. (London, 1907), p. 131.
13 Wills, H. *Pillboxes: A Study of UK Defences 1940* (London, 1985), pp. 15–39.
14 PRO WO/199/2527.
15 Ibid.
16 PRO WO/199/2.
17 PRO WO/199/36.
18 PRO WO/32/11674.

Chapter three

1 *VCH Kent*, ii, p. 284.
2 *L & P*, xiv (1), 655.
3 Colvin, H. M., *The History of the King's Works*, iv (2), p. 602.
4 BL Add. MSS 16,370, no. 4.
5 *Cal SP Dom*, 1547–65, xi, p. 424.
6 Colvin, p. 603.
7 Ibid.
8 *VCH Essex*, ii, p. 273.
9 Saunders, A. T., "Tilbury Fort and the development of artillery fortifications in the Thames Estuary", *Antiquaries Journal,* 40 (1960), p. 155.
10 BL Add. MSS 44,839.
11 Colvin, p. 604.
12 Mattingly, G., *The Defeat of the Spanish Armada* (London, 1959), pp. 327–329.
13 Saunders, p. 155.
14 Hakluyt, R. *The Principal Navigations of the English Nation* (Glasgow, 1903), p. 208.
15 Colvin, p. 604.
16 Saunders, p. 156.
17 *Cal SP Dom*, 1625–26, p. 194 & 202.
18 *Cal SP Dom*, 1629–31, p. 282.
19 *Cal SP Dom*, 1631–33, p. 96.
20 *Cal SP Dom*, 1636–37, p. 275.
21 *Cal SP Dom*, 1631–33, p. 295.

22 *Cal SP Dom*, 1649–50, p. 156.
23 *VCH Essex*, ii, p. 233.
24 Saunders, A. D., *Tilbury Fort* (HMSO, 1977), p. 11.
25 *VCH Essex*, ii, p. 233.
26 Ibid., p. 289.
27 *Cal SP Dom*, 1667, p. 278.
28 Ibid., p. 239.
29 Printed in Saunders "Tilbury fort and the development of artillery fortification in the Thames Estuary", as plate xxx.
30 Ibid., plate xxix.
31 Ibid., plate xxxi.
32 Ibid.
33 Ibid., p. 161.
34 Ibid., p. 163.
35 De Beer, E. S., ed. *The Diary of John Evelyn*, 6 vols. (Oxford, 1955), iii, p. 609.
36 Defoe, D. *Tour Through the Eastern Counties* (Ipswich, 1949), p. 18.
37 Saunders, *Tilbury Fort*, p. 14.
38 Saunders, "Tilbury Fort and the development of artillery fortifications", p. 164.
39 Ibid., p. 165.
40 Saunders, *Tilbury Fort*, p. 15.
41 BL Add. MSS 22,875. The number was the same in 1766, see PRO SP/41/39.
42 Saunders, "Tilbury Fort and the development of artillery fortifications", p. 164.
43 Saunders, *Tilbury Fort*, p. 18.
44 *Report on the Fortifications in the Medway Division, June 6th, 1778*. BL King's xvii, 16.b.
45 Saunders, *Tilbury Fort*, p. 15.
46 Saunders, "Tilbury Fort and the development of artillery fortifications", p. 165.
47 PRO WO/55/2589.
48 PRO WO/30/72.
49 Saunders, *Tilbury Fort*, p. 18. For details of the Trinity House contribution see Woodman, R., *Keepers of the Sea* (Lavenham, 1983), pp. 23–26.
50 Smith, V. T. C., *Defending London's River* (Rochester, 1985), p. 20.
51 PRO WO/44/614.
52 *Report of the Commissioners Appointed to Consider the Defences of the United Kingdom* (London, 1860), xliv, 129.
53 Ibid., xiv, 133.
54 Hogg, I. V., *The Coast Defences of England and Wales* (Newton Abbot, 1974), p. 100.
55 Ibid.
56 *Report of the Royal Commission with Reference to the Progress Made in the Construction of Fortifications for the Defence of the Dockyards and Naval Arsenals etc. of the United Kingdom* (London, 1868), ixc.
57 PRO CAB/7/6/9.
58 Hogg, pp. 98–99.
59 White, W., *Eastern England, from the Thames to the Humber*, 2 vols. (London, 1865), i, p. 278.
60 Ibid., p. 277.
61 Smith, p. 27.
62 Saunders, "Tilbury Fort and the development of artillery fortifications", p. 171.
63 Smith, p. 29.
64 Elton, Lord, *General Gordon* (London, 1954), p. 99.
65 PRO WO/30/106 II (139).
66 Elton, p. 99.
67 White, i, p. 254.
68 PRO WO/33/47/A96.
69 *Hansard*, 3rd Series, cccxxvi, 1046.

70 PRO WO/33/47/A96.
71 Ibid. and WO/32/744.
72 Smith, p. 36.
73 PRO CAB/7/6/9.
74 PRO WO/78/5725.
75 Portway, D., *Militant Don* (London, 1961), p. 42.
76 Wilson, J. D. "Later Nineteenth Century Defences of the Thames", *Journal of the Society for Army Historical Research*, 40.
77 PRO WO/33/395.
78 Information supplied by Major Tony Hill.
79 PRO WO/33/395.
80 PRO WO/33/593.
81 PRO WO/192/48.
82 PRO WO/33755 A1917.
83 PRO WO/78/4410.
84 Saunders, *Tilbury Fort*, p. 15.
85 PRO WO/78/5134.
86 PRO WO/192/190.
87 Collier, *The Defence of The United Kingdom*, p. 104n.
88 PRO WO/192/191.
89 PRO WO/78/5134.
90 PRO WO/199/2553.
91 PRO WO/199/1113.
92 PRO WO/199/2608.

Chapter four

1 *VCH Essex*, ii, p. 259.
2 Colvin, H. M., *The History of the King's Works*, iv (2), p. 470.
3 Ibid.
4 A total of £2,717 was spent on seven fortifications in Essex and on Landguard Point, so £400 is a rough average. Colvin, p. 470.
5 Jordan, W. K., *The Chronicle and Political Papers of King Edward VI* (London, 1966), p. 147.
6 From a map of 1656 printed in Sier, L. C., "The Fort, West Mersea", *Essex Review*, 30 (1921).
7 BL Cotton MSS Augustus. I.i.68.
8 APC, 1552–1554, p. 286.
9 Murdin, W., ed., *Burghley Papers*, 2 vols. (London, 1740–1759), ii, p. 541.
10 *APC*, 1625–1626, p. 294, and *VCH Essex*, ii, p. 281.
11 De Beer, *The Diary of John Evelyn*, iii, p. 177.
12 Cromwell, T., *History and Description of the Ancient Town and Borough of Colchester* (London, 1825), i, p. 110.
13 See map printed in Ross, Lieut. Col. W. G., *Military Engineering during the Great Civil War: 1642–49* (London, 1984), p. 139.
14 *Cal SP Dom*, 1648–1649, p. 136.
15 Ibid., 1651–1652, p. 604.
16 Ibid., 1655, p. 229.
17 Ibid., p. 389.
18 PRO WO/30/59 (73–119).
19 PRO WO/55/1548/1.
20 PRO WO/55/1548/2 and Maurice, Major-General Sir J. F., ed., *The Diary of Sir John Moore* (London, 1904), i, p. 266.
21 PRO WO/55/733.
22 *VCH Essex*, ii, p. 303.

23 PRO WO/30/100(123).
24 Ibid, (120)
25 Ibid, (164). A full description of the position is given in Ibid. (107–113).
26 PRO WO/55/733 Letter of 25 April, 1805.
27 PRO WO/55/1548/2.
28 PRO WO/55/733.
29 Ibid.
30 Walker, K., "Martello Towers and the Defence of North East Essex in the Napoleonic Wars." *Essex Review*, 47 (1958) p. 184.
31 *VCH Essex*, ii, p. 299.
32 Sutcliffe, *Martello Towers*, p. 106.
33 PRO WO/55/1548/4.
34 PRO WO/33/25.
35 PRO WO/33/329.
36 NAM Folio–7203–11.
37 PRO WO/33/50 A138.
38 PRO WO/33/51 A203.
39 PRO WO/78/2806.
40 The defence lines were based on the plans of the London Position set out in the *Handbook for the London Position* (War Office, 1903), see also Smith, V. T. C., "Chatham and London; The Changing Face of English Fortification, 1870–1918", *Post Medieveal Archaeology*, 19 (1985) p. 143.
41 Ibid.
42 PRO WO/33/872.
43 PRO WO/33/828.
44 Ibid.
45 PRO WO/192/85 and WO/192/60.
46 PRO WO/192/66.
47 PRO WO/199/85.
48 PRO WO/199/110 and WO/199/2556.
49 PRO WO/199/2608.
50 PRO WO/166/1909.
51 PRO WO/199/625.
52 Ibid.
53 PRO WO/199/2452.

Chapter five

1 Collier, *The Defence of the United Kingdom*, p. 322.
2 PRO WO/32/11064.
3 Mallory K., & Ottar, A., *The Architecture of Aggression* (London, 1973), p. 137.
4 Ibid., p. 143.
5 Ibid., p. 147.
6 *East Anglian Daily Times*, 21st August, 1967.

Chapter six

1 Wren, W. J., *Ports of the Eastern Counties* (Lavenham, 1976), p. 151.
2 Taylor, S., *The History and Antiquities of Harwich and Dovercourt Continued by S. Dale* (London, 1792), p. 18.
3 Turner, H. L., *Town Defences in England and Wales* (London, 1972), p. 126.
4 *VCH Essex*, ii, p. 269.
5 Weaver, L. J., *The Harwich Story* (Harwich, 1975), p. 13.
6 Wren, p. 152.
7 BL Cottonian MSS. Augustus I.i.56.
8 *APC*, 1552–54, p. 139.

9   *Cal SP Dom*, Addenda, 1547–65, vi, p. 424.
10 Weaver, p. 13.
11 Taylor, p. 27.
12 *VCH Essex*, ii, p. 272.
13 Ibid.
14 *APC*, 1576–77, p. 302.
15 *VCH Essex*, ii, p. 272.
16 Murdin, *Burghley Papers*, ii, p. 540–541.
17 Weaver, p. 13.
18 Ibid.
19 ERO D/DE/557/1.
20 Weaver, p. 25.
21 *VCH Essex*, ii, p. 224.
22 *APC*, 1625–26, p. 71.
23 *VCH Essex*, ii, p. 281.
24 *APC*, 1625–26, p. 71.
25 Ibid.
26 Ibid., p. 233.
27 *Cal SP Dom*, 1653–54, p. 84.
28 *VCH Essex*, ii, p. 288.
29 *Cal SP Dom* , 1667, p. 275.
30 Tomlinson, H., "The Ordnance Office and the King's Forts, 1660–1714", *Architectural History*, 1973, p. 3.
31 *VCH Essex*, ii, p. 293.
32 Trollope, C., "The Defences of Harwich", *Fort*, 11 (1983), p. 18.
33 *VCH Essex*, ii, p. 293.
34 Taylor, p. 236.
35 *VCH Essex*, ii, p. 300.
36 PRO WO/30/59 (73–119).
37 PRO SUPP/5–46.
38 PRO WO/30/78(5).
39 PRO WO/55/1548/2.
40 Trollope, p. 20.
41 Ibid.
42 PRO CAB/7/6/6.
43 Lindsey, W. H., *A Season at Harwich* (London, 1856), p. 74.
44 PRO WO/55/740.
45 Trollope, p. 21.
46 PRO WO/33/25.
47 Ibid.
48 PRO CAB 7/6/6.
49 PRO WO/33/48 A118.
50 PRO WO/78/5141.
51 Weaver, p. 147.
52 PRO WO/33/329 A940.
53 PRO CAB/7/6/9.
54 Ibid.
55 Trollope, p. 21.
56 PRO CAB/16/1(21).
57 NRO TC/34/1/10–13.
58 PRO WO/33/755 A1917.
59 *Norwich Mercury*, 30th August, 1914.
60 PRO WO/78/5135.
61 PRO WO/192/211.
62 Bates, M., *The Regional Military Histories; East Anglia* (Reading, 1974), p. 143.
63 Collier, *The Defence of the UK*, map facing p. 15.

64   Ibid., pp. 499–500.
65   Ibid., p. 480.
66   "A Radar Problem", *Casemate*, 13 (1983), p. 8.
67   PRO WO/192/206.
68   PRO WO/199/1173.
69   Ibid.
70   PRO WO/192/211.

Chapter seven

1   PRO WO/1548/3 (61–64).
2   PRO WO/1548/2.
3   An 1826 survey shows towers O and S as well as battery R (PRO WO/1548/18),
     but by 1839 they had all disappeared (PRO WO/55/1548/4).
4   PRO WO/55/740.
5   PRO WO/33/25.
6   Trollope "The Defences of Harwich", p. 23.
7   PRO WO/33/25.
8   Ibid.
9   Ibid. and Clarke, *Fortification*.
10   PRO CAB/7/6/6.
11   PRO CAB/7/6/9.
12   Sutcliffe, *Martello Towers*, p. 110.
13   Trollope, p. 25.
14   PRO CAB/17/109.
15   PRO WO/192/205.
16   PRO WO/78/4423.
17   PRO WO/33/942.
18   *Hansard*, 5th Series, (184) 1756.
19   PRO WO/192/205.
20   Trollope, p. 25.
21   PRO WO/199/1173.
22   PRO WO/192/205.
23   PRO WO/192/73.
24   PRO WO/199/625.
25   Collier, *The Defence of the United Kingdom*, p. 482.

Chapter eight

1   *L & P*, XIV (1), 655.
2   *L & P*, XVIII (1), 662, 740.
3   BL Cotton MSS Augustus I.i.56.
4   *APC*, 1552–54, pp. 139–140.
5   Leslie, J. F., *The History of Landguard Fort in Suffolk* (London, 1898), p. 5.
6   Trollope, "The Defences of Harwich", p. 10.
7   Jordan, *The Chronicle and Political Papers of King Edward VI*, p. 147.
8   BL Cotton MSS Augustus I.i.61 and Cotton MSS Augustus I.i.68.
9   *Cal SP Dom*, 1547–65, vi, p. 424 and *APC*, 1552–54, p. 286.
10   *APC*, 1556–58, p. 322.
11   *VCH Suffolk*, ii, p. 220.
12   PRO SP 12.206 (32).
13   PRO SP 12.208 (23).
14   Hist MSS Comm 8, 9th R. I, p. 250.
15   PRO SP 12.221 (23d).
16   PRO PC1 3/45.
17   *Cal SP Dom*, 1625–26, p. 92.

18 Ibid., p. 102.
19 *VCH Suffolk*, ii, p. 226.
20 *APC*, 1625–26, p. 241 and 335.
21 *APC*, 1627–28, p. 62.
22 PRO SP 16.37 (64) I.
23 *Cal SP Dom*, 1627–28, p. 582.
24 *Cal SP Dom*, 1629–31, p. 16.
25 *Cal SP Dom*, 1627–28, pp. 91–92.
26 *Cal SP Dom*, 1635, p. 121.
27 *Cal SP Dom*, 1635–36, p. 467.
28 *Cal SP Dom*, 1644–45, p. 527.
29 Leslie, p. 30.
30 *Cal SP Dom*, 1656–57, p. 282.
31 Hist MSS Comm 39, Hodgkin, p. 301.
32 *VCH Essex*, ii, p. 288.
33 Leslie, p. 41.
34 Hussey, F., *Suffolk Invasion* (Lavenham, 1983), p. 95.
35 Accounts of the attack on the fort are to be found in Hussey, pp. 61–106,
    Leslie, pp. 44–49 and *VCH Suffolk*, ii, 233.
36 *Cal SP Dom*, 1667, p. 272.
37 Ibid., p. 263.
38 Ibid.
39 Ibid.
40 Ibid., p. 267.
41 Ibid., p. 272.
42 *Cal SP Dom*, 1672–73, p. 384.
43 *Cal SP Dom*, 1683–84, p. 325.
44 PRO PC1 3/45.
45 Ibid.
46 *Cal SP Dom*, 1671–72, p. 4992.
47 *Cal Treasury Papers*, 1708–14, p. 66.
48 PRO PC1 3/45.
49 BL King's xxxix 62.A and PRO WO/78/320.
50 PRO WO/2269.
51 PRO WO/78/320.
52 BL King's xiii.5.
53 Leslie, pp. 70–76.
54 Ibid., p. 130.
55 PRO SP 41.39.
56 BL King's xvii.16.b.
57 BL King's xxxix, 62.b.
58 BL Add. MSS 15,533.
59 Trollope, p. 14.
60 Maurice, *The Diary of Sir John Moore*, i, p. 266.
61 PRO WO/55/1548/2.
62 PRO WO/33/100 (132).
63 PRO WO/30/78.
64 Trollope, pp. 11–12.
65 PRO WO/55/733.
66 Trollope, p. 14.
67 PRO WO/55/1548/4.
68 PRO WO/55/740.
69 Ibid.
70 PRO WO/33/25.
71 Leslie, p. 80.
72 White, W., *Eastern England from the Thames to the Humber*, p. 147.

73 *VCH Suffolk*, ii, p. 237.
74 PRO WO/33/25.
75 Leslie, p. 83.
76 *Hansard*, 3rd Series, (218) 983.
77 *Hansard*, 3rd Series, (238) 153.
78 Leslie, p. 86.
79 PRO WO/78/5156 and CAB/7/6/6.
80 Leslie, p. 87.
81 Clarke, *Fortification*.
82 PRO WO/78/2735.
83 PRO WO/33/47 A80.
84 PRO WO/78/5137.
85 Trollope, p. 14.
86 Leslie, p. 89.
87 PRO CAB/7/6/9.
88 Ibid.
89 PRO WO/78/5137.
90 PRO WO/78/5136.
91 PRO WO/78/5139.
92 Leslie, p. 49.
93 Wood, D. A., *Landguard Fort: Felixstowe* (Felixstowe, 1983), p. 30.
94 PRO WO/78/4162.
95 They were sold to a scrap firm, Messrs Forester of Swansea, *Hansard*, 5th
    Series (6), 687.
96 Boulton, D., *Objection Overruled* (London, 1967), p. 164–165.
97 PRO WO/78/5137.
98 PRO WO/192/209.
99 Ibid.
100 PRO WO/192/206.
101 PRO WO/199/1173.
102 PRO WO/192/209.

Chapter nine

1 Gardner, T., *An Historical Account of Dunwich* (London, 1754), p. 179.
2 Kenyon, J. R., "Early Artillery Fortifications in England and Wales," *Archeological Journal*, 138 (1981), p. 227.
3 *L & P*, XIV (1), 398.
4 *VCH Suffolk*, ii, p. 212.
5 *L & P*, XX (1), 717.
6 *Framlingham Castle* (HMSO, 1977), p. 19.
7 *APC*, 1586–87, p. 414.
8 PRO SP 12.208 (23).
9 Hist MSS Comm 32, 13 R IV, p. 443.
10 Ibid.
11 Hist MSS Comm 4, 5th R, p. 67.
12 Redstone, L. J., *Ipswich Through the Ages* (Ipswich, 1969), p. 145.
13 BL Add. MSS 23,655.
14 Ibid.
15 PRO WO/30/59 (73–119).
16 PRO WO/55/1548/3 (61–64).
17 PRO WO/30/67 (82).
18 PRO WO/1548/2 and *VCH Suffolk*, ii, p. 241.
19 Gillingwater, E., *An Historical Account of the Ancient Town of Lowestoft* (London,
    1790), p. 430.
20 Sutcliffe, S., *Martello Towers*, p. 111.

21   Adair, Lieut.-Col. Shafto, "The Defence of East Suffolk by Militia Artillery", *Lectures on National Defence* (London, 1871), part III, pp. 3–15.
22   PRO WO/33/25.
23   PRO WO/33/329 A940.
24   PRO WO/33/25.
25   Ibid.
26   PRO WO/192/217.
27   PRO WO/192/56.
28   PRO WO/199/2.
29   Collier, *The Defence of the United Kingdom*, p. 392.
30   *Eastern Daily Press*, 20th January, 1954.

Chapter ten

1   BL Cotton MSS Augustus I i.58.
2   *L & P*, XX (1), 717.
3   *APC*, 1578–80, p. 379–380.
4   Hist MSS Comm 55, Var. Coll. IV, p. 302–303.
5   Ibid., p. 303.
6   *APC*, 1586–87, p. 379–380.
7   Ibid.
8   *Cal SP Dom*, 1547–80, i, p. 643.
9   *APC*, 1586–87, p. 414.
10   Ibid.
11   *APC*, 1587, p. 313.
12   Hist MSS Comm 55, Var. Coll. IV, p. 290.
13   BL Add. MSS 22,249, fol. 53.
14   BL Add. MSS 11,802 n.
15   *Cal SP Dom*, 1625, p. 226.
16   Hist MSS Comm 31, 13th R IV, p. 443.
17   Clodd, H. P., *Aldeburgh; the History of an Ancient Town* (Ipswich, 1959), p. 114.
18   *APC*, 1627–28, p. 88.
19   Ibid., p. 184.
20   PRO SP 16. 245 (49).
21   *VCH Suffolk*, ii, p. 227.
22   Ibid.
23   Hale, N. F., *Notes about Aldeburgh* (London, 1870), p. 54.
24   Hist MSS Comm 31, 13th R IV, p. 310.
25   *Cal SP Dom*, 1667, pp. 223–224.
26   PRO SP 41. 49.
27   BL Add. MSS 8,987 art. 137.
28   PRO WO/30/67.
29   PRO WO/1548/3.
30   PRO WO/55/733.
31   PRO WO/55/1548/2.
32   Sutcliffe, *Martello Towers*, p. 112.
33   Anon. *Aldeborough Described* (London, 1820), p. 15.
34   Ibid., p. 14.
35   PRO WO/33/35.
36   Clodd, p. 121.
37   James, M. R., *A Warning to the Curious*.
38   Sutcliffe, p. 113.
39   PRO WO/192/214.
40   Ibid.
41   Ibid.
42   Ibid.
43   Ibid.

Chapter eleven

1   BL Cotton MSS Augustus I i.58.
2   *APC*, 1577–80, p. 643.
3   Ibid.
4   *Cal SP Dom*, 1547–80, p. 643.
5   *APC*, 1586–87, p. 114.
6   PRO SP 12.208 (23).
7   Hatfield MSS CP 142/98 (1).
8   Ibid.
9   PRO MP F 138.
10 Hist MSS Comm 31, 13th R IV, p. 443.
11 *Cal SP Dom*, 1625–26, p. 274.
12 Ibid., p. 296.
13 *APC*, 1625–26, p. 396.
14 Ibid.
15 PRO SP 16. 245. 49.
16 *VCH Suffolk*, ii, pp. 227–228.
17 *Cal SP Dom*, 1667, p. 219.
18 Hist MSS Comm 55, Var. coll. VII p.116.
19 Gardner, T., *An Historical Account of Dunwich* (London, 1754).
20 Macksey, P. J., *The Southwold Guns* (1st ed. no date) p. 1.
21 Ibid., p. 3. There is a persistent and absurd belief that these guns were given to Southwold by the Duke of Cumberland after he had captured them from the Jacobites at Culloden. This myth, fostered by Gardner, has been demolished by P. J. Macksey. The Privy Council ordered that Southwold be granted artillery early in November, 1745, and the guns were delivered in January, 1746. The battle of Culloden was not fought until 16th April, 1746. The legend might arise from the possibility that Cumberland landed at Southwold on his way back from Belgium in October, 1745. If he did so, then it must be certain that the town's dignitaries rushed to meet him and sought his aid in obtaining guns from the Ordnance.
22 Ibid., p. 5.
23 PRO WO/30/67 (75).
24 PRO WO/55/1548/3 (61–64).
25 Wake, R., *Southwold and its Vicinity; Ancient and Modern* (Yarmouth, 1839), p. 268.
26 Hist MSS Comm 55, Var. coll. VII, p. 117.
27 Ibid.
28 Wake, p. 268.
29 Ibid.
30 Macksey, p. 7.
31 PRO WO/55/1548/4.
32 Macksey, p. 8.
33 Baker, M. J., *The Story of Southwold* (Southwold, 1948), p. 133.
34 Ibid.
35 Ibid., p. 137.
36 PRO WO/192/79.
37 Macksey, p. 9.
38 PRO WO/192/79.
39 Baker, p. 138.
40 IWM H 40432.

Chapter twelve

1   *VCH Suffolk*, ii, p. 199.

2   *L & P*, XIII (1), 1405.
3   *L & P*, XV, 196.
4   *L & P*, XVI, 1488 (3), *L & P*, XVII, 220 (37). A contemporary plan (BL Cotton MSS Augustus I.i.58) shows a small crenellated tower with three guns firing through letterbox embrasures on the Ness as well as a three-gun earth battery on the cliff behind. This chart also shows a great number of works that were never built, including a similar blockhouse at Corton. The draughtsman of the plan knew that there was a fortification at Lowestoft; a note on the chart refers to "the blockhouse made at Lowestoft Rode", but he had never seen it and so put down a conventional representation of an artillery tower.
5   *L & P*, XX (1), 717.
6   Ibid.
7   Anon. [Hunt, B. P. W. S.] *Pakefield; The Church and Village* (Lowestoft, 1938), p. 49.
8   Ibid.
9   Gillingwater, E., *Historical account of the ancient town of Lowestoft* (1790), p. 416.
10 *APC*, 1578–1580, p. 379–380.
11 *APC*, 1586–1587.
12 PRO SP 12.208 (23).
13 Gillingwater, p. 416.
14 *VCH Suffolk*, ii, p. 221.
15 Ibid., p. 417.
16 Ibid., pp. 418–419.
17 *Cal SP Dom*, 1655–1656, p. 332.
18 Gillingwater, p. 420.
19 Ibid. The text is printed here in full.
20 Ibid., p. 421.
21 Ibid., p. 422.
22 *Cal SP Dom*, 1665–1666, p. 276.
23 Hist MSS Comm 29, Portland II, p. 267.
24 PRO PC 1/1/239.
25 Gillingwater, p. 415.
26 PRO SP 41/39.
27 Gillingwater, p. 422.
28 Ibid., p. 433.
29 Ibid.
30 BL King's, xvii.16.b.
31 PRO WO/30/59.
32 Ibid.
33 Gillingwater, p. 425.
34 Ibid., p. 426.
35 Ibid.
36 Ibid., p. 427.
37 Ibid., pp. 427–428.
38 Ibid.
39 PRO SUPP/5–46.
40 Ibid., p. 427.
41 Ibid., p. 433.
42 PRO WO/30/67 (99).
43 Ibid.
44 PRO WO/55/1548/3 (61–64).
45 PRO WO/30/100 (191) and PRO WO/55/733.
46 *VCH Suffolk*, ii, p. 240.
47 PRO WO/55/1548/4.
48 *An Act for the Improvement and Regulation of the Town of Lowestoft*, 10 July 1854, 17 & 18 Victoria Cap CLXI.
49 PRO WO/33/25.

50 PRO WO/44/63.
51 PRO MP.HH.340.
52 PRO WORK 43/1438 (13).
53 Bignold, Canon R., *The Chronicles of Carlton Colville* (Lowestoft, 1982), p. 12.
54 Hammerton, J. A., *The War Illustrated* No. 90, Vol. 4, p. 312.
55 Bignold, p. 14.
56 *Norwich Mercury*, Saturday, 29th April, 1916, p. 3.
57 PRO WO/33/776 (6).
58 Bignold, p. 81.
59 They were found in 1970 and restored the following year.
60 PRO WO/192/59.
61 PRO WO/192/216.
62 PRO WO/199/1167.
63 Ibid.
64 Ibid.
65 PRO WO/192/63.
66 PRO WO/199/1167.
67 PRO WO/192/216.
68 PRO WO/192/218.
69 PRO WO/192/215.
70 PRO WO/199/1167.
71 PRO WO/192/59.
72 Ibid.
73 PRO WO/199/2980/B.
74 Jenkins, F., *Port War* (Ipswich, 1946), p. 9.
75 PRO WO/199/119.
76 PRO WO/192/216.
77 PRO WO/192/218.
78 PRO WO/199/2452.

Chapter thirteen

1 Bradfer-Lawrence, H. L., *Castle Rising, a Short History & Description of the Castle with Illustrations* (King's Lynn, 1934), p. 2.
2 Hudson, W. and Tingey, J. C., *The Records of the City of Norwich*, 2 vols (Norwich, 1906), ii, p. 48.
3 Howlett, R., "Norwich artillery in the fourteenth century", *Norfolk Archaeology*, 16 (1907), p. 55.
4 Kenyon, J. R., "Early artillery fortifications in England and Wales", *Archaeological Journal*, 138 (1981), p. 211.
5 Blomefield, F., *An Essay towards a Topographical History of the County of Norfolk*, 11 vols (London, 1805–10), iv, p. 402.
6 Kenyon, p. 211.
7 Ibid., pp. 226–227.
8 Ibid.
9 Wright, J. A., *Brick Building in England* (London, 1972), p. 116.
10 Ibid., p. 119.
11 *L & P*, XIV (1), 116.
12 BL Lansdowne MSS 58 no 66 or Hatfield Plans vol. 2, p. 36.
13 Cozens-Hardy, B., "Norfolk coastal defences in 1588", *Norfolk Archaeology*, 26 (1938), p. 312.
14 Blomefield, iii, p. 229.
15 Hillen, H. J., *History of the Borough of King's Lynn*, 2 vols (Norwich and London, 1907), i, p. 294.
16 O'Neil, B. H. St. J., "The fortification of Weybourne Hope in 1588," *Norfolk Archaeology*, 27 (1945) p. 253.

17 Ibid.
18 Ibid., p. 252.
19 Ibid.
20 Cozens-Hardy, p. 310.
21 BL Lansdowne MSS 58 no 66 or Hatfield Plans, vol. 2, p. 36.
22 BL Lansdowne MSS 58 no 66 or Hatfield Plans, vol. 2, p. 36.
23 O'Neil, p. 256.
24 O'Neil, p. 262.
25 *APC*, 1588, p. 116.
26 *Cal SP Dom*, 1589, p. 273.
27 Cozens-Hardy, p. 312.
28 Ibid.
29 Dunn, R. M., ed., "Norfolk Lieutenancy Journal: 1660–1676," *Norfolk Record Society*, 45 (1977), p. 100.
30 Blomefield, iii, p. 383.
31 Ibid.
32 Ibid.
33 Ibid.
34 Armstrong, J. M., *History and Antiquities of Norwich* (Norwich, 1781), p. 165.
35 Kirkpatrick, J., *Notes Concerning Norwich Castle* (London, 1847), p. 3.
36 Ibid.
37 Dunn, p. 90.
38 Ibid., p. 133.
39 PRO WO/30/59 (73–119).
40 Ibid.
41 Dutt, W. A., *The Norfolk and Suffolk Coast* (London, 1909), pp. 220–221.
42 PRO WO/30/58 (5).
43 PRO WO/30/100 (152).
44 Ibid.
45 Ibid.
46 Ibid.
47 Matchet, J. and Stevenson, H., *The Norfolk and Norwich Remembrancer and Vade Mecum*, 2nd edition (Norwich, 1822), p. 74.
48 PRO WO/30/100 (152).
49 Ibid.
50 Matchet and Stevenson, p. 102.
51 Ketton-Cremer, R. W., *Norfolk Portraits* (London, 1949), p. 166.
52 Ibid.
53 PRO WO/13/4474.
54 PRO WO/55/1548/4.
55 PRO WO/33/25.
56 Ibid.
57 PRO WO/33/329/A940.
58 Campbell Erroll, A., *A History of Sheringham and Beeston Regis* (Norwich, 1970), p. 74.
59 PRO WO/33/779(6).
60 PRO WO/33/828.
61 Churchill, W. S., *My Early Life* (London, 1958), p. 167.
62 Balfour, G., *The Armoured Train; Its Development and Usage* (London, 1981).
63 Rawlinson, A., *The Defence of London* (London, 1923), p. 132.
64 PRO WO/33/828.
65 *Eastern Daily Press*, files for 1937.
66 Collier, *The Defence of the United Kingdom*, p. 83.
67 PRO WO/199/85.
68 Ironside, W. E., Kelly, D. and Macleod, R., eds, *The Ironside Diaries, 1937–1940* (London, 1962), p. 368.

69 Collier, p. 131.
70 PRO WO/199/1113.
71 PRO WO/33/1861.
72 PRO WO/192/67.
73 PRO WO/192/62.
74 NRO N/EN/8/23.
75 Ibid.
76 Collier, p. 479.
77 Ibid., p. 217.
78 Ibid., p. 229.
79 Ibid., p. 321.
80 Mallory and Ottar, *The Architecture of Aggression*, p. 131.
81 PRO WO/199/2592.
82 PRO WO/199/2452.
83 *Eastern Daily Press*, 3 October, 1958.

Chapter fourteen

1 Kenyon, "Early artillery fortifications in England and Wales", *Archaeological Journal*, 138 (1981), p. 213.
2 Rutledge, P., ed., "Great Yarmouth Assembly minutes; 1345–1538", *Norfolk Record Society*, 39 (1970), p. 53.
3 *L & P*, I (1), 686–687.
4 *L & P*, XXI (2), 456.
5 BL Cotton MSS Augustus I.i.58.
6 *L & P*, XX (1), 717.
7 Ibid.
8 Palmer, *The History of Great Yarmouth*, p. 155.
9 Swinden, H., *The History and Antiquities of the Ancient Burgh of Great Yarmouth in the County of Norfolk* (Norwich, 1772), p. 46.
10 Castle, Major M. A., *The History of the Yarmouth Battery: 1569–1926* (Norwich & Great Yarmouth, 1927) p. 2.
11 Manship, H., C. J. Palmer, ed., *The History of Great Yarmouth* (Great Yarmouth, 1854), p. 46.
12 BL Cotton MSS Augustus I.i.74.
13 Ibid.
14 Swinden, p. 96.
15 Ibid., p. 101.
16 Bodleian Library, Tanner MSS vol. 241 fol. 60.
17 Swinden, p. 102.
18 Ibid.
19 O'Neil, B. H. St. J., "A plan of the fortifications of Yarmouth in 1588", *Norfolk Archaeology*, 28 (1945), p. 4.
20 BL 186 h i (37).
21 PRO WO/78/1402 and Manship, p. 47.
22 Swinden, p. 98.
23 de Gomme's map of Great Yarmouth, 1688, PRO MR 487.
24 Manship, p. 48.
25 Ibid.
26 PRO MR 487.
27 Palmer, C. J., *The Perlustration of Great Yarmouth*, 3 vols (Great Yarmouth, 1875), i, p. 94 and Swinden, p. 108.
28 Palmer, *The Perlustration of Great Yarmouth*, i, p. 94.
29 Swinden, p. 110.
30 Manship, pp. 276–277.
31 *APC*, 1625–1626, p. 320.

32   Swinden, p. 162.
33   PRO WO/55/1548/15.
34   Swinden, p. 162.
35   *Cal SP Dom*, 1625–1626, I, p. 305.
36   Hedges, A. C., *Yarmouth is an Antient Town* (Norwich, 1959), p. 29.
37   Castle, p. 15.
38   Swinden, p. 129.
39   Manship, p. 277.
40   Manship, p. 434.
41   Palmer, *The Perlustration of Great Yarmouth*, iii, p. 219.
42   *Cal SP Dom*, 1655–1656, p. 332.
43   *Calendar of Treasury Books*, vii (2), p. 820.
44   *Cal SP Dom*, 1667, p. 224.
45   Ibid.
46   Palmer, *The Perlustration of Great Yarmouth*, iii, p. 220.
47   Ibid.
48   Ibid.
49   Hist MSS Comm 75, Downshire II, p. 539.
50   PRO WO/55/1548/15.
51   Ibid.
52   Ibid.
53   BL King's xvii 16 b.
54   NRO C/36/20 (9).
55   Palmer, *The History and Antiquities of Great Yarmouth*, p. 82.
56   PRO WO/30/59 (73–119).
57   PRO WO/30/67.
58   PRO WO/30/101 (29).
59   PRO WO/30/67.
60   PRO WO/30/101 (21).
61   PRO WO/30/67.
62   Ibid.
63   PRO WO/30/100(165).
64   Ibid.
65   PRO WO/30/100(19).
66   PRO WO/55/733 and PRO WO/55/734.
67   PRO WO/55/1548/18.
68   Preston, I., *The Picture of Yarmouth* (Great Yarmouth, 1819), p. 144.
69   PRO WO/44/62.
70   Ibid and PRO WO/55/740.
71   Ecclestone, A. W. and J. L., *The Rise of Great Yarmouth* (Great Yarmouth, 1959), p. 56.
72   PRO WO/55/1548/4.
73   Ibid.
74   Crisp, W. F., *A Chronological History of Great Yarmouth* (Great Yarmouth, 1885), p. 47.
75   PRO WO/33/10 and *Yarmouth Archaeology*, vol. 2 No 3, p. 92.
76   Palmer, *The Perlustration of Great Yarmouth*, iii, p. 220.
77   *Yarmouth Archaeology*, vol 2 No. 3, p. 90.
78   Ibid., p. 94.
79   PRO WO/33/25.
80   Ibid.
81   PRO MP HH 368.
82   Ecclestone, *The Rise of Great Yarmouth*, p. 9.
83   Ecclestone, A. W., *Great Yarmouth: 1886–1936* (Great Yarmouth, 1977), p. 88.
84   Holmes, J. S., *Diary of the Norfolk Artillery: 1853–1909* (Norwich, 1909), p. 121.

85   Ibid., p. 156.
86   NRO TC 34/1/10–13.
87   Ibid.
88   Holmes, p. 121.
89   Castle, p. 30.
90   Ibid., p. 32.
91   NRO TC 34/1 (11).
92   Ibid.
93   PRO WO/78/4405.
94   Banks, A., *A Military Atlas of the First World War* (London, 1975), p. 286;
     Chamberlain, G., *Airships Cardington* (Lavenham, 1984), pp. 33–37.
95   PRO WO/33/828.
96   *Eastern Evening News*, 24 July, 1948.
97   PRO WO/192/225.
98   PRO WO/192/57.
99   PRO WO/192/226.
100 Ibid.
101 PRO WO/33/10376.
102 PRO WO/192/57.
103 PRO WO/199/1120.
104 PRO WO/192/1121.
105 NRO Y/TR 650 1.
106 Ibid.
107 Ibid.
108 Ibid.

Chapter fifteen

1   Wren, *Ports of the Eastern Counties*, p. 41.
2   Carter, A. and Clarke, H., *Excavations in King's Lynn, 1963–1970* (London,
    1977), p. 435.
3   Smith, T. P., "The medieval town defences of King's Lynn". *Journal of British
    Archaeology* 33 (1970), p. 62.
4   Kenyon, J. R., "Early artillery fortifications in England and Wales". *Archae-
    ological Journal*, 138 (1981), p. 213.
5   *L & P*, XIV (1), 655.
6   *L & P*, XVII (1), 1405.
7   *L & P*, XV, 372 and XVI, 456.
8   Carter and Clarke, p. 436.
9   Harrod, H., *Report on the Deeds & Records of the Borough of King's Lynn* (King's
    Lynn, 1874), frontispiece.
10 Hillen, *History of the Borough of King's Lynn*, ii, p. 763.
11 Cozens-Hardy, "Norfolk coastal defences in 1588", *Norfolk Archaeology*, 26
    (1938), p. 311.
12 Ibid., p. 312.
13 *Post-Medieval Archaeology*, 2 (1969), p. 177.
14 Carter and Clarke, p. 436.
15 Hillen, i, p. 333.
16 *Cal SP Dom*, 1627–28, p. 156.
17 *APC*, 1625–26, p. 433.
18 *Cal SP Dom*, 1627–28, p. 156.
19 *Cal SP Dom*, 1629–31, pp. 222, 248 and Hillen, i, p. 333.
20 Hillen, i, p: 349.
21 Ibid.
22 Carter and Clarke, p. 437.
23 Hist MSS Comm 6, 7th R, I, p. 559.

24 Blomefield, *History of Norfolk*, iii, p. 387.
25 *Post-Medieval Archaeology,* II, p. 177.
26 Ibid.
27 Hist MSS Comm 6, 7th R, I, p. 564.
28 Hillen, i, p. 362.
29 NRO BL/4/14/17.
30 Hist MSS Com 5, 6th R, p. 15.
31 *Cal SP Dom*, 1652–53, p. 280.
32 *Martial Lore* (King's Lynn, 1918), p. 9.
33 *Cal SP Dom*, 1652–53, p. 574.
34 Richards, W., *The History of Lynn* (King's Lynn, 1812), ii, p. 845 and PRO PC2/98.
35 Defoe, *Tour through the Eastern Counties*, p. 100.
36 PRO PC2/98.
37 Hillen, ii, p. 489.
38 Ibid., p. 764.
39 Ibid., p. 765.
40 Ibid., p. 764.
41 PRO WO/30/100 (65).
42 PRO WO/30/100 (84).
43 Richards, ii, p. 717.
44 Carter and Clarke, p. 438.
45 PRO WO/30/100 (163).
46 Cooke, G. A., *A Topographical and Statistical Description of the County of Norfolk* (London, 1822), p. 94.
47 Hillen, ii, p. 764.
48 PRO WO/55/1548/4.
49 Ibid.
50 PRO WO/33/25.
51 White, W., *Directory of Norfolk*, 1890.
52 Hogg, *Anti-Aircraft; a History of Air Defence*, p. 33.
53 PRO WO/199/1110.
54 Ibid.
55 Collier, *The Defence of the United Kingdom*, p. 514.

Chapter sixteen

1 Kenyon, "Early artillery fortifications in England and Wales", *Archaeological Journal* 138 (1981) p. 228.
2 *L & P*, XIV (1), 655.
3 Hist MSS Comm 23, Cowper, I, pp. 20–21.
4 *Cal SP Dom*, 1625–26, p. 117.
5 Kingston, *East Anglia in the Civil War*, p. 98.
6 Ibid., p. 233.
7 Hist Mon Comm *Hunts*, p. 214.
8 Muir, R. and Taylor, C., *Visions of the Past* (London, 1983), p. 172. See also Harrington, P., "English Civil War fortifications", *Fort* 15 (1987).
9 Hist Mon Comm *Hunts*, pp. 20–21.
10 Ibid.
11 Kingston, p. 91.
12 Hist Mon Comm *Cambridge*, ii, p. 305.
13 Kingston, p. 91.
14 Hist Mon Comm *Cambridge*, ii, p. 306.
15 Kingston, p. 115.
16 Hist Mon Comm *Hunts*, p. 162.

17 Kingston, p. 215.
18 Rogers, A., *A History of Lincolnshire* (Henley, 1970), p. 44.
19 Rogers, p. 155.
20 Kingston, p. 106.
21 Rogers, p. 155.
22 *VCH Lincolnshire*, ii, p. 282.
23 PRO WO/30/62.
24 PRO WO/192/233.
25 Ibid.
26 Ibid.
27 Ibid.
28 PRO WO/199/1110.
29 Hudson, T. J., *Evaluation of the Remains of Coast Defence Positions at Horseshoe Point* (unpublished MS).
30 Ibid.
31 Ibid.

Bibliography

Adair, Lieut.-Col., S. *Lectures on National Defence*. London, 1871.

Anon. *Aldeborough Described*. London, 1820.

Armstrong, J. M. *History and Antiquities of Norwich*. Norwich, 1781.

Balfour, G. *The Armoured Train; Its Development and Usage*. B. T. Batsford, London, 1981.

Baker, M. J. *The Story of Southwold*. Southwold, 1948.

Banks, A. *A Military Atlas of the First World War*. Heinemann, London, 1975.

Bartlett, C. J. *Great Britain and Sea Power: 1815–1853*. Oxford University Press, Oxford, 1963.

Bates, M. *The Regional Military Histories: East Anglia*. Osprey, Reading, 1974.

Bignold, Canon R. *The Chronicles of Carlton Colville*. Lowestoft, 1982.

Blomefield, F. *An Essay towards a Topographical History of the County of Norfolk*, 11 vols. London, 1805–10.

Boulton, D. *Objection Overruled*. London, 1967.

Bradfer-Lawrence, H. L. *Castle Rising, a Short History and Description of the Castle with Illustrations*. King's Lynn, 1934.

Campbell Erroll, A. *A History of Sheringham and Beeston Regis*. Norwich, 1970.

Callender, G. *The Naval Side of British History*. Christophers, London, 1924.

Carter, A., and Clarke, H. *Excavations in King's Lynn; 1963–1970*. London, 1977.

Castle, Major M. A. *The History of the Yarmouth Battery*. Jarrold and Sons, Norwich, 1927.

Clarke, G. S. *Fortification: Its Past Achievements, Recent Developments and Future Progress*. 2nd ed., London, 1907.

Clodd, H. P. *Aldeburgh; the History of an Ancient Town*. Ipswich, 1959.

Churchill, W. S. *The Second World War*. Cassell, London, 1950.

Collier, B. *The Defence of the United Kingdom*. Her Majesty's Stationery Office, London, 1957.

Colvin, H. M. *The History of the King's Works*, 5 vols. Her Majesty's Stationery Office, London, 1982.

Cooke, G. A. *A Topographical and Statistical Description of the County of Norfolk*. London, 1822.

Cozens-Hardy, B. "Norfolk coastal defences in 1588", *Norfolk Archaeology*. 26 (1938).

Crisp, W. F. *A Chronological History of Great Yarmouth*. Great Yarmouth, 1885.

Cromwell, T. *History and Description of the Ancient Town and Borough of Colchester*. London, 1825.

De Beer, E. S., ed. *The Diary of John Evelyn*, 6 vols. Oxford University Press, Oxford, 1955.

Defoe, D. *Tour through the Eastern Counties*. East Anglian Magazine, Ipswich, 1949.

Duffy, C. *Siege Warfare*. Routledge and Kegan Paul, London, 1979.

Dunn, R. M., ed. "Norfolk Lieutenancy Journal: 1660–1676", *Norfolk Record Society* 45 (1977).

Dutt, W. A. *The Norfolk and Suffolk Coast*. London, 1909.

Ecclestone, A. W. *Great Yarmouth: 1886–1936*. Great Yarmouth, 1977.

Ecclestone, A. W. and J. L. *The Rise of Great Yarmouth*. Great Yarmouth, 1959.

Elton, Lord. *General Gordon*. London, 1954.

Gardner, T. *An Historical Account of Dunwich*. London, 1754.

Gillingwater, E. *An Historical Account of the Ancient Town of Lowestoft*. London, 1790.

Glover, R. *Britain at Bay*. George Allen and Unwin, London, 1973.

Hakluyt, R. *The Principal Navigations of the English Nation*. Glasgow, 1903.

Hale, N. F. *Notes about Aldeburgh*. London, 1870.

Hammerton, J. A. *The War Illustrated*. 9 vols, Amalgamated Press, London, 1914–19.

Harrington, P. "English Civil War fortifications", *Fort* 15 (1987).

Harrod, H. *Report on the Deeds and Records of the Borough of King's Lynn*. King's Lynn, 1874.

Hedges, A. A. C. *Yarmouth is an Antient Town*. Great Yarmouth Corporation, 1959.

Hillen, H. J. *History of the Borough of King's Lynn*, 2 vols. Norwich and London, 1907.

Hogg, I. V. *Anti-Aircraft; A History of Air Defence*. Macdonald and Jane's, London, 1978.

Coast Defences of England and Wales. David and Charles, Newton Abbot, 1974.

Holmes, J. S. *Diary of the Norfolk Artillery: 1853–1909*. Jarrold and Sons, Norwich, 1909.

Howlett, R. "Norwich artillery in the fourteenth century", *Norfolk Archaeology*, 16 (1907).

Hudson, W., and Tingey, J. C. *The Records of the City of Norwich*, 2 vols. Norwich, 1906.

Hughes, Q. *Military Architecture*. Hugh Evelyn, London, 1974.

Hussey, F. *Suffolk Invasion*. Terence Dalton, Lavenham, 1983.

Jenkins, F. *Port War*. W. S. Cowell, Ipswich, 1946.

Jordan, W. K. *The Chronicle and Political Papers of King Edward VI*. London, 1966.

Kenyon, J. R. "Early artillery fortification in England and Wales", *Fort*, 1 (1976).

"Early artillery fortifications in England and Wales", *Archeological Journal*, 138 (1981).

Ironside, W. E., 1st Baron Ironside. *The Ironside Diaries, 1937–1940*, ed. Kelly, D. and Macleod, Col. R. Constable, London, 1962.

Ketton-Cremer, R. W., *Norfolk Portraits*, Faber and Faber, London, 1949.

Kingston, A. *East Anglia in The Civil War*. London, 1902.

Kirkpatrick, J. *Notes concerning Norwich Castle*. London, 1847.

Leslie, J. F. *The History of Landguard Fort in Suffolk*. Eyre and Spottiswoode, London, 1898.

Lewis, J. F. *Fortification for English Engineers*. Chatham, 1890.

Textbook of Fortification and Military Engineering Part II. War Office, London, 1893.

Lindsey, W. H. *A Season at Harwich*. London, 1856.

Macksey, P. J. *The Southwold Guns*, 1st ed. No date.

Mallory, K., and Ottar, A. *The Architecture of Aggression*. Architectural Press, London, 1973.

Manship, H. (ed. C. J. Palmer). *The History of Great Yarmouth*. Great Yarmouth, 1854.

Matchet, J., and Stevenson, H. *The Norfolk and Norwich Remembrancer and Vade Mecum*, 2nd ed. Norwich, 1822.

Mattingly, G. *The Defeat of the Spanish Armada*. Jonathan Cape, London, 1959.

Maurice, Maj.-Gen. Sir J. F. *The Diary of Sir John Moore*, 2 vols. London, 1904.

Muir, R., and Taylor, C. *Visions of the Past*. London, 1983.

Murdin, W., (ed.) *Burghley Papers*, 2 vols. London, 1740–1759.

O'Neil, B. H. St J. *Castles and Cannon: A Study of Early Artillery Fortifications in England*. Oxford University Press, Oxford, 1960.

"The fortification of Weybourne Hope in 1588", *Norfolk Archaeology*, 27 (1941).

"A plan of the fortifications of Yarmouth in 1588", *Norfolk Archaeology*, 28 (1945).

Palmer, C. J. *The History of Great Yarmouth Designed as a Continuation of Manship's History*. Great Yarmouth, 1858.

The Perlustration of Great Yarmouth, 3 vols. Great Yarmouth, 1875.

Portway, D. *Militant Don*. London, 1961.

Porter, Maj.-Gen. W. *History of the Corps of Royal Engineers*, 2 vols. London, 1889.

Preston, I. *The Picture of Yarmouth*. Great Yarmouth, 1819.

Rawlinson, A. *The Defence of London*. London, 1923.

Redstone, L. J. *Ipswich through the Ages*. East Anglian Magazine, Ipswich, 1969.

Richards, W. *The History of Lynn*, 2 vols. King's Lynn, 1812.

Rogers, A. *A History of Lincolnshire*. Henley, 1970.

Ross, Lieut.-Col. W. G. *Military Engineering during the Great Civil War: 1642–49.* Ken Trotman, London, 1984.

Saunders, A. D. "Tilbury Fort and the development of artillery fortification in the Thames Estuary", *Antiquaries Journal*, XL (1960).
   Tilbury Fort. Her Majesty's Stationery Office, London, 1977.

Sier, L. C. "The Fort, East Mersea", *Essex Review*, 30, (1921).

Smith, T. P. "The Medieval town defences of King's Lynn", *Journal of British Archaeology*, 33 (1970).

Smith, V. T. C. "Chatham and London; The changing face of English fortification, 1870–1918", *Post Medieval Archaeology*, 19 (1985).
   Defending London's River. North Kent Books, Rochester, 1985.

Strang, Lord, *Britain in World Affairs.* André Deutsch, London, 1961.

Sutcliffe, S. *Martello Towers.* David and Charles, Newton Abbot, 1972.

Swinden, H. *The History and Antiquities of the Ancient Burgh of Great Yarmouth in the County of Norfolk.* Norwich, 1772.

Taylor, S. *The History and Antiquities of Harwich and Dovercourt continued by S. Dale.* London, 1730.

Tomlinson, H. "The Ordnance Office and the King's Forts, 1600–1714", *Architectural History*, (1973).

Trollope, C. "The defences of Harwich", *Fort*, 11 (1983).

Turner, H. L. *Town Defences in England and Wales.* London, 1972.

Wake, R. *Southwold and its Vicinity; Ancient and Modern.* Yarmouth, 1839.

Walker, K. "Martello towers and the defence of north east Essex in the Napoleonic Wars", *Essex Review*, 47 (1958).

White, W. *Eastern England from the Thames to the Humber.* London, 1865.

Wills, H. *Pillboxes: A Study of UK Defences 1940.* Leo Cooper, London, 1985.

Wilson, J. D. "Later nineteenth century defences of the Thames", *Journal of the Society for Army Historical Research*, 41.

Weaver, L. J. *The Harwich Story.* Harwich, 1975.

Wood, D. *Landguard Fort: Felixstowe.* Felixstowe, 1983.

Wren, W. J. *Ports of the Eastern Counties.* Terence Dalton, Lavenham, 1976.

Wright, J. A. *Brick Buildings in England.* London, 1972.

Glossary

Banquette	Footstand for infantry behind a parapet.
Barbette	A mound or platform from which guns fire over a parapet without requiring the cutting of an embrasure.
Barbican	An outer fortification protecting a gateway.
Bartizan	A turret projecting from the top of a tower or wall.
Bastion	A projection from the side of a fortification from which flanking fire can be directed.
Berm	A ridge below a parapet to prevent earth falling into the ditch.
Blockhouse	Small detached fort.
Bomb-proof	A building or a part of the defences constructed to withstand cannon balls or shells.
Bulwark	A loose term applied to a bastion, a battery or a blockhouse.
Caponier	A chamber or sheltered passage across the ditch providing flanking fire.
Casemate	A vaulted chamber providing an emplacement for artillery.
Cavalier	A raised platform for guns.
Citadel	The main fortress of a town, placed to dominate or protect it.
Cordon	A horizontal moulding beneath the parapet of a curtain wall.
Counterscarp	The outer side of a ditch.
Covered way	A broad space on the top of the counterscarp protected by a parapet.
Cunette	A small outer moat at the foot of the glacis.
Cupola	Armoured dome for guns, searchlights or observation equipment.
Curtain	A section of wall or rampart between towers or bastions.
Embrasure	An opening in a parapet through which a gun can be fired.

Enceinte	Main line of fortifications surrounding a town, castle or fort.
Expense magazine	A store near the gun emplacements containing enough ammunition for immediate use.
Fausse-braye	Secondary enceinte outside the main rampart and at a lower level.
Flanker	Casemate or embrasure sited to provide flanking fire along the line of a curtain wall.
Fleche	A small arrow-shaped work.
Gabions	Large baskets filled with earth providing protection for men and guns.
Glacis	The slope outside a ditch or wall.
Gorge	The rear of a fortification.
Half-moon	Outwork, often rounded or segmented in plan.
Loop	An opening in a wall through which a gun can be fired.
Lunette	A large advance work shaped like a bastion.
Murderer	Casemate or emplacement for a cannon to provide flanking fire.
Orillons	Projections at the rear corners of a bastion designed to mask the embrasures covering the adjoining flanks.
Palisade	A fence of strong timber stakes set in the ground.
Parapet	Low wall or mound of earth along the front edge of a rampart.
Place d'armes	Space for troops to assemble on the covered way.
Platform	The floor or surface on which guns are mounted.
Postern	A secondary entrance to a fort or castle
Rampart	A mass of earth formed behind the curtain wall.
Ravelin	An outwork, normally triangular in shape, in front of a curtain.
Redan	A triangular outwork, similar to but slightly larger than a fleche.
Revetment	Retaining wall in a ditch, built to face earthen ramparts.
Salient	The outward point of a bastion.

Sally-port	Subsidiary gateway, often concealed, through which troops can make a "sally" or attack on besieging forces.
Scarp	The inner side of a ditch.
Sconce	A detached fort.
Tenaille	Small low-lying work, placed between adjoining bastions to provide additional cover for the curtain wall.
Terreplein	Level ground behind a parapet providing a platform for guns.
Trace	The plan of a fortification.
Traverse	Mound of earth thrown up to stop enfilade fire.
Twydall profile	Gentle slope from the crest of a fortification to about fifteen feet below ground level with a steel fence and barbed wire at its foot.
Vamure	A parapet, often of turf, erected on the forward edge of a rampart.

Abbreviations

AA	Anti-aircraft.
AT	Anti-tank.
BL	Breech-loader.
BLC	Breech-loading converted (converted from QF to BL).
BOP	Battery observation post.
CASL	Coast artillery searchlight.
CP	Central pivot.
GHQ	General headquarters.
HP	Hydro-pneumatic.
IGF	Inspector-General of Fortifications.
ML	Muzzle-loader.
QF	Quick-firer.
RML	Rifled muzzle-loader.
SB	Smooth-bore.

Artillery

THE variety of artillery pieces was enormous. This appendix does not intend to be exhaustive but only to give the average details of each particular type. It has been limited to the guns that were emplaced in East Anglia and does not include details of rarer weapons that were installed elsewhere.

Sixteenth and seventeenth century cannon

By the mid sixteenth century the types and titles of the more common guns in use had been roughly standardised.

Type of gun	Approx. weight	Weight of shot	Calibre	Extreme range
Base	200 lb.	0.33 lb.	1.25 in.	800 yards
Robinet	300 lb.	0.75 lb.	1.5 in.	900 yards
Falconet	400 lb.	1.25 lb.	2.25 in.	1,000 yards
Sling	600 lb.	2.5 lb.	2.5 in.	1,100 yards
Falcon	700 lb.	2.5 lb.	2.75 in.	1,200 yards
Minion	1,200 lb.	3.25 lb.	3.25 in.	1,400 yards
Sakeret	1,200 lb.	3.25 lb.	3.25 in.	1,400 yards
Saker	1,500 lb.	5.25 lb.	3.75 in.	1,500 yards
Demi-culverin	2,400 lb.	10.5 lb.	4.5 in.	1,800 yards
Culverin	4,500 lb.	20 lb.	5.5 in.	2,000 yards
Demi-cannon	6,000 lb.	36 lb.	6.75 in.	1,600 yards
Cannon	8,000 lb.	64 lb.	8 in.	1,500 yards
Basilisk	9,000 lb.	60 lb.	8.75 in.	1,800 yards

Smooth-bore artillery

In the eighteenth century guns were known simply by the weight of shot fired. The size and weight of the gun varied greatly, the projectile being the only constant.

18-pounder	4,250 lb.	18 lb.	5.3 in.	1,580 yards
24-pounder	5.600 lb.	24 lb.	5.8 in.	2,630 yards
32-pounder	7,000 lb.	32 lb.	6.41 in.	1,620 yards
42-pounder	6,300 lb.	42 lb.	7 in.	1,660 yards
68-pounder	12,500 lb.	68 lb.	8.12 in.	1,840 yards

Smooth-bore shell guns

In the eighteen-thirties smooth-bores firing spherical explosive shells were introduced. These guns, unlike those firing solid shot, were known by the diameter of their bore.

8-inch SB	6,000 lb.	82 lb.*	8 in.	2,900 yards
10-inch SB	7,400 lb.	65 lb.*	10 in.	2,500 yards

Shell weights varied. The bursting charge was 1–3 lb. of black powder.

Converted smooth-bores

These were old smooth-bore guns converted to RMLs by the insertion of rifled liners on Palliser's system.

Type of gun	Approx. weight	Weight of shot	Calibre	Effective range
64/32-pounder	6,500 lb.	64 lb.	6.3 in.	1,500* yards
80/68-pounder	11,200 lb.	80 lb.	6.3 in.	1,500* yards

Rifled muzzle-loaders

Introduced from the mid eighteen-sixties, they formed the staple armament of most forts. Some remained in service until the early twentieth century.

7-inch	7 tons	115 lb.	7 in.	1,500* yards
9-inch	12 tons	250 lb.	9 in.	1,800* yards
10-inch	18 tons	400 lb.	10 in.	2,000* yards
11-inch	25 tons	535 lb.	11 in.	2,000* yards
12-inch	25 tons	600 lb.	12 in.	2,000* yards
12-inch	35 tons	700 lb.	12 in.	2,000* yards
12.5-inch	38 tons	800 lb.	12.5 in.	2,000* yards

* These ranges are effective ranges. The guns could fire much further but their powers of penetration declined rapidly.

Breech-loaders

The first breech-loaders were introduced in 1882 but they did not begin to replace the RMLs in large numbers until the eighteen-nineties. Breech-loading guns were of two kinds: quick-firers (QF) loaded both cartridge and shell in one unit while breech-loaders (BL) used a separate charge and shell.

QF Guns				
3-pounder	560 lb.	3 lb.	1.85 in.	5,000 yards
6-pounder	672 lb.	6 lb.	2.224 in.	5,500 yards
12-pounder	1,344 lb.	12 lb.	3 in.	9,000 yards
4-inch	4,700 lb.	28 lb.	4 in.	14,300 yards
4.7-inch	4,600 lb.	45 lb.	4.7 in.	13,000 yards
5.25-inch	9,600 lb.	80 lb.	5.25 in.	25,200 yards

BL Guns				
4-inch	4,700 lb.	31 lb.	4 in.	17,000 yards
5-inch	3 tons	60 lb.	5 in.	13,000 yards
5.5-inch	6 tons	82 lb.	5.5 in.	17,300 yards
6-inch	7 tons	100 lb.	6 in.	20,200 yards
9.2-inch	28 tons	380 lb.	9.2 in.	34,000 yards
10-inch	29 tons	500 lb.	10 in.	18,900 yards

Index

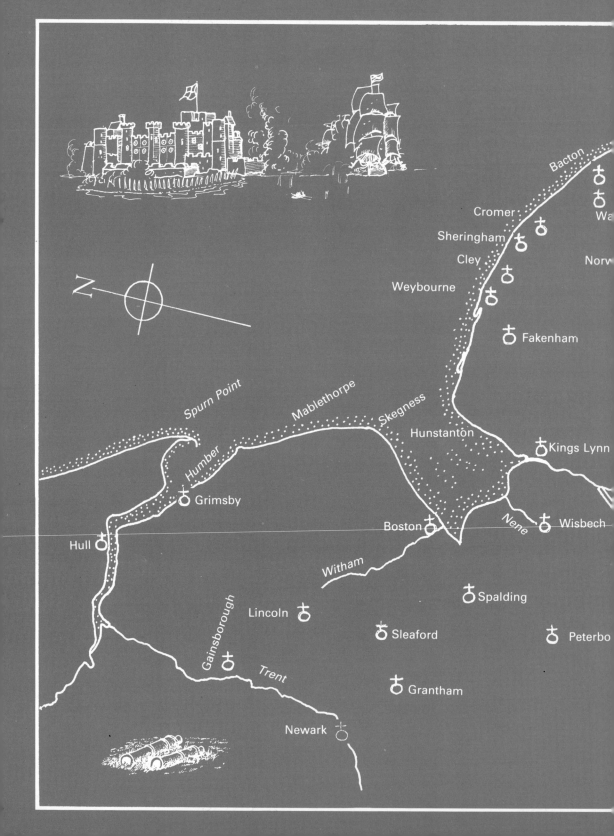